# CHEAP

# CHEAP

## THE HIGH COST OF DISCOUNT CULTURE

### ELLEN RUPPEL SHELL

THE PENGUIN PRESS | NEW YORK | 2009

THE PENGUIN PRESS
Published by the Penguin Group
Penguin Group (USA) Inc., 375 Hudson Street, New York, New York 10014, U.S.A. · Penguin
Group (Canada), 90 Eglinton Avenue East, Suite 700, Toronto, Ontario, Canada M4P 2Y3 (a
division of Pearson Penguin Canada Inc.) · Penguin Books Ltd, 80 Strand, London WC2R oRL,
England · Penguin Ireland, 25 St. Stephen's Green, Dublin 2, Ireland (a division of Penguin Books
Ltd) · Penguin Books Australia Ltd, 250 Camberwell Road, Camberwell, Victoria 3124, Australia
(a division of Pearson Australia Group Pty Ltd) · Penguin Books India Pvt Ltd, 11 Community
Centre, Panchsheel Park, New Delhi - 110 017, India · Penguin Group (NZ), 67 Apollo Drive,
Rosedale, North Shore 0632, New Zealand (a division of Pearson New Zealand Ltd) · Penguin
Books (South Africa) (Pty) Ltd, 24 Sturdee Avenue, Rosebank, Johannesburg 2196, South Africa

Penguin Books Ltd, Registered Offices:
80 Strand, London WC2R oRL, England

First Published in 2009 by The Penguin Press,
a member of Penguin Group (USA) Inc.

LIBRARY OF CONGRESS CATALOGING IN PUBLICATION DATA
Shell, Ellen Ruppel
Cheap : the high cost of discount culture / Ellen Ruppel Shell.
p. cm.
Includes bibliographical references and index.
ISBN 978-1-59420-215-5
1. Discount houses (Retail trade)—United States. 2. Consumer behavior—United States. I. Title.
HF5429.215.U6S54 2009
381'.1490973—dc22 2009009503

Printed in the United States of America
1 3 5 7 9 10 8 6 4 2

Designed by Marysarah Quinn

TO JO, ALI, AND MART . . . PRICELESS

I do not prize the word "cheap." It is not a badge of honor.

| PRESIDENT WILLIAM MCKINLEY

# CONTENTS

# NOTE TO READERS

This book is about America's dangerous liaison with Cheap.

In a market awash in increasingly similar—even identical—goods, price is the ultimate arbiter; the lower, the better. I know this because I live it. I buy $10 bootleg watches from street vendors, repressing the suspicion that in six weeks' time said timepiece is as likely to sprout wings as to tell time. I buy three-for-$15 underwear at Target, and discontinued glassware at the outlets. I graze the home section of discount stores to stock up on key chains and flashlights and "mini tool boxes" and other cool stuff too cheap to resist.

Like almost everyone, I have a wobbly budget to balance and a torrent of bills every month. But thrift doesn't explain this behavior. How thrifty is it to buy a watch with a two-month life span, or a Lilliputian hammer "just in case"? I would drive an extra mile to save a few pennies a gallon on gasoline but wouldn't dream of driving any distance to retrieve a fallen quarter from the sidewalk. No, this isn't about thrift. The craving for bargains springs from something much deeper. Low price is an end and a victory in itself, a way to wrestle control from the baffling mystery that is retail.

Alas, that control is largely illusory and those "unbelievable deals" all too believable. The underpants shred in the dryer. The hammer is too small to bang in a nail. The watch stops. Still, these "deals" are irresistible.

Knowing that bargains are ephemeral doesn't diminish our desire for them. It doesn't keep us from leaving a warm bed on Black Friday morning to elbow through the post-Thanksgiving mob. It doesn't stop us from draining gas and time to save two bucks on a case of diapers or Coke at the Big Box store. And it doesn't prevent us from cluttering our homes, garages, and rented storage units with cheap stuff we may have forgotten we own.

As a nation, we've come to assume that low price powers both productivity and the gross national product. Under this logic, the ebb and flow of cheap goods underlies progress and rewards us with good jobs and bright futures. Historically, key economists have endorsed this view, as have legislators. And while a smattering of consumer advocates, labor unionists, and social scientists grumble, outside of the predictable jabs at Wal-Mart few have dared to publicly challenge this orthodoxy. In these trying times, who but a hopeless elitist would suggest that low price is not an unassailable good?

I plead not guilty to that elitist charge. For most of my life, the phrase "cheap thrill" did not constitute an oxymoron. My personal devotion to cheap stretches back to a college diet of ramen noodles and brown rice—bought in bulk. I cultivated a tolerance (though never a taste) for horse meat, thanks to its incredibly low price. Though I no longer eat palomino, until beginning this project I did comparison shop for chicken thighs, and rarely passed a jumble bin of half-priced anything—jeans, dress shirts, plumbing fixtures, gloves, coffee mugs—without giving it a good tumble. My bliss was driving into Manhattan late on a Friday afternoon and slipping into an unmetered parking spot free for the entire weekend.

What changed me was the boot incident. A couple of years ago I needed a pair of dress boots to complement a New Year's Eve outfit I'd purchased on super sale at Bloomingdale's (you would not believe how much I saved). I went to my local shoe store—a mini-outlet—and had a look around. The selection was just so-so. I asked the salesman whether he had anything special, and he brought over a gorgeous pair of boots from Italy. The leather was buttery, the look great, the fit perfect, but the price well out of my range. I settled for some Chinese imports selling for about one quarter the price. The boots were clunky and so uncomfortable that on New Year's Day I tossed them to the back of my closet, where they landed in a heap of other unwearable "good deals" in bad colors or unflattering shapes: a bargain hunter's pile of shame.

The footwear fiasco got me thinking about all those cheap gloves and socks and T-shirts and "Guess how much I saved?" gizmos cluttering my family's life. How much of this stuff had we used once or not at all and then packed away, given away, thrown away? Why were we doing this? It was time to take a hard look at this behavior, a behavior that on its face seemed not quite rational. And why was there such a scarcity of things reasonably priced? It seemed that almost all consumer goods were cheap, like the Chinese boots, or extravagant, like the Italian boots. Where, I wondered, was the solid middle ground that offered safe footing not so very long ago?

Ferreting out the answer to these seemingly simple questions led to a fascinating journey, from the hinterlands of Sweden to the back alleys of Shanghai to the shipyards of Los Angeles. I met with psychologists, economists, farmers, marketers, designers, historians, cultural theorists, mathematicians, and retailers large and small. I spent a couple of years wandering a world of consumer choices driven by a system that creates the desire it claims to sate. This book explores that world and what role we—as consumers and citizens—play in it.

LIKE ALL sensible journeys, this one begins with a look backward to history. Retail giant John Wanamaker's inventions from the white sale to the price tag changed forever the way we shop. Also playing a role were Frank W. Woolworth, the sickly farm boy who built his "Cathedral of Commerce" one hairpin at a time, and appliance salesman Eugene Ferkauf and his wildly successful creation, Korvettes. The rise of technology-enabled globalism enabled a shift in power away from manufacturers and workers and onto giant retailers and their stockholders. Low price became king and the consumer its willing pawn. Simple but clever inventions like the shopping cart and the bar code abetted the shift from full service to self-service, further reducing the need for skilled staff and offloading more responsibility onto consumers. Over time, choice became restricted by price—what could not be sold cheaply, like the Chinese boots, became a de facto luxury, like the Italian boots. Discounting reshuffled America's demography, hastening the collapse of cities and the flight to the suburbs. In the "distribution upheaval" of the early 1960s, hundreds of merchants were put out of business by the looming discount behemoths. By the late 1970s, discounting had infiltrated every market segment, and the emergence of "category killers" in hardware, toys, and furniture had killed off more than half of existing retail chains. Millions of jobs were shipped overseas as discounters leaped at every opportunity to buy from foreign suppliers. Prices crashed, consumer debt soared, and Americans put their futures on the installment plan.

What does this have to do with us today? Well, quite a lot. From the day we open our first lemonade stand, most of us understand that price is a relative matter, one that can infuriate, surprise, sadden, or delight. As Harvard Business School professor Gerald Zaltman told me, "Price is typically a number, but there is nothing more subjective." Who knew that the way prices are positioned on a menu can influence what we eat for lunch or that some numbers trigger in our minds the flashing light of good deal, while others send signals of rip-off? Looking deep inside the human brain, neuroscientists have discovered that the very anticipation of a "bargain" sets our neural networks aquiver. The manipulation of price can confuse us, block the thinking part of our brain and ignite the impulsive, primitive side, the part that leads us to make poor decisions based on bad assumptions. Ever wonder why you'll drive five miles out of your way to save a buck on a six-pack of beer or, for that matter, a tank of gas? Or why you'll snap up a sweater "marked down" from $150 to $50 but pass up the very same sweater selling for "full price" at $50? Or why you'd prefer to pay more for an item than witness someone else pay less? Ever wonder why your own closet is cluttered with ill-fitting shoes and T-shirts in unbecoming shades? As we will see, science has the answer.

Factory outlets are America's number-one tourist destination, the fastest-growing segment of not only the retail industry but also the travel industry. In Las Vegas we see the point that outlets can be as dicey as the slots, treacherous places for those who don't know the landscape. At the outlets a "designer" necklace, a pair of Levi Strauss jeans, a Coach bag are often mere decoys, name brands in name only. Who's to know? And it's not only outlets that lead us astray. Merchants of rugs, mattresses, jewelry, and almost everything else use similar strategies to make bad deals irresistible. Even Harvard University dilutes its brand to capitalize on the human penchant for bargains. When the price is right, what's in the box seems to matter far less than what is on the label.

In the world of Cheap, "design" has become a stand-in for quality. Companies such as Target, H & M, and Zara offer consumers the look they love at a price they can live with—but at what true cost? In Sweden we visit IKEA, the global furniture retailer made famous and fabulously successful by a scheme of designing not just *for* low price but *to* low price. The consequences of this are both obvious and subtle. IKEA makes furniture available to all at a low price, which means college students, young couples, and others on a budget can furnish their homes in style. But IKEA does not overly concern itself with what Homer Simpson calls "fall-apart." The company designs for easy construction, uniformity, cheap production, and transportability around the globe. Ultimately, what it markets is disposable, with everything that implies. The genius of IKEA and other cheap-chic purveyors is that they have made fashionable, desirable, and even lovable objects nearly devoid of craftsmanship. The environmental and social implications of this are insidious and alarming.

Taking a hard look at the impact of discounting on the family budget raises the inevitable question: Does shopping at Wal-Mart and its like make us wealthier? Discounters have helped to keep inflation at bay, and that in itself is a victory. But the Great Depression was characterized not by inflation but by deflation, particularly wage deflation. In recent decades, wage stagnation and growing debt made discounting all the more compelling. Yet discounts don't compensate for the staggering and rising costs of essentials—housing, education, and health care. A terrific deal on tube socks does not keep foreclosure and bankruptcy at bay. Nor will it sustain us.

Food reflects our culture, traditions, and values; nothing is more personal or more intimate. But what we put in our mouths often comes down to price. Americans pay less for food than do citizens of any other developed nation. The puzzle of how restaurants can possibly turn a profit selling one-dollar cheeseburgers and "all you can eat" shrimp platters led me to the question of how food is grown, processed, and sold in America and around the world. While small family farms are no longer adequate to supply the burgeoning global population, overreliance on factory-farmed and factory-processed foods has made food scarce in many parts of the developing world while forcing down the price of food in the United States to unsustainable levels. As agricultural economist Peter Timmer told me, "I'm quite concerned about what the large food companies are doing to the quality and safety of our diet."

Without China, there would be no Cheap. Still, predictable generalizations about this vast and fascinating nation do not apply. In Shanghai and Taizhou the role American business interests have played in keeping prices low and conditions difficult is crystal-clear. The Chinese call those who make, sell, and profit from substandaard and counterfeit goods the *heixin*, or "small, black-hearted ones," and as we will see, the *heixin* come in many nationalities. What I hope to convey is that we have more in common with the people of China than many of us would like to believe. As one trade expert told me: "The severe exploitation of China's factory workers and the contraction of the American middle class are two sides of the same coin."

Cheap fuel, cheap loans, cheap consumer goods do not pave the road to salvation. On the contrary, our Faustian pact with bargains contributed to the worst recession of two generations. The economics of Cheap cramps innovation, contributes to the decline of once flourishing industries, and threatens our proud heritage of craftsmanship. The ennoblement of Cheap marks a radical departure in American culture and a titanic shift in our national priorities. Tracking the trail of the low price imperative, I've tried to take an unflinching look at the roots, the reasons, and the consequences of bargain hunting—as hobby, as public policy, and, most of all, as blood sport.

On a personal note, I can honestly report that writing this book has changed me. I approach factory outlets with trepidation, and remainder racks with extreme caution. I no longer comparison shop for chicken thighs or buy wristwatches from street vendors. But I am still a thrifty person. I save papers bags and rubber bands and gift wrap; haunt flea markets and vintage stores. As for nabbing a free parking spot in New York on a late Friday afternoon? Well, for me that is and will always be priceless.

# CHEAP

# INTRODUCTION

# GRESHAM'S LAW

If you know how to spend less than you get, you have the
philosopher's stone.

| BENJAMIN FRANKLIN

Our pleasures are not material pleasures, but symbols of
pleasure—attractively packaged but inferior in content.

| ALAN WATTS

Airport Mesa is a popular spot to gather in Sedona, Arizona, especially
at dusk. It is a mystical time when the faithful perch on sandstone boul-
ders and meditate as the sun slips below the western horizon. Native
Americans believe Sedona is sacred, and for good reason. How else to
explain its stark unearthly beauty and the splendor of its red-rock vistas
and sandstone canyons?

Or, more to the point, how else to explain the vortexes? Vortexes, I'm
told, are where the earth's magnetic lines merge into a tingling energy
that frees the mind and renews the spirit. A staunch empiricist, I try
hard not to believe this. But as the sun burns down to a fuchsia smudge,
the earth cools and my will weakens. Reluctantly, I'm sensing the vibe.
At the same time, though, I can't help but be distracted a little by the
loot gleaming like trophies from Navajo blankets strewn fetchingly across
the rocks. There are necklaces and rings and bracelets made of silver and
semiprecious stones, crafted by the same weathered hands that hold them
up for inspection. A silver chain hung with a turquoise pendant costs
eight bucks! Who can resist? I chose one for each of my daughters. The

Native American artisanal jewelry maker drops them into a plastic sandwich bag. "For you, two for fifteen dollars," she says, smiling. Ah, a bargain.

On the drive back to our hotel, a colleague confides that what I took to be silver and turquoise appears to be tin and glass. He estimates the worth of these trinkets at just a bit more than the Baggies they're carried in. Although I feign disappointment, this revelation is no surprise. I wasn't really expecting quality jewelry; quality wasn't the point. Maybe I didn't get value, but I did get a "good deal." Those very same trinkets, I reasoned, would have cost much more at a tourist boutique in downtown Sedona. Most important, I hadn't done the unthinkable. I hadn't paid *full* price.

Americans are enamored of bargains, a love that does not go unrequited. Paying retail today is a sucker's game. There are more discount and warehouse stores, more bargain basements, more dollar stores and closeout stores than ever before in our history. Most of us buy many things at discount every week—from discounted laundry detergent to two-for-one Ram trucks. Given this reality, one would think that shoppers would believe what we've been told for decades: that the consumer is king and queen of the marketplace. But despite discounts galore, Americans habitually fret that we are paying too much. Lisa Bolton, a professor of marketing at the Wharton School of Business, said there is good reason for this confusion. Most of us, she said, have absolutely no idea of what goes into setting a price. "Consumers don't think about the costs behind what they buy," she said. "They link price to profit, and they grossly overestimate profit margins."

The skyrocketing cost of fuel and food in mid-2008 seemed to confirm our deepest fears that unchecked inflation would be our ruin. Now we really were paying too much! And how could we not worry given that in recent years corporate profits and wages had become a zero-sum game? Despite astonishing productivity growth, median family income, adjusting for inflation, dropped by $1,175 between 2000 and 2007, at the same time that average family spending on basic expenses grew $4,655. Meanwhile, corporate profits doubled. As the gross domestic product ballooned, ordinary Americans lost both ground and faith—and rising prices seemed to be at the heart of the matter.

As financier Leon Levy once wrote, "Change creeps upon us incrementally . . . often as not rationalized but as part of business as usual. Only later do we realize that the world has been turned on its head." This especially holds true when it comes to money. The fear of inflation-driven price hikes is so deeply engrained in the national psyche that many of us believe we pay far more for goods and services than our parents or grandparents. We barely notice that prices of most consumer goods—even food and fuel—have been trending downward for decades. The rather astounding facts are these: Compared with the early 1970s, in 2007 we spent 32 percent less on clothes, 18 percent less on food, 52 percent less on appliances, and 24 percent less on owning and maintaining a car.

TECHNOLOGY-DRIVEN GLOBALIZATION has pushed real prices to rock bottom in almost every category—a trend that verged on the desperate in late 2008 when even tony retailers such as Saks and Nordstrom engaged in an orgy of price slashing so extreme that it threatened to tarnish the reputation of their own brands. Meanwhile, television beams into our living rooms the handiwork of entire networks devoted to feeding the frenzy of more for less. The Internet bristles with bargains. And why not? Isn't the bargaining instinct branded into society's DNA? Where would civilization be without the haggling rug merchants of Istanbul or the teeming bazaars of Marrakesh? Are these venerable institutions so different from Home Shopping Network, Filene's Basement, and eBay?

In a word, yes. The ancient marketplace was built on a balance of power between buyer and seller that is all but gone today. A cascade of corporate scandals and screwups from Enron to Halliburton to Citibank to Michael Madoff's audacious Ponzi scheme has shaken whatever faith we once held in corporate responsibility, and this mistrust has dripped down to the retail level. Even on the sacred rocks in Sedona, it seems, we get taken for a ride.

Martin Neil Baily, senior fellow at the Brookings Institute, said that the suspicion that we are being charged more than we should be is entirely rational. After all, plenty of retailers charge staggering sums for their goods. "The consumer economy is bipolar," he said. "Some of us count our pennies, while others pay $2,500 for a handbag at Barneys."

To be fair, most of us have barely heard of Barneys, let alone shopped there. Still, many of us hold the belief that retailers from supermarkets to hardware stores follow Barneys' pricing strategy. That is, we believe that merchants habitually overcharge us just because they can, and the difference among products represents not a difference in quality but in the varying ability of salesmen to fool us. There is a general consensus that "prices are unfairly high," said Lisa Bolton. "People really believe they are being ripped off."

Such mistrust leads to miscalculation. Anthropologist Clifford Geertz once wrote that information in the traditional marketplace is "poor, scarce, mal-distributed, inefficiently communicated, and intensely valued. The level of ignorance about everything from the product quality and going prices to market possibilities and production costs is very high, and . . . the search for information is the central experience of life in the bazaar." Geertz's insights into the Middle Eastern bazaar apply even more emphatically today. Poorly informed shoppers (which is to say most shoppers) instinctively attribute differences in price among stores not to differences in service or quality or design or materials, but to what we believe are variances in salesmanship. The formulation, essentially, is that the greedier the retailer, the higher the price. Bolton calls this a "sticky" belief, a belief that persists despite rather than because of the facts. "It's very difficult to dislodge the idea that prices—very reasonable prices—are unfair," she told me. Muddling things even more is that in our "bipolar" marketplace the disparity between the value of the product and the asking price is sometimes quite real. Take that Barneys handbag, a leather confection that cost the store far, far less than the selling price. (While retailers guard their markups like state secrets, luxury handbags at some stores sell for more than thirteen times their production price.) Barneys will fight hard to keep its buying price low, but Barneys' customers have no such leverage: No ordinary customer can haggle with sales associates to get a break on that brazen markup.

The traditional marketplace had no such limitations. Bazaar culture assumes a symbiosis between buyer and seller, because whether or not they trust each other, the buyer and seller need each other. Each is a member of the same community, and the game of offer and counteroffer is a ritual over which each exerts a high level of control. The traditional marketplace relies on both buyers and sellers benefiting from transactions for the good of the community at large. Wrote Geertz, "Whatever the relative power, wealth, knowledge, skill or status of the participants—and it can be markedly uneven—clientship is a reciprocal matter, and the butcher or wool seller is tied to his regular customers in the same terms as he to them." Overcharge a man for your lamb, and he's sure to overcharge you for his pots or give you a bad haircut when you patronize his barbershop. Merchants in the bazaar want the best possible price, of course, but they also rely on return customers—and those customers are their neighbors, family, and friends. As those of us who have visited bazaars well know, tourists and other outsiders not in on the game are easily and frequently fleeced.

It is easy to conjure a scenario that mimics this dichotomy in our own everyday experience. Imagine you are looking for a used car of a particular year, make, and model. Now imagine that your good friend and neighbor is selling just such a car, as is a dealership 50 miles from your home. It is likely (though not certain) that you would prefer to buy the car from your neighbor for several reasons. Hopefully, you trust this neighbor, but even if you don't, you know where he lives and it's not far. Also, by buying his car you enrich him and therefore your neighborhood; perhaps your neighbor will apply the proceeds toward fixing his sagging garage or patching his roof. Purchasing your car from the dealership, by contrast, enriches only the dealer and his business while exposing you to a number of unknowns. There are pluses and minuses to each option, of course, but it boils down to this: When we buy a used car from a friend or neighbor, we feel like an insider. When we buy a used car from a dealer we don't know, we feel like a tourist.

In the Age of Cheap we are all tourists, blindly reliant on the seller to wring out the best price from his suppliers and to reliably pass those savings on to us. Retailers, and in particular discount retailers, reliably betray this trust. Nobel Prize winner in economics George Akerlof illustrates the problem with a thought experiment. Imagine that a quart of high-quality milk wholesales for $1.00, and a quart of watered-down milk wholesales for 60 cents. A typical buyer might willingly pay up to 80 cents for the watered-down milk and up to $1.20 for the pure milk. In either case, mutual gains would be made from the transaction: Both the buyer and the seller know what he or she is getting, and both end up with what might be considered a fair deal. But if the customer is unable to distinguish quality, both grades of milk must sell for the same price—about 90 cents a quart. Under this system, honest brokers of pure milk go bankrupt, while corrupt watered-down milk sellers flourish. So, logically enough, soon all surviving merchants are watering their milk and pocketing large profits, and consumers believe they are getting a bargain when in fact they are being ripped off. Economists call this Gresham's law, after Sir Thomas Gresham, a sixteen-century merchant who persuaded Queen Elizabeth to restore the debased currency of England. Its guiding principle is this: Bad money drives out good.

In America today, Gresham's law rules, with sweeping consequences both obvious and subtle. The way we shop, the way we do business, and the way we think about money all reflect this new reality. The global economy challenges us to do more with less every day, a challenge both bracing and daunting. It is an intriguing time and a treacherous one for those caught unawares. It is my hope that this book will serve as both cautionary tale and road map, pointing out the road blocks and dangerous turns, the falling rocks and speed traps, while never losing sight of the scenery.

# CHAPTER ONE

# DISCOUNT NATION

We must have cheap labor or we cannot sell cheap goods.
When a clerk gets so good she can earn better wages
elsewhere, let her go.

| FRANK W. WOOLWORTH, QUOTED IN JOHN K. WINKLER,

*FIVE AND TEN: THE FABULOUS LIFE OF F. W. WOOLWORTH*

American history is replete with tales of celebrated bargains. Manhattan was purchased for a pile of trinkets, and the Louisiana Purchase for three cents an acre. But these were real estate deals at a time when our boundaries seemed limitless. In early America, beyond land, water, and air, very few things came cheap.

Until the industrial revolution, backbreaking, heart-aching labor was behind the production of almost everything we made, and objects of all kinds were scarce. As author Robert Kanigel writes of the pre–Civil War period: "The beautiful things, the useful things, the conveniences and comforts—were in short supply, cost too much, or couldn't be had at any price. A wagon wheel was no trifle; neither was a stove. The great mass of people, at least by the standards of our time, had little. You could . . . point to inequities in the distribution of wealth and indirect capitalism. But with equal justice, you could point simply to how much trouble it was, how much labor and material it took, to make a plow, or dig a ton of coal, or generate even as much power as a horse."

Precisely when we came unyoked from the harnesses of manual labor is a matter of debate, but historians tend to link our liberation to the army's frantic scramble for firepower in the latter half of the eighteenth century. It is hardly surprising that guns were among the first mass-produced objects in America. Munitions were critically important in military and domestic life; farmers, ranchers, storekeepers, and nearly everyone else needed a firearm for peace of mind if not survival. Yet the amount of work that went into making guns was stunning, and their production was painstakingly slow. A skilled gunsmith making a flintlock musket or Kentucky long rifle began by hand-forging and reaming the barrel; he then carved the stock, assembled the locking mechanism, and finished each gun (again by hand) often with the help of an apprentice. Making a really fine piece took more than three hundred hours of labor, and the resulting product cost $40—about three times what the average person of the time made in a month. A fine firearm might have been well worth the price, but it was beyond the reach of the American rank and file. Most soldiers of the time would have been happy with a gun that reliably fired in the direction in which it was pointed. Unfortunately, not many had that luxury.

The revolution was waged with a hodgepodge of backfiring muskets and rifles, "fowling pieces," pistols, and blunderbusses. Shortages were so severe that some soldiers were reduced to fighting with swords or axes. General George Washington lamented this, as did Benjamin Franklin, who early in 1776 wrote that "both arms and ammunition are much wanted." While weapons imported from France were of high quality, most American guns were so shoddy that militias were accompanied in the killing fields by armorers, dodging enemy fire as they worked gamely to nurse busted muskets. This was, to say the least, an awkward approach to doing battle and a precarious one. Not surprisingly, the American arms industry felt pressed to do better. In 1794, fretting over the possibility of yet another war with England, now President George Washington proposed a bill to create public facilities to manufacture and supply the military with reliable weapons. The bill was passed and arsenals established in Springfield, Massachusetts, and Harpers Ferry, Virginia. Contracts were also opened to private companies. Two of the successful bidders, Simeon North and Eli Whitney, proposed to improve the quality and speed of gun manufacture through sophisticated mechanization.

Whitney, the better known of the two, was nearly broke at the time, having failed to retain financial control over his famous cotton gin. He desperately needed the gun-making contract but was so distracted by ensuing litigation that he neglected to pay much attention to the enterprise. A tireless self-promoter, he managed to take and get credit for being the first to mechanize gun manufacture through the use of interchangeable parts, a distinction for which he is known to this day. Unfortunately for schoolchildren everywhere, this distinction was unearned. As one scholar put it, "Except for Whitney's ability to sell an undeveloped idea, little remains of his title as father of mass production."

The real hero here was Simeon North, a steady and humble maker of scythes and other small agricultural implements who pioneered both interchangeable parts and its corollary, mass production. Using a manufacturing technique that would later be linked to efficiency expert Frederick Winslow Taylor, North broke down the gun-building process into a series of basic tasks and distributed the work among a group of semi-skilled laborers. This radical departure from traditional gun making led to a cheaper and more consistently reliable product. As North reported in 1808, "To make my contract for pistols advantageous for the United States and to myself I must go to a great proportion of the expense before I deliver any pistols. I find that by confining a workman to one particular limb of the pistol until he has made two thousand, I save at least one quarter of his labor, to what I should provided (that) I finished them by small quantities; and the work will be as much better as it is quicker made." This "de-skilling" of the gun-making process transformed gunsmithing from a masterly craft to a well orchestrated routine, thereby growing efficiencies well beyond expectations. North not only fulfilled the terms of his contract within his deadline, but was awarded another one to produce an additional twenty thousand pistols, the components of which were "to correspond so exactly that any limb or part of one pistol may be fitted to any other pistol of the twenty thousand." The first contract known to stipulate interchangeable parts, it was a resounding step in the inexorable march toward low price.

---

WHITNEY'S FAMOUS GIN, though not the font of mass production he claimed, nonetheless played a critical role in lowering the price of textiles. The gin separated cotton fiber from seed, cleaning more cotton in minutes than a battalion of humans could in a day. With the adaptation of James Watt's steam engine as a power source, cotton cleaning became almost entirely mechanized, and within a few years of the gin's patenting in 1774, the blizzard of cotton fiber spread beyond New England's booming textile industry to Europe and as far away as Russia. The value of the U.S. cotton crop rose from $150,000 to more than $8 million in a decade.

World demand for fabric that was cheaper than linen and cooler than wool made cotton a very desirable commodity, accounting for more than 50 percent of all American exports by the middle of the nineteenth century. Once the gin made cleaning cotton fiber so cheap, the expectation grew that cotton itself would be cheap. The cotton gin reduced the labor required to extract and remove seeds, but planting and picking remained a distinctly human chore. To meet the expectation of low price, the farming and picking of cotton had to be cheap as well, and this meant cheap labor. There is no cheaper labor than the slave variety, and it makes sense that the cotton gin led to an emphatic boost to the slave trade. The American South was by then growing 60 percent of the world cotton supply, and nearly three-quarters of all slaves were involved in cotton production. By the time those slaves were set free shortly after the Civil War, the mass merchandising of textiles and other "dry goods" was well under way, and the expectation of cheap fabric was deeply ingrained in the American psyche.

To imply that the cotton gin or interchangeable revolver parts changed everything would be to overreach. North's and Whitney's innovations planted the early seeds of systematized mass production, but it took more than half a century for those seeds to take root and sprout. "I don't like the word "revolution," Merit Roe Smith, historian at the Massachusetts Institute of Technology, told me. "It's misleading. Real industrialization didn't happen overnight. It began after the War of 1812 and took about forty years to really take off."

By the waning days of the nineteenth century, mass manufacture was a given, accounting for more than 50 percent of the nation's production. This dramatic shift in the way things were made led to a striking reduction in the price of consumer goods, as well as to a sharp decline in the status and power of craftsmen. Craftsmanship was still important, of course, but in many cases it was not quite as important as it was before the advent of industrialization. One observer wrote, "As low cost is the main object of American industry, no premium is placed on craftsmanship for its own sake. Only so much accuracy and refinement of finish are put into the article as are necessary if it is to meet the standard of the quality range for which it was originally designed."

AS AMERICA'S population shifted away from ranches and farms, thickening the concentration of people and capital in urban centers, there was a growing demand for a new kind of store to match the nation's speeded-up system of manufacture. Philadelphia haberdasher John Wanamaker was there to meet that demand. A deeply religious man, Wanamaker considered good business his ministry, attacking even the smallest transaction with Calvinistic fervor and an ambition deeper even than his piety. In 1861 he and his brother-in-law, Nathan Brown, opened Oak Hall, a men's clothing store, at Sixth and Market Streets on the site of George Washington's executive mansion. (Even this early in his career, Wanamaker displayed a knack for the dramatic.) Oak Hall prospered based on Wanamaker's then-radical policy: "One price and goods returnable." In 1869, he opened his second store at 818 Chestnut Street, and capitalizing on both the untimely death of his brother-in-law and his own growing reputation, he renamed the company John Wanamaker & Co. Both enterprises were extremely successful, but Wanamaker had in mind something even grander, something on the scale of London's Royal Exchange or Les Halles in Paris. In 1875 he bought an abandoned Pennsylvania Railroad freight depot, an enormous, sprawling structure big enough to hold his vision. He renovated the space spectacularly into what he called in overheated advertisements "the Grand Depot for merchandise." If not America's first department store, historians agree, it was certainly its first grand department store.

Forever the evangelical, Wanamaker summarized his entrepreneurial vision in "The Evolution of Mercantile Business," an address he gave at an annual meeting of the American Academy of Political and Social Science. "The evolution in trade was inevitable, because it was waterlogged by old customs that overtaxed purchasers; that there was at work for a long time a resistless force moving towards the highest good of humanity; that the profit therefrom to individuals who have risked their own capital, as any man may still do if he chooses, has been insignificant, compared to the people benefited both by the cheapening of the comforts of life and by the improved condition of persons employed . . . "

Wanamaker's Philadelphia store was an eye-popping colossus, and his Manhattan store even more so. Hailed as "the largest space in the world devoted to retail selling on a single floor," it featured 129 circular counters around a central gas-lit tent where customers were treated to shows of women's ballroom fashions. By the early 1890s, improved manufacture and transportation systems had made available a boggling array of consumer goods both domestic and imported, and for the first time customers of nearly every socioeconomic bracket could afford a spectrum of mass-produced and increasingly streamlined everyday wear and sportswear, imitation jewels, artificial silk and furs, cheap perfume—all new on the market and all geared to make the working and middle classes feel rich. Wanamaker offered all of these and more, and in 1911 he expanded with a 150-foot-high Grand Court featuring the world's second largest organ and a great eagle statue from the 1903 St. Louis World's Fair. Topping it all off (quite literally) was a rooftop wireless station, the first telegraph office to receive word when the *Titanic* sank.

The opportunity to buy in bulk offered unbeatable economies of scale that, in Wanamaker's words, was the "most powerful factor yet discovered to compel minimum prices." Critics decried him as a bottom-feeding monopolist, a vulture whose insistence on low prices was putting smaller merchants out of business. Wanamaker deflected even the most biting critiques, arguing that, on the contrary, by cutting out the "middle man" and passing savings directly to his customers, he was creating opportunities and a better life for his fellow Americans. He made this case eloquently in the Evolution speech, forecasting what discounters would argue decades in the future.

*Perhaps some one will ask what effect reduced prices of merchandise have upon labor. It is a noticeable fact that lowered prices stimulate consumption and require additional labor in producing, transporting and distributing. The care of such large stocks, amounting in one single store upon an average at all times to between five and six millions of dollars, and the preparation of and handling from reserves to forward stocks, require large corps of men.*

*Under old conditions of storekeeping a man and his wife or daughter did all the work between daylight hours and midnight. The new systems make shorter hours of duty and thus the number of employees is increased, while many entirely new avenues of employment for women are opened, as typewriters, stenographers, cashiers, check-clerks, inspectors, wrappers, mailing clerks and the like. The division of labor creates many places for talented and high-priced men, whose salaries range alongside of presidents of banks and trust companies and similar important positions.*

Wanamaker's argument was lofty and self-serving, of course, and a touch misleading; for one thing, he employed many more low-priced clerks than "high-priced men." But to be fair, he had experienced firsthand the power of low price to better the lives of ordinary citizens. During his early years in business, he dreaded having to temporarily lay off clerks each year when the inevitable post-Christmas doldrums slowed business to a near halt. Disheartened by the hardship suffered by his employees and those of his textile suppliers during those bleak winter months, he determined to brighten them, purchasing bed linens and other white goods in bulk and putting them on sale at a price just slightly above cost. This innovation, eventually recognized as the first January White Sale, was a huge hit. Customers poured in, employees stayed employed, and America got a new retailing tradition. The success of this high-volume/

low-price gambit inspired Wanamaker to add July Midsummer Sales and February Opportunity Sales. These regular and expected discounting periods whet consumer expectations for cost reductions and made regular low-price sales a department store standard.

Retailing was for Wanamaker not only a career but a calling, and he seemed to believe that making consumer goods affordable to all was the key to heaven. Recognizing that everyone was equal before God, he preached that all should be "equal before price." (Equating God and price is a stretch we can perhaps forgive as rhetorical flourish.) In Wanamaker's day, prices were not fixed but fluid, and those in the know haggled, just as they had in the ancient bazaars. Less sophisticated shoppers or those out of favor paid more. To level the playing field, Wanamaker invented what was arguably his most enduring creation: the price tag. Those bite-sized paper dangles made an indelible impression on retail history, fixing price so that pauper and king, insider and naïf, all paid equally, at least in theory. The tags did not foreclose the possibility of negotiation, of course, but they did set an upper limit, making it more difficult for merchants to overcharge and more likely they would set the lowest possible prices to attract customers. Price tags also generated a daunting problem that vexes pricing experts today: how to fix a price that is seductive to bargain hunters and at the same time wrings every possible penny out of the odd spendthrift?

WANAMAKER was not the only nineteenth-century entrepreneur to recognize the power of low price to enrich market share. In 1878, Frank W. Woolworth, a sickly farmer's son, cut the ribbon on a "five-and-dime" in Utica, New York, the first of over a thousand such stores he would christen in his lifetime. Unlike Wanamaker, who stumbled upon discounting, Woolworth was a low-price man from the start. He had learned the retail trade as an apprentice at Moore and Smith's, a dry goods store in Watertown, New York. At that time dry goods were stored behind the counter and pulled out for inspection at the customer's request. Woolworth, who was only a passable salesclerk, found this process tiresome and inefficient. The story goes that one day during a slow spell his boss asked him to arrange a selection of five-cent items in full view on a self-service table display. The cheap stuff sold out in a single day and with little fuss; the customer picked it up, held it, had a close look, and made a decision. No clerk was necessary to make the sale. Woolworth found this both sensible and appealing. When he went on to open his own stores, low price and convenience became the cornerstone of his business.

A Harvard don once noted that "one of the very first psychological lessons learned was that the 5 and 10 business was faddish and promotional—new lines of goods had to be continually added." Woolworth had an almost instinctual knack for this, giving bargain hunters what they wanted even before they knew what that was. He traveled the globe in search of ornaments, hair ribbons, buttons, fasteners—anything mass-manufactured and cheap. The crushing 1893 depression allowed him to add other things to his stock, such as leather goods. Everyone needed these things, and if they didn't, they might buy them anyway, given they could purchase them for pocket change.

Europe at the time was far ahead of the United States in adopting and adapting the basic tenets of mass manufacturing and was therefore more efficient. So rather than pay more for American-made goods, Woolworth scoured European factories for bargains; consolidated and packaged them in his warehouses in Sonneberg, Germany, and Calais, France; packed them into crates; and shipped them across the Atlantic to his American stores. During one European buying trip he wrote: "Today I made up my mind to find some bargains . . . and I have succeeded, although it was awfully hard work . . . thermometers on wood, imported, $7.50 per gross. . . . Thermometers are not so good as the domestic goods, but make a bigger show." Woolworth was not looking for thermometers; he was looking for a bargain, and he found a terrific one. Sure, it was of low quality, but that was beside the point. Woolworth understood then what discounters know now: In selling everyday commodities, price generally trumps value.

Woolworth was endlessly inventive, tireless, and single-minded. When World War I made it impractical to do business overseas (in his diary and letters home he complained of U-boats getting in the way), he determined to bring cheap production closer to home. He studied the manufacturing process used by his European suppliers and taught these methods to a number of American suppliers, at least one of which he then bought outright. Woolworth now had an even cheaper source of goods: American factories versed in European-style mass-manufacturing techniques. Hailed as the "Napoleon of Commerce" for helping American industry catch up with its European rivals and become self sufficient in cheap goods, Woolworth established himself as the king of American mass production.

Woolworth's and similar chains such as S. S. Kresge Company and W. T. Grant focused on offering the absolutely lowest price even if it meant things would need replacing a lot sooner than they once did. This pushed hard against the American tradition of frugality, where price was only one consideration. Historically, Americans sought durable long-lasting goods that they could pass among themselves and down to their children. Shoes were reheeled, socks darned, and hems let out to fit generations of brothers and sisters. Discounters gave the common man and woman the opportunity to eschew the cobbler and the darning needle, to break in a brand-new pair of shoes or socks when their toes poked through the old ones. Discounters made ordinary folks feel rich by putting a wide selection of goods within easy reach of all but the most meager budgets. Someone had to pay, of course, but that someone need not be the customer.

Woolworth hired only the cheapest labor to serve on the store floor, and most of the time that meant young, unmarried women. In the chain's early years he paid these clerks two or three dollars a week, not a living wage even then. Woolworth knew this, for as he once wrote in a memo to his managers, it was part of his plan. "It may look hard to some of you for us to pay such small wages but . . . one thing is certain: we cannot afford to pay good wages and sell goods as we do now, and our clerks ought to know it." Woolworth proudly rewarded his star (and always male) managers; by 1929 a few were paid as much as $50,000 annually. But the vast majority of his employees were low-skilled and low-paid cashiers. Understandably, these jobs were not considered real careers, and the company was plagued by rapid turnover; a problem with which overworked managers were constantly forced to grapple. Still, these low-level managers were not given the tools to solve this or other problems because they, too, were discouraged from thinking too hard for themselves or being "over-ambitious." Treated like naughty children, they were constantly admonished to be obedient and abstemious in their professional as well as in their personal lives.

Woolworth himself harbored neither of these virtues and lived like a potentate. His Xanadu was the Woolworth Building in lower Manhattan, the tallest building in the world at the time of its completion in 1913. Woolworth's personal office in this "Cathedral of Commerce" was a close replica of the Empire Room of Napoleon's palace at Compiègne. The difference was this: Where Napoleon settled for wood, Woolworth demanded marble.

Woolworth's nickel-and-dime empire had several competitors, some of them fierce. In 1895, Richard Warren Sears published his 332-page *Book of Bargains,* setting in motion a mail-order business that put an astonishingly comprehensive selection of low-priced "consumables" within reach of everyone from the farthest flung cowhand to the girl he loved back home. In this first of his many catalogs, Sears promised, "By comparison of our prices with those of any thoroughly reliable house, you can save money on everything you buy from us." Catalog prices were indeed very low, sometimes half or even less that of department stores. Sears managed this by driving hard bargains with manufacturers and sometimes buying them. By 1906, Richard Sears owned a major piece of sixteen manufacturing plants, including producers of stoves, furniture, agricultural implements, plumbing equipment, and cameras.

Mainstream retailers, too, were cutting prices and opening special discount sections in their stores. In 1917 the *New York Times* wrote that the

*establishment of a five, ten, and twenty-five cent department, under proper management, in almost any retail dry goods store would be a profitable venture is not doubted by men who are close to the business and who knew cheap goods and the profits that can be made out of them.*

The article went on to praise the

*cheap merchandise department [as doing a] triple service. Not only is it expected to make a straight profit on the goods it offers, but it is expected to attract customers to the store to buy other lines, who under different circumstances might become patrons of competitors. Lastly, it is expected to furnish such merchandise to the regular departments as will attract and hold the attention of the customers it brings into the store.*

Mass production made onetime luxuries, such as clocks, sewing machines, and typewriters almost everyday things. This trend was not universally admired. While some reveled in these bargains, others scorned the infiltration of cheap goods as suspect, even subversive. Critics derided mass-manufactured "cookie-cutter" goods as "low-priced trash . . . ugly, short-lived . . . abominations." They railed against the "senseless, vicious, yes criminal tendency to cheap goods." John Hargreaves, an early president of the Retail Merchants Association, argued that cut-rate prices "reduced the value of labour, and have destroyed the purchasing power of many classes, thereby affecting all classes." Shopkeepers who advertised low prices to attract business were derided as "common cutters" and "gutter merchants," and social reformers pointed to the "vile, awful sweatshop" where "plenty of the bargains" were made. Chain stores in particular came under fire as citizens coast to coast banded together to halt what they considered a vicious and cutthroat corporate invasion.

Despite this protest, chain stores rose to prominence with startling speed after World War I, growing in number from an estimated 50,000 in 1920 to 141,492 in 1929. Many Americans found this alarming. The independent, freestanding retailer who knew and valued his customers was a cherished component of the nation's economic and social life, and integral to its concept of community. It is hard to imagine where either Wanamaker or Woolworth would have ended up had they started their careers as clerks in a chain rather than in an independent store. Because chains did away with the local proprietor, funneled money away from the local community, and traded skilled employees for stock boys and "order takers," they were seen as waging a direct assault on the American way of life. Anti-chain protesters in the 1920s represented close to three hundred local and national organizations, comprising roughly 7 percent of the country's population. Editorialists railed against the chains, as did many trade organizations. The National Association of Retail Druggists decried chain store owners as "privilege-seeking tycoons [and] would-be dictators." Station KWKH owner and operator William K. "Old Man" Henderson of Shreveport, Louisiana, proud forefather of the modern shock jock, warned listeners of the "ruinous and devastating effect of sending the profits of business out of our local communities to a common center, Wall Street. We have appealed to the fathers and mothers—who entertain the fond hope of their children becoming prosperous business leaders—to awaken to a realization of the dangers of the chain stores' closing this door of opportunity. We have insisted that the payment of starvation wages such as the chain-store system fosters must be eradi- cated." To raise funds for his campaign, Henderson sold coffee over the air for more than twice its normal price. And populist politicians built their reelection platforms on a foundation of anti-chain sentiment. Loui- siana Governor Huey P. "Kingfish" Long groused that he would rather admit thieves and gangsters to his state than the operators of chain stores.

Representative Wright Patman of Texas was perhaps less provocative than Long, but no less vehement. In an impassioned statement he railed: "The wide distribution of economic power among many independent proprietors is the foundation of the Nation's economy. Both Franklin and Jefferson feared that industrialization would lead to a labor proletariat without property or hope. Small-business enterprise is a symbol of a society where a hired man can become his own boss. . . . History shows that the elimination of the independent businessman has been the first step in the development of totalitarianism."

In the view of Patman and others, a thriving small-business sector was essential to thin out and redistribute the thick, concentrated power of big business. Several state and municipal legislatures responded to these concerns by charging steep licensing fees and imposing heavy graduated taxes on the chains. They put caps on the number of stores a corporation could open in a single community and even tried to make chain stores themselves unlawful. And it was not just brick-and-mortar chains that got the bruising. Shopping through mail-order-house catalogs carried such a powerful stigma that Sears shipped merchandise shrouded in plain brown wrappers.

As the new century emerged, a crescendo of critics voiced alarm at the growing trend toward Cheap, in particular as it applied to the production of America's most iconic object: the automobile. Even efficiency guru Frederick Winslow Taylor seemed to think things had gone too far when he scoffed at the mass-produced Model T Ford as "very cheaply and roughly made." Henry Ford, who famously pioneered the moving assembly line in 1914, could only marvel at this criticism. His assembly plant in Highland Park, Michigan, dubbed the "Crystal Palace" for its abundant windows, was a model of scientific management. As did North before him, Ford broke each step of his production process into individual tasks and assigned workers to perform just one. Where before a skilled mechanic and a couple of helpers would build an automobile engine, now the engine block was pulled down the line past a hundred workers, each contributing his own little bit. One line worker would ream bearings, one bearing every other second; another would file the bearings, one every fourteen seconds; another would put the bearings on the camshaft, one every ten seconds, all day long, day after day, bearing after bearing. The automated assembly line allowed a division of labor that took the brain work out of building a car. While one out of every three workers had once required special skills, now only one out of every five workers required skills. Ford needed fewer mechanics and craftsmen, and he hired more unskilled immigrant laborers, many of whom did not speak English. To prevent slowdowns, managers walked the assembly line, stopwatch at the ready. Sales skyrocketed from 10,600 in all of 1909 to 16,000 a month in 1913. And as demand increased, the assembly line sped up and the pressure boiled over. Ford paid his workers $2.25 for a nine-hour shift, which was pretty good money at the time but not good enough to keep his overstressed workforce happy. In 1913 the company was rehiring between 40 and 60 percent of its workforce *every month*. Unlike Woolworth, Ford did not consider his workers disposable. To slow the stratospheric turnover, he designed the "$5 a day" plan, a profit-sharing scheme that offered bonuses to employees who stuck to the job. This sounded too good to be true, and in a sense it was. Not everyone received the bonus, only those who passed muster with a sort of vice squad of thirty Ford employees who followed workers around to make sure they didn't gamble, drink, or have wives who worked outside the home. Incredibly, few workers objected to this Big Brother treatment, and the plan resulted in an extremely stable workforce. It also increased wages across the industry, as other automakers were forced to follow suit. As Carnegie Mellon historian of technology David Hounshell wrote, "Ford had given the world the first system, in the fullest sense of the expression, of mass production: single-purpose manufacture combined with the smooth flow of materials; the assembly line; large-volume production; high wages initiated by the five-dollar day; and low prices."

THANKS TO THESE increased efficiencies, the sticker price of a Model T dropped from $850 in 1908 (the same price as a Cadillac) to $290 in the early 1920s. Ford's "$5 a day" enabled some of his workers to purchase the fruits of their own labor (at least theoretically), offering yet another steady if not exactly gushing customer stream. Gradually, semiskilled, blue-collar laborers came to recognize their power not only as workers but as consumers. Rather than being mere "cogs in a wheel," they were now in a position to get themselves their own wheels, wheels that properly balanced, might set the entire nation rolling into prosperity. By satisfying their own individual material desires (a new car) these workers were boosting the economy not only by their labors but through their purchases. In his book *Sold American*, historian Charles McGovern argues persuasively that in the early decades of the twentieth century Americans "came to understand spending as a form of citizenship, an important ritual of national identity in daily life. . . . Americans embraced a material nationalism that placed goods and spending at the center of social life."

The mass manufacture of consumer goods and the lowering of prices led eventually to what Harvard historian Lizabeth Cohen called "a consumer's republic," an economy, culture, and politics built "around mass consumption linked both to an enhanced material life and to the promise of greater freedom, democracy and equality." These so-called citizen consumers were not satisfied watching other, richer Americans get the goods; they demanded affordability, and it became the worker's patriotic duty to provide it. Writing in the mid-1920s, Yale economist Walton Hamilton, an advisor to Franklin Delano Roosevelt, suggested that industrial laborers greet their friends and neighbors not with "Good morning" or "How are you?" which he considered relics of an agricultural past, but with the more forward-looking "Low prices." Americans formed coalitions such as the National Consumers League, asserting themselves as much through their power to purchase as through their power in the voting booth. The suspicion then, as it had been since the dawn of industrialization, was that prices were too high, and that protections were needed to keep corporate greed-heads from pushing them even higher.

In 1930 more Americans lacked a car, a radio, and a washing machine than owned one, but it seemed that nearly every American believed that he or she had a claim to ownership. A growing national media and advertising industry made popular the idea that purchasing goods of all kinds was not a privilege but a right, even a patriotic duty. An advertisement for General Motors that appeared in the *Saturday Evening Post* in 1936, for instance, argued against government controls on business, reasoning that America "outstripped the nations of the world because the energy and enterprise of our people were free to *multiply* wealth, to *go forward* instead of 'stabilize,' to succeed in the productive task of making *more* things at *lower* prices for *more* people. . . . Today in America more people want and need better things than ever before! In the satisfying of these wants is America's opportunity to serve progress." As historian Charles McGovern wrote, "Market replaced polis in a new communal public life characterized not by geography, religion, or politics, but by spending."

There was something thrilling, even patriotic, about the Sears catalog making available to Americans from Texas to Maine the same brand of blanket or sewing machine or overalls at the very same low price. Mass production had led to such a proliferation of affordable consumer goods that the challenge became not making things but convincing consumers to buy them. "The key to economic prosperity," General

Motors researcher and inventor Charles Kettering declared in 1929, just days before the stock market crash, "is the organized creation of dissatisfaction." Dissatisfaction was well within reach, although not the sort Kettering envisioned. The tidal wave of unemployment and fiscal misery brought by the Great Depression reshaped the nation's economic landscape and dimmed its optimism. Wanamaker's claims notwithstanding, the presumed link between godliness and unfettered capitalism came under fire. There was a growing and understandable distrust of large corporations, and the government strove to rally economically weak groups to balance out more powerful interests. With unemployment peaking at over 20 percent, prices were fixed to prevent large retailers from forcing smaller ones out of business. As part of the New Deal, the National Industrial Recovery Act set codes of conduct for business, including guidelines for hours worked, wages paid, and fair-trade practices. Low prices, it was feared, would force a dip in wages and profits, pushing more businesses into bankruptcy. To help minimize this, Congress passed the Robinson-Patman Act of 1936, one of several fair-trade laws designed to forestall predatory price cutting by prohibiting chain stores from entering into exclusive contracts with manufacturers. A year later Congress passed the Miller-Tydings Act to exempt fair-trade laws from antitrust legislation. Under this law, manufacturers could set minimum retail prices for products that carried their brand name, thus setting a legal floor that not even huge conglomerates could undercut. Although not consistently enforced, the law offered some protection against escalating price competition and downward spiraling prices.

That year a General Motors promotional film, *From Dawn to Sunset*, featured scenes of happy assembly line workers in coveralls building Chevrolets, picking up their paychecks, and all but dancing off with their families to unleash their "fresh buying power" in a thriving downtown marketplace. To a stirring soundtrack the narrator trumpeted "the tens of thousands of men on one single payroll . . . [having] the pleasure of buying, the spreading of money, and the enjoyment of all the things that paychecks can buy." The film depicts worker-consumers in symbiotic synch with the company, one big happy family on an inexorable march to prosperity. Bargains were most decidedly not part of that triumphant picture, as workers and consumers were considered one and the same. If cheap goods are made by cheap men, then the goods these men and their families were buying—everything from violins to cars—were anything but cheap. In this fleeting homage to capitalism, workers earned fair wages and paid fair prices for high-quality goods. What went unmentioned was that these very same Chevrolet workers had earlier that year waged a successful sit-down strike in Flint, Michigan, to protest unfair and unsafe working conditions, and low wages. The strike helped prompt the creation of the United Auto Workers, arming employees with unprecedented control of their working lives and unprecedented political and economic power. As the car unions won successively larger concessions for their membership in the mid-1930s, Detroit ranked first in the nation in private home ownership.

WORLD WAR II blotted out this happy picture with the double whammy of scarcity and inflation. There was little on offer, and what was available was priced out of reach for many Americans. Car manufacture came to a halt in 1942, to make way for the war effort, and the price of textiles shot up nearly 30 percent, the cost of farm products more than 40 percent. While before the war the government had set legislation to keep prices from falling too low, now it struggled to stave off price gouging. In 1942 the Office of Price Administration and Civilian Supply issued the General Maximum Price Regulation, requiring merchants to set ceilings on the price of what eventually grew to be 90 percent of all goods. There was rationing of rubber, sugar, gasoline, heating oil, milk, coffee, soap, nylon stockings, and even used cars. The merrily dancing worker/spender bees were gone; thrift, not the "spreading of money," became the desired norm. The "Consumer's Pledge," sung to the tune of the "Battle Hymn of the Republic," urged Americans to eschew canned goods in favor of "fresh fruits and vegetables [to] save tons of tin" and to "take the best care of your wearables, and mend them when they tear." Waste was reviled, and recycling elevated to a patriotic duty. Interestingly, despite this enforced frugality, most Americans managed to live well, far better than they had in the roaring twenties when there was enormous income disparity. In 1944 the average factory worker's pay had grown by 80 percent in five years, while, thanks in part to government-imposed price controls, living costs had climbed only 24 percent. And in 1945 personal savings reached an astonishing 21 percent of disposable income, compared to a mere 3 percent two decades earlier.

In the boom years following World War II, soldiers returned flush with optimism and eager to set up new homes and new lives. Consumers saved to buy their chunk of the American dream, typically a detached single-family home, preferably in the suburbs. No one argued that wages should be kept low to keep prices low. Indeed, social thinkers of the time reasoned that high wages were critical to the nation's growing prosperity. As one wrote, "There can be no high levels of production unless the products of industry are bought by workers" with their generous slice of the American pie.

As America moved into the Eisenhower era, wartime frugality lifted as the rank and file shared in the postwar prosperity. *Fortune* magazine gushed that "the union has made the worker to an amazing degree a middle-class member of a middle-class society." Workers were encouraged to derive increasing satisfaction and status from their lives outside of the office or factory. Thanks to high wages and solid benefits, they had both the time and the means to invest in outside interests such as sports, gardening, and travel. They could move uptown for better schools or to a larger home in a leafier suburb for more space. Equality meant not access to the means of production (well out of reach for most workers) but to a growing range of consumer goods. Cultural historian Christopher Lasch noted, "The tired worker, instead of attempting to change the conditions of his work, seeks renewal in brightening his immediate surroundings with new goods and services."

To meet the needs of this growing consumer class, discounting was quietly on the rise. By this time many manufacturers had stopped even trying to set minimum retail prices, since the fair-trade laws were difficult to enforce and critics accused them of being discriminatory and anti-American, and worse. A decade earlier, in 1937, Harvard Business School Professor Malcolm P. McNair had railed against the laws in the pages of a Duke University Law School journal: "The sentiment which furthered the Robinson-Patman Act and its various blood relatives has in it more that is reminiscent of the beginnings of the Nazi movement in Germany, where the same zeal was displayed to protect the small business owner from large corporations. Ultimately, perhaps both may lead to a totalitarian state." McNair did not explain how enforcing manufacturers' minimum prices would lead America down the totalitarian path, but by the early 1950s the public had lost its stomach for price minimums.

New technologies—television in particular—radically altered America's relationship with the material world. In 1948, only 350,000 homes had television sets. Five years later, in 1953, television ownership had exploded reaching 25 million homes. Suddenly, half of all American households had a hulking brown cube in their living rooms through which merchants cycled a steady stream of promotional messages. A wave of lively and sometimes aggressive advertising rolled over the country and spurred record levels of consumption. Advertising expenditures soared, prompting progressive economist John Kenneth Galbraith to decry the creation of "desires . . . to bring into being wants that previously did not exist." Television advertising was particularly vital for the low-service discount chains that, with no experienced salesforce to push product, relied on the customer to come to their stores pre-loaded with wants.

The postwar boom of the late 1940s and 1950s found the working and middle classes actively seeking better homes, better furniture, more and better medical care, fancier cars, and more exotic travel. As war shortages faded into memory, the challenges of industry remained not in the production of goods but in the selling of them. There was more than enough stuff to go around; the challenge was unloading it at a profit. As the 1950s bled into the 1960s, further increased efficiencies cleared the way for still more products to be made, sparking still more price competition. Computers, although laughably primitive by today's standards, were in the early 1960s nothing short of miracles. The room-sized card-fed IBM behemoth stored more information and processed more data than could small armies of humans. Described as a "wondrous combination of the traveling salesman, mathematical genius, and the Sears, Roebuck catalogue," the computer vastly streamlined distribution, giving retailers still more power. Thanks to the new technology, store owners no longer had to wait five days or more for their merchandise; they could demand next-day delivery and get it. And because of this remarkable "just-in-time" distribution capability, suppliers were no longer free to dump piles of goods into a customer's warehouse with the understanding that the retailer would eventually find the market. It was now up to the manufacturer, not the retailer, to manage inventory and to pay the price if supply got out of sync with demand. The trick was to hold inventories to a minimum without getting caught short. If a manufacturer couldn't provide the right item at the right price, the retailer simply went elsewhere. Manufacturers felt great pressure to keep their own inventories well stocked—at significant cost to themselves—while at the same time offering retailers the lowest possible wholesale price.

Food stores offer a particularly vivid example of this trend. Before the "supermarket revolution" of the 1930s, roughly 110,000 retail food sellers accounted for 70 percent of the business. Thirty years later a mere 30,000 retailers accounted for the same volume. And the large, centralized supermarkets wielded enormous power. As a General Foods executive told a reporter at the time, "If one [chain store] makes a decision not to carry our brand, this could be a sizeable chunk of our business." The obvious corollary is that General Foods tried very, very hard to keep the chain stores happy by keeping wholesale prices as low as possible.

While this may seem a subtle change, it was not. In the 1930s and 1940s, American manufacturers seemed invincible—muscular bastions of technological sophistication and efficiency, in sharp contrast to the puny, low-tech, and somehow feminized world of retail. The manufacturers called the tune, and the retailers danced to it. Suppliers signed exclusive contracts with individual store managers with the understanding that theirs would be the only store in a given region to carry a particular brand. If the store didn't perform or reduced the size of its order, it lost the contract. But in the 1950s, federal laws severely restricted the scope of these exclusive deals, and department stores began poaching competitors' best-selling merchandise. As the goods became more generic—as one coffeepot or sewing machine or bicycle was considered just as good or nearly as good as another—the manufacturers lost their edge. At the same time, locally owned hardware stores, clothing stores, and electronics dealers were giving way to the large, centrally controlled chains. The gradual consolidation in the retail sector led to stores being gobbled up by larger stores like so many minnows in the sea.

By the late 1950s legal barriers to price-cutting were gone. Retailers of every stripe—department stores, specialty shops, supermarkets—reconsidered their business models, rethought their distribution systems, and worked hard to offer at least a semblance of the discount experience. They lowered their prices and lengthened store hours. With the exodus to the suburbs and the improved highway system, shopping became decentralized. Discounters took advantage, drawing customers from within a five-mile radius of urban centers and a twenty-five-mile radius in rural areas. Soon every corner of the country had its own discount operation: Spartan, Zayres, Mammoth Mart, Bradlees, Shoppers World, Two Guys, W. T. Grant, The Giant Store, among scores of others. These chains catered to the growing legion of suburbanites by cultivating a "family fair" environment with acres of free parking, piped-in music, and aisles wide enough for the ubiquitous shopping cart. They cut overhead costs by maintaining little or no stored inventory. Everything in stock was laid out on the store floor within sight and easy reach of customers. Self-service further reduced costs by eliminating the need for salesclerks, and it sped up the shopping process. A newly informal shopping environment attracted a growing number of male shoppers—especially blue-collar workers who felt out of place in the stodgy downtown department stores. Evening and Sunday hours were added to encourage working stiffs to stroll the aisles with their homemaker wives. Men were highly desired customers, for it was thought that they, not women, were the most impatient and impulsive shoppers, prone to making purchases based on visual and visceral appeal. To capitalize on this, discounters prominently displayed tempting selections of auto supplies, shaving accessories, and other manly goods at the end of shopping aisles, poised for easy launch into shopping carts and baskets.

Far from being sated with this growing feast of goods and services, as John Kenneth Galbraith predicted they would be, Americans' desire for what money could buy grew faster than their incomes. Third-party universal credit cards, introduced in 1949, would in ten years' time enable the conversion of frugal America to a nation in debt. Despite growing prosperity, the new middle class found it increasingly difficult to keep up, and, as do many of us today, started to "trade down" to "trade up." Middle-class consumers who wanted a showy car or a boat or a trip to Paris saved for these luxuries by cutting corners where they could on commodities such as children's clothes, toiletries, hardware, and even food. As more and more respectable people sought low price, discount shopping lost its stigma. It would gradually become the norm. In the words of one anonymous retail guru of the time, "The discount house is producing the greatest deflation of stuffed shirts ever to hit American business." As the Eisenhower administration drew to a close, three thousand discount chains littered the country with annual sales of an astonishing $5 billion. Discounters became the leading retailers for children's clothes and toys; the second largest sellers of sporting goods, auto accessories, garden products, and housewares; and third in health and beauty aids, women's clothing, shoes, furniture, and jewelry. Stuffed shirts or no, discounting had changed the face of retail indelibly and forever. There would be no turning back.

# CHAPTER TWO

# THE FOUNDING FATHERS

Cheap Merchandise means cheap men, and cheap men mean
a cheap country, and that is not the kind of Government our
fathers founded, and it is not the kind their sons mean to
maintain.

PRESIDENT WILLIAM MCKINLEY

In 1962, Harvard's Malcolm P. McNair drew up a list of the six greatest
merchants in American history. Frank W. Woolworth made the cut, as
did John Wanamaker, J. C. Penney, General Robert E. Wood of Sears,
Roebuck, and Michael Cullen, the first "supermarketeer." Perhaps least
known of these notables was Eugene Ferkauf, founder and controlling
stockholder of E. J. Korvette, then the nation's largest discount store. With
his hardscrabble upbringing and all-American good looks, Ferkauf is
sometimes likened to Sam Walton. In truth, the men had very few things
in common. A quick look at their personal histories offers clues that they
probably thought quite differently on pressing issues of the day. For start-
ers, the name *Ferkauf* is an Ellis Island contortion of *ferkoyf,* which means
"sell" in Yiddish. *Walton* means "walled town" in Old English. Putting
personal history aside, the two did share one defining character trait:
Each was unimaginably cheap.

Sam Walton drove the obligatory junk car and wore off-the-rack suits
from his stores, price tag dangling. Wal-Mart executive offices were furnished with mismatched furniture samples from vendors, some of it lawn
furniture. The company still charges suppliers for incoming phone calls,

and its notorious reimbursement policy allows for tips no higher than 10 percent.

Ferkauf's brand of parsimony was no less severe, but it tended toward the personal. He maintained no office, paid no secretary, and reportedly took important business clients to lunch at a hot dog stand. (It's unclear who paid for the franks.) From all available evidence he never dictated a letter or made a speech. He shunned credit cards. He spent weekends with his family and workdays making surveillance runs through his stores, tidying up piles of merchandise and interrogating customers. In a 1962 cover story, *Time* magazine described the forty-one-year-old CEO as "probably the most unorthodox tycoon in the land."

Unorthodox, maybe, but at the same time familiar. Ferkauf's biography reads like a caricature of a self-made man. He was born in Brooklyn, the cherished son of Rumanian immigrants. An indifferent and dreamy student, college was not for him. After high school he hopped the subway every morning to midtown Manhattan, where he managed one of his father's two small luggage shops. He enlisted in the army during World War II, served four years as a sergeant in the Signal Corps, and returned home to a hero's welcome and the family business. He sold belts and bags at the expected 40 percent markup, netting about $80 a day. This brought a decent living, but it was not enough for Gene, who had grown in both confidence and ambition in the military. Slash that markup in half, he reasoned, and leather goods will fly out the door. His father, Harry Ferkauf, was not so sure. Harry was a cautious, careful man who recalled the Great Depression with dread. Low prices, he warned his son, would anger other merchants. Civility and comradeship, not profit, came first. Gene ignored his father, cut prices, and stood back as the customers poured in. Soon he was selling $500 worth of merchandise a day. Harry pleaded with him to up his prices. He was antagonizing the competition, and, in any case, why sell more than you need to make a decent living? In 1948, Gene could stand the kvetching no longer. He plowed $4,000 into his own business selling discounted leather goods out of a second-story loft on East 46th Street. He named the store E. J. Korvette.

E. J. KORVETTE is sometimes mistaken as a contraction of "eight Jewish Korean War veterans." This blunder is understandable, given that Ferkauf hired his army pals to run the place, but these were veterans of a different era. Korvette opened its doors before the Korean War began. The *E.* stands for Eugene and the *J.* for Ferkauf's friend and partner Joe Zwillenberg. *Korvette* is an allusion to the famed Canadian World War II sub-chaser, the Corvette. (Ferkauf changed the *C.* to a *K.* to avoid legal hassles with the navy.)

Korvette started in leather because Ferkauf knew leather. But he also knew that leather wasn't sexy, at least when it took the shape of wallets and luggage. Customers needed wallets and luggage, of course, but this was not the stuff of which dreams were made. Postwar America was bursting with pent-up eagerness and enthusiasm for the new, especially technology. People loved the shiny stuff—especially large appliances: washing machines, vacuum cleaners, and refrigerators. Everyone wanted the biggest and the best, and in hot new colors like avocado green. The media had cast these mechanical marvels as freedom machines, transformers of the dreary into the fabulous. Washing machines banished the drudgery of "washing day"; freezers made the dream of TV dinners come true. To cite but one remarkable example, General Electric ran an advertisement entitled "Things My Bill Has a Right to After It's Over," referring to the postwar world as seen through the eyes of the wife of a young soldier. The blushing bride says her Bill has a right to all the coffee he wants from her spanking new G.E. Coffee Maker, all the ice he wants from her G.E. "zoned" refrigerator, and "no more K.P.," thanks to the new G.E. electric sink that "will let us forget that kitchen drudgery forever." Suddenly, actions once taken by hand—mixing a cake batter, opening a tin can—were jobs for a machine. "Electronic servants" loosened apron strings and gave women more leisure to—what else?—shop for more low-price goods. Set free from their domestic doldrums, women were drenched in newfound leisure, or at least that's how the story was told. Advertisements advised them to spend all that free time wisely, as in this *Ladies' Home Journal* advisory: "Time to watch the papers for announcements of special sales. Time to be constantly alert for special bargains. Time to shop around and secure the utmost for their money."

But not everything came cheap. Appliances were costly things in 1950. A freezer sold for close to $400 when a loaf of bread cost only 14 cents, and the median annual income for a family was $3,319. Customers wanted discounts on what they desired most: refrigerators, deep freezers, and 20-inch color television sets. So Ferkauf bought piles of appliances, slashed the prices to just above cost, and stood back once again. His store did $700,000 in sales its first year, an incredible volume.

Ferkauf was well acquainted with the anti-price-cutting provisions of the Miller-Tydings Act. His dodge was clever: making Korvette technically a "membership store." To qualify for this loophole, Korvette was closed to the general public, but only by a nose. The threshold to membership was low: There was no application policy or admissions fee or initiation rite. Flashing a union card or a driver's license was validation enough but even customers without identification could join, since Ferkauf and his wife Estelle blanketed nearby office buildings with thousands of free "membership cards." Korvette employees passed out more cards to passersby on the street. It was almost impossible to walk down 43rd Street and not become a Korvette member; indeed, avoiding it required a powerful act of will. Yet, thanks to its members-only status, Korvette could legally skirt fair-trade laws and accept deep discounts from its suppliers— deep discounts that were forbidden to competing department stores such as Macy's and Gimbels.

Ferkauf's cut-rate logic was this: If he could make a one-dollar profit selling one refrigerator, he could make a million-dollar profit selling a million refrigerators. Such arrogance did not endear him to the competition. Traditional retailers scorned Ferkauf as a "parasite and a bootlegger" and, most degrading of all, a "discounter." Understandably, they feared for their livelihoods. This offended Ferkauf. An almost pathologically honorable man, his aim was simply to help customers who were unwilling or unable to shop at full-price stores. Many people could not afford to pay retail for an electric mixer or a suitcase, he reasoned, and for these poor folks low prices were simply realistic. Unsure of their ability to compete with such "realism," rival department stores pressured distributors to stop selling to

Ferkauf, and some did. When these sanctions threatened to reduce his inventory, Ferkauf simply switched suppliers. Many manufacturers and wholesalers were happy to do business with him, because they knew that attempts to enforce the fair-trade laws were easily thwarted. Over a period of five years Ferkauf dodged nearly a hundred lawsuits. The threat of impending litigation seemed only to encourage him. Newspaper reports of the lawsuits were essentially free advertising, leading potential customers to suspect that Ferkauf was hawking hot goods. (A similar scenario is played out by urban street vendors today who claim that the Rolex and Cartier watches lining their jackets are not counterfeits but somehow "fell off a truck" on their way to Neiman Marcus.) By 1950, Korvette was turning over $2 million worth of merchandise a year, and Ferkauf was plowing a good portion of the profits into new stores on more leased sites.

Most discount houses of the time were buried deep in urban centers, dark dens with a whiff of the illicit about them. But the mass urban exodus of the 1950s lured retail out of the city centers and into suburban malls, and eventually, discounters followed. The malls were something new. No one knew what to expect of them, and discounters found them particularly congenial. Ferkauf was among the first to follow the money. In addition to his four Manhattan locations he had a store in White Plains and another in Hempstead. But to Ferkauf's eyes the Hempstead store was a dump; it occupied a former Grand Union supermarket and faced a cemetery. He wanted better.

Ferkauf saw his future in suburbia serving a burgeoning young middle class shrugging off the stale values of their parents. Dealing with this new generation was not, as it had been for his father, a lengthy give-and-take in which merchants knew their customers' specific needs and met them. These buyers had big new homes to fill and knew perfectly well what they wanted to fill them with. Ferkauf rushed to their service with a 90,000-square-foot "super store" in Westbury, Long Island, complete with an appliance store, a supermarket, and a toy store. It was one-stop shopping, just the thing for young families on the go. December 2, 1953, was opening day, and more than a thousand customers showed up. By Christmas the place had done an almost inconceivable $2 million in sales.

FERKAUF pulled a low-margin, low-service, high-turnover, down-and-dirty discount model out of the shadows and onto the cover of *Fortune* magazine. Many others were to follow. Upstarts such as Two Guys, G.E.M. G.E.X., Zayre, Spartan, FedMart, and Bargain City built sprawling 70,000- to 200,000-square-foot discount stores in New York, Philadelphia, Detroit, and Chicago, and in medium-sized cities such as Canton, Mississippi, and Yakima, Washington. Like Ferkauf many of these operators leased their land and buildings. This freed up capital and made it easy to pick up and move when and where the shoppers did. These stores were free agents without loyalty to any particular community, and they held no loyalty to any particular supplier. Price was the determining factor in most of their transactions. Massive amounts of merchandise moved through the system. For the first time in history observers enthused; the United States had matched mass manufacture with mass distribution: Retailers could sell stuff as fast as manufacturers could make it. When his chain caught Professor McNair's attention in 1962, Ferkauf's operations boasted $240 million annually in sales. The immigrant's boy from Brooklyn was worth $50 million.

Not to be outdone, well-established companies such as Grand Union, Allied Stores, and S. S. Kresge either acquired or created their own discount chains. (Kresge's bargain division was, of course, Kmart.) Dayton Hudson opened Target stores, and J. C. Penney christened its Treasure Island stores. In its 1961 annual report, Woolworth Company, then the country's seventh largest retailer, described the "consumer willingness to dispense with certain services in exchange for cash saving and the shopping for all manner of goods under a single roof, with self-selection and checkout counters." Responding to this trend, the company announced the opening the following year of Woolco Department Stores, a low-margin, self-service, mass-merchandising chain geared mostly to the suburban trade. In its report, Woolworth outlined some of the major elements then emerging as the discounting standard: an oversized freestanding store with acres of free parking and the promise of one-stop shopping for a wide selection of merchandise at the lowest possible price. Typically the décor was Spartan; cement wall exteriors encasing cavernous warehouse-like spaces with exposed metal roof beams striped with fluorescent light fixtures and pipe rack shelving piled wide with merchandise. Dignity was not a priority. Loudspeakers barked intermittently to announce fifteen-minute specials (in the case of Kmart, "blue light specials" signaled revolving police-style lighting fixtures) sending impulse buyers from one end of the store to another in a Pavlovian stampede. Labor-intensive customer service was replaced by customer *self* service, not all of it felicitous.

In traditional department stores, electronic cash registers were thoughtfully positioned department by department to expedite the checkout process for customers. Clerks, many of them quite experienced and knowledgeable, worked with "clients" to help them find precisely what they wanted in the right color, size, and style. The sales staff then held the purchases until the customer's shopping was complete, packaged everything carefully for transport home, and rang up the sale. Sometimes the loot was actually carried to the customer's car. (Letitia Baldrige, White House social secretary and chief of staff to Jackie Kennedy, offered in the pages of the *New York Times* a quaintly nostalgic if somewhat frightening look back at how department store sales staff once treated their clients. "The salespeople never forgot you. They made little notes on you, your family and where you were in life each time you stopped to buy or to custom order their merchandise. It was such a safe, predictable world. It was also intensely personal—everything directed at you and no one else.")

At discount chains, customers paid with their time. Sales assistants were sometimes ignorant or absent. Cash registers were clumped at the exits, supermarket style, and in some cases customers were herded through a labyrinth of roped-off "squeeze shoots," like so many cattle. Purchases were not wrapped and certainly not carried to the customer's car. Still, many consumers—particularly younger ones—preferred this. They had confidence in their ability to make their own purchasing decisions, a confidence boosted by advertising. They knew—or thought they knew—what they wanted and enjoyed foraging on their own without having to cope with a hovering sales staff.

THE BEAUTY PART was this: By cutting back on customer service and most other frills, discounters not only saved money but created the impression that their merchandise was cheap due not to low quality but to low overhead. This was partially true. Discount stores had the advantage of being relatively inexpensive to run and certainly less expensive to build and operate than other stores. In the 1960s construction costs of discount stores ran $5 to $10 a square foot compared with $14 to $18 a square foot for standard department stores. Payroll at the stores was tightly controlled, with wages and benefits set at just 6 to 7 percent of sales compared with about 18 percent at traditional stores. And thanks to their size and reach, discount chains were in a powerful position to bargain with wholesalers, and they used that power to strong-arm ever lower wholesale prices. Long before Wal-Mart was born, suppliers were being continually pressured to wring out every drop of cost from their products before they reached the store floor.

WHETHER ALL or even most of these savings trickled down to consumers in the form of good deals was a matter of heated debate. Discounters boasted of prices that were 30 percent or more below department store prices, and to the customer on the store floor this appeared to be a valid claim. But competing merchants argued that this was a specious comparison since discounters stocked lots of off-brand and store-brand merchandise, the actual price of which was anyone's guess. And discounters carried only 40 to 50 percent of the assortment carried by the full-service department stores. Consider shirts, for example. Macy's boasted 129 different men's styles, priced from $1.99 to $14.09. Korvette, by contrast, stocked only 35 styles of men's shirts, priced from $1.49 to $6.99. While it was difficult to pin down precise numbers, Korvette's "bargain" prices were at least in part a reflection of its relatively paltry selection. Neither the $1.99 shirt from Macy's nor the $1.49 shirt from Korvette was likely to be of the highest quality, and it was impossible to know which of the two offered the best value. But Macy's customers had the opportunity to compare a $1.99 shirt with a $14.09 shirt, while Korvette shoppers were limited to the low end of the category. For Korvette this had the advantage of shielding customers from top-of-the-line goods that by comparison may have made their largely low-end lines appear shabby. For Korvette customers to make truly informed buying decisions was nearly impossible.

The discount store of the 1960s adapted many principles from the classic supermarket model, most notably the self-service ideal. Charles Saunders, who opened the first fully self-service grocery in 1916 in Memphis, showed how costs could be dramatically lowered by eliminating butchers, bakers, and experienced clerks. Stock workers simply piled the shelves and refrigerator cases with factory-packaged goods, and customers helped themselves. Shopping carts, also adapted from supermarkets, were a discount store staple and a surprisingly effective one. Sylvan Goldman, owner of the Humpty Dumpty supermarket chain in Oklahoma City, introduced the carts in 1937 to ward off the problem of shoppers retreating to the checkout line when their arms were too tired from carrying handheld baskets. His original design involved a metal folding chair rigged out with wheels, but the device tended to collapse whenever it snagged as much as a misplaced hairpin. Goldman successfully stiffened the design and touted his invention as the "no basket carrying plan." Customers were not impressed; men found the carts effeminate, and women found them insulting. As one female customer complained, "I've pushed my last baby buggy." A keen student of the "monkey see, monkey do" school of human nature, Goldman hired burly men and attractive women to pose as customers and dutifully roll shopping carts up and down the aisles of his stores. The ruse worked: Customer reluctance faded, and later that year Goldman founded the Folding Basket Carrier Corporation. Soon shopping carts were commonplace, although not in department stores where they were considered undignified, and impractical because they tended to get stalled on escalators and took up too much space in elevators. But discount stores, with their stripped-down ambience, sprawling single-floor layout, and acres of parking, were perfectly suited to shopping carts and adopted them with relish. The impact of the carts was immediate and profound: Analysts estimate that shoppers buy on average one more item per visit when they have a shopping cart to put it in. Today few discount stores operate without them.

The supermarket model of self-service was not new in 1960. What was new was how rapidly the discount format proliferated and dominated the general merchandise sector. Almost overnight discounters reversed the venerable retailing practice of offering customers precisely what they wanted. Rather, discounters offered customers what was available at the lowest possible price and positioned these goods in such a way—both physically and psychologically—as to convince customers they were getting the very best deal. The focus switched from the object to the deal: If the deal was good, the object under consideration became less critical to the transaction. Nearly half a century earlier, Frank W. Woolworth had set the stage for this parlor trick when he scoured the globe for almost anything cheap: hair ribbons, buttons, and poorly made wood-backed thermometers. Fifty years later the country had changed dramatically. Far fewer Americans lived on farms, and the great exodus from cities to suburbs was well under way. Advertising had transformed citizens into consumers, persuading them that wants were needs. But the discounting formula remained the same: Sell it cheap, buy it cheaper, and convince consumers that low price trumps all. A full-page 1960 advertisement placed by the long-defunct Des Moines Shoppers World Discount Department Store promotes its 36-inch dolls at $8.97, its transistor radios at $9.88, its bulky Orlon sweaters at $3.67, and 2-pound fruit cakes at 88 cents, but offers not a clue to the brand or provenance of these items. This motley assortment of merchandise seems almost flea market random, and it may well have been. The one constant is low price. As two business scholars of the time wrote, "Merchandising emphasis was predominantly on items that could be bought under exceptionally favorable circumstances, rather than upon planned assortments."

Planned assortments tailored toward the needs and desires of a particular clientele were a luxury that discounters could not afford. They could not have merchandise on the shelf that didn't turn over quickly, and they could not afford to buy small lots from wholesalers. Retailing theorists agree that 5 to 8 percent of items in any given product line generate about 90 percent of sales. The remaining 92 to 95 percent of the items are essentially specialty goods, there for some customers but not for all. These specialty goods sell far less quickly, yet item for item they take up as much shelf space as fast sellers and also tie up capital for much longer periods of time. Slow sellers can languish, go stale, out of season, or out of style. Discount chains eliminated as many as possible of these slow performers and stocked what amounted to the lowest common denominator of products—essentially what most people sought or could be persuaded to buy most of the time. As one observer put it, "Instead of the traditional department store motto of 'Thick on the best, thin on the rest,' the discount operator says, 'Thick on the best, to hell with the rest.' "

What this means to customers even today is that a trip to a discount store often begins with high hopes, moves on to a frustrated search, and ends happily in a surprising number of unanticipated purchases. The paradoxical coupling of frustrated customers and expanded profit is perhaps unique to the discount model, but the logic behind it is not complex. While almost all customers require commodities such as soap, socks, and laundry detergent—making those things consistent sellers— most shoppers also require one or another of tens of thousands of other items that other shoppers do not need or want. Take sporting goods: Many people participate in sports but not necessarily any particular sport. So the market for sporting goods is fragmented; some people want softballs, others need fishing gear, while still others want ice skates or surfboards. Different sports enthusiasts prefer different brands. Stocking any one of these items, and certainly any particular brand of one of these items, is risky, because not everyone needs or wants it. Therefore, large discount department stores are far less likely to carry any particular brand of football or softball or tennis ball than they are to carry store brands, off brands, or the low end of a national brand line. But this lack of variety does not necessarily interfere with a discounter's sales volume. Customers tend not to window-shop their way through discount stores as they do in traditional department stores. They go to buy. If they can't find what they are looking for, they'll pick up what is available—if not tennis balls for themselves, then maybe a jump rope and football for their kids. And while they are at it, maybe some diapers, laundry detergent, and a couple of cans of motor oil.

HALF A CENTURY AGO when gas cost $4 a tankful, discount stores were seen through unjaded eyes as 65,000 to 120,000 square feet of possibility within a 50-cent Saturday morning drive. Discount customers liked not having to cope with a daunting array of high-end merchandise and stuck-up salesclerks. And there was comfort in the idea that shopping no longer required a wardrobe. Those who can remember the sixties may recall getting dressed up to go downtown; some older women even wore hats and gloves. Discount customers could—and did—wear anything they chose. On Friday night Dad could come straight from work, no matter his work clothes, and Mom could bring her toddlers dressed for bed in their feet pajamas. This working family could afford to buy more and with confidence because the choice—based on price—had already been made for them. Adding to these advantages was that the discount mall offered a glimmer of novelty, even a carnival atmosphere with maybe a balloon stand or a hot dog vendor. Sometimes there were raffles, and occasionally there were even bigger surprises: When Consumer Mart of America opened a 132,000-square-foot store in Phoenix, Arizona, it staged a personal appearance by sex goddess Jayne Mansfield. "The discount store's growth is not so much due to its prices," speculated an industrial designer of the time, "as to its fireworks." There was a grain of truth to this, but only a grain. Pyrotechnics might draw customers initially, but the low prices kept them coming.

The impact of the low-price juggernaut in the post-Sputnik era is difficult to overstate. Discounters shuffled the American demographic, abetting the further decline of already troubled city centers by luring still more customers to the suburbs and beyond. Department stores had for some time felt the pinch of urban flight, but many could at least rely on their suburban branches to sputter some revenue back into their city locations. Typically, these suburban stores were expensively constructed and carried merchandise priced at least as high as downtown stores.

Discounters undercut prices at both the urban and suburban locations, and choked off the money flow. And discounters were promiscuous, carrying anything that could be bought cheap and sold in large lots. Increasingly these things were made outside the country's borders.

Discounters leaped at every opportunity to buy from foreign suppliers, particularly in Asia. In 1965 the United States ran its first postwar trade deficit with Japan. The deficit was small, only $334 million, and largely traceable to the importation of cheap goods, primarily low-quality steel targeted at the bottom tier of the American steel market. The remaining imports were also on the low end of the quality spectrum: transistor radios, portable black-and-white televisions, fabrics, toys, clothing, and glass products—things that customers might trip over in those flea market collections at Shoppers World in Des Moines. While some domestic producers complained of unfair competition, there was no overriding concern that these imports posed a real and sustained threat to American business interests or job security. Rather, these flimsy, cheap imports were considered a validation of the widely held view that Japan was far behind the United States in manufacturing sophistication and business savvy. Labor unions were surprisingly sanguine. Confident of the superiority of American products, United Steelworkers Union president David McDonald actually approved of the importation of steel from Japan. Years earlier he had testified before Congress, saying, "If I had the slightest feeling that increased trade, particularly imports, would be injurious to the American working man, I wouldn't be supporting a policy of trade liberalization." McDonald could not imagine that Japanese imports might pose a threat to his constituency.

But even a tinny-sounding radio is a radio, after all, and American teenagers were happy to put up with static for the opportunity to enjoy the Beatles in private rather than huddle with their parents around a bulky American-made vacuum tube set. Gradually, America grew accustomed to the compromises embedded in low price and showed a growing willingness to trade cost for quality. This trend toward "value" (often a thinly disguised euphemism for cheap) gave discounters of the 1960s a substantial edge over traditional stores, where product quality and service were integral to the business model. And it gave low-wage manufacturers a huge edge over high-wage manufacturers unprepared to compete on price. But this was not—as it is often portrayed—a sudden titanic clash of first- and third-world manufacturers, with workers getting crushed in between. American corporations were by then deeply invested abroad and had factories scattered throughout the developing world and Europe. The line between American-made and other goods was already smudged. Essentially, many American firms were already multinational, and so-called Buy American appeals, some bordering on the jingoistic, were more often than not an attempt to blur this inescapable reality. Speaking at a meeting of the AFL-CIO in 1961, United Textile Workers Union President George Baldanzi worried about what this trend would mean to American workers. "When there are all these corporate interests . . . investing billions of dollars in the Common Market of Europe that are establishing plants that are more modern than our own today, unless we get some safeguard against wholesale importation into this country, there is no guarantee that in five years from now these same automated factories that are being built by American capital in many parts of the world that are using slave labor, that they will not curtail operations in this country and dump all the cheap goods right back here in the United States." Baldanzi's concern was well founded; five years later, in 1966, U.S-based corporations employed nearly one-third of their workforce overseas, many of them in low-wage industries that pumped out low-grade products—Orlon sweaters! eighty-eight-cent fruitcakes!—for the discount trade.

In 1962, *Fortune* magazine ran a four-part series entitled "The Distribution Upheaval," describing in some detail the growing dominance of the discount sector and its overwhelming and potentially disturbing influence on American life. More than three thousand discounters—both individual stores and chains—were in operation at the time, totaling 40 million square feet of floor space and with combined sales topping $6 billion, accounting for more than a third of all department store sales. The larger discounters were now competing not just with full-price department stores but with one another. Kmart, Wal-Mart, Zayre, and Target feverishly grew their assortment of merchandise and achieved unheard-of economies of scale, enhanced by "lean retailing" techniques that were soon to become a hallmark of the discount trade and, eventually, of most

American business. Successful merchants have always been known to tailor their offerings to their most loyal customers, but lean retailers refined and enlarged this concept, making all their stores consistently responsive across a diverse range of products. Such precision required a fluid adjustment of inventory to the ebb and flow of consumer demand. Since discount chains had little personal knowledge of their customer base, they relied heavily on technology—optical scanning devices and computers—to track products from factory to warehouse to distribution center to individual store and every stop along the way. Accomplishing this required a precision operation bordering on the militaristic. Typically on Sunday evenings, information was gathered from each store on desired products—ncluding size, style, model, and color—and reorders transmitted to the appropriate supplier. The supplier sent out the items the next day in containers tagged for scanning at the buyer's distribution center where it was unloaded and routed to a truck for delivery to the designated store. To maintain efficiencies across their supply chains, discounters required that suppliers tag their products at the factory or warehouse, thereby pulling manufacturers and wholesalers—some kicking and screaming—into the stark new computer age. This just-in-time model reduced the problem of languishing inventory. It also meant that manufacturers had to play by the retailers' rules, limiting their production to items that discounters could sell at low prices and in vast volumes. Options for both manufacturers and consumers narrowed: Manufacturers had much less discretion in what they could produce or how they could produce it, and consumers, although treated to what seemed like an ever-expanding variety of merchandise, were in fact being offered less variety and more variations on a theme.

THE AMERICAN clothing market reflected those changes then as it does today. Peter Doeringer, a professor of economics at Boston University and an expert on global textile and garment markets, said that the culture of mass consumption sharply influenced the variety and quality of goods. "Ninety percent of Americans buy clothing from a limited array of mass marketers, and spend a smaller percentage of their income on clothing than consumers in most other developed countries," he said. "They tend to buy more clothes at lower prices. If your marketing strategy is low price, standardization is key." Which means, Doeringer said, that selection is narrowly limited to styles that can be produced quickly and easily. Technically, the quality of the clothing is high: Patterns match, the seams are tight, and there is little color variation from lot to lot. What is sacrificed is drape, feel, and design. "Mass manufacturers tend to stick with durable fabrics, simple patterns, and much less style," he said. "Advertisers created an image that people accepted: a less stylish image that leant itself to standardization. Consumers were actually marketed away from style and induced and seduced with low price."

America in the 1970s could not have been more receptive to the concept of swapping style, variety, and durability for price. "Stagflation," a bitter brew of unemployment and inflation coupled with an unnerving energy crisis, had eroded consumer confidence. Gas lines were long, tempers were short, and everyone was trying to save a buck. As labor unions lost traction, the Keynesian ideal of well-paid workers powering a thriving mass economy in which all could share and prosper began to falter. Late in the decade, President Jimmy Carter warned "too many of us now tend to worship self-indulgence and consumption" and that the "piling up of material goods" led to an "emptiness of lives which have no confidence or purpose." Carter found particularly noxious "a mistaken idea of freedom [as] the right to grasp for ourselves some advantage over others."

His warning came too late: For better or for worse, that "mistaken idea" had already taken hold. Gradually the consumer had become disassociated from the worker/citizen, as though those who consumed were an entirely separate species from those who worked or voted. Warehouse clubs, off-price retailers, and specialty discounters in electronics, toys, office supplies, and home improvement swelled the discounting ranks, while mass merchandisers such as Sears, Ames, The Limited, and the Gap began to operate on the discount model. In announcing its ambitious plans for Kmart to its stockholders, Kresge characterized discounting as "the fastest growing force in retail merchandising. . . . These self-service stores, eliminating most customer services . . . in economically constructed but functional buildings, have gained impressive public acceptance." By the decade's end, Kmart and the other "big three" discounters surpassed even supermarket chains in technological and organizational integration, and their approach was adopted by a growing number of retailers. The line between the discount industry and "full price" retailers had blurred long ago, with retailers of every stripe promising to sell at the lowest possible price. This led to still fiercer competition, a further lowering of prices, and a smackdown. Department stores in particular had difficulty surviving the onslaught of low-price competitors. Their inability to adapt to changing consumer tastes and the emergence of new retail channels that targeted specific market segments—the so-called category killers in hardware, toys, and furniture—deeply eroded their market share. While in the 1960s and 1970s most clothing was sold in full-service department stores, by 1990 such stores accounted for only 29 percent of sales. Many family-run operations were wiped out, and even giants such as Macy's, Gimbels, Saks Fifth Avenue, Federated, and, yes, the venerable Wanamakers filed for bankruptcy. Of the forty-two department store chains in operation in 1980, only twenty survived that decade. Advances in information technology, further consolidation in the retail sector, and the rise in global competition converged, shifting the power center still further away from the manufacturer and toward the merchant. Major discounters strove to squeeze out still more efficiencies by reorganizing their entire supply chain, from raw material to customer. Previously, planning inventory was guesswork. To avoid running short of desirable items and alienating customers, many merchants bought in large quantities and if sales were slower than expected, "pushed down" the goods by stepping up advertising and price cuts. Emerging information technologies removed some of the uncertainty by allowing retailers to track sales, monitor inventories across stores, and take deliveries from a centralized warehouse. One ingenious invention in particular, the bar code, was transforming.

Entire books have been devoted to extolling the rich technical history of the bar code and its myriad virtues. This will not be one of them, but it's tough to overstate the impact of this ingenious innovation. Bar codes were first popular with supermarkets, which had relatively few items to tag. (The first product branded with a Uniform Product Code [UPC] was a double pack of Wrigley's chewing gum in 1974.) Department stores, which had literally hundreds of thousands of different items (think colors and sizes in addition to brands), were understandably more circumspect about adopting the technology. But once Kmart adopted bar codes in the early 1980s, Wal-Mart and a number of other chains caught the fever, pressuring suppliers to tag all their products with the little black bars before delivering them to stores or warehouses.

Scanners made it possible to monitor customer preferences in "real time" so that discounters could quickly sort the slow-moving merchandise from the fast moving and fine-tune their orders. Less merchandise loitering in warehouses meant lower real estate costs, fewer handling costs, and higher inventory turnover, resulting in a smoother flow of capital. The widespread automation of discount retailers' distribution centers in the 1990s created an environment in which all but the smallest retailers were forced to update their supply chain technology to remain even remotely competitive. Wal-Mart grew famous for its technological wizardry, and for this it was richly rewarded: In 1992, three decades after Sam Walton opened his first store, the chain became the nation's largest private employer and the largest retailer in the world with $191 billion in revenue.

American productivity—the level of output per hour worked—grew from 1996 to 2000 at nearly double the rate of the previous two decades. Productivity growth in the retail sector grew even faster. Several factors contributed to this: the almost universal adoption of computers and related information technology, a better educated and trained workforce, a high demand for goods, and the fierce battle for primacy by competitors here and abroad. Through all this Wal-Mart surpassed all takers by focusing relentlessly on a single core value: low price. It undercut local competition by making notoriously shrewd deals with suppliers and empowering local managers to react instantly to price fluctuations in their markets. This unflinching focus on low price gave the chain an edge with which no small dealer could compete and that even competing discount chains—Kmart in particular—found daunting.

Discount chains not only put untold numbers of small retailers out of business, they reshaped the American demographic. Since retail traditionally had one of the lowest median rates of pay, the expansion of discount retailers that paid even lower wages contributed to a spurt in poorly paid jobs. Discounters tended to flatten the employment hierarchy that once characterized full-service department stores such as Macy's and Bloomingdale's, limiting access to the career track leading from stock clerk to salesperson to buyers and managers. At discount stores the term "career ladder" no longer applied as an ever-growing base of minimum- and low-paid workers supported a much smaller number of loftier posts. Workers did and do rise to management status at discount chains, but fewer workers and—outside of top management—at lower pay.

Harvard cultural historian Lizabeth Cohen has pointed out that mass-market consumption offers the *façade* of social equality without forcing society to go through the hard work of redistributing wealth. Low prices lead consumers to think they can get what they want without necessarily giving them what they want—or need. The ancient Roman phrase for this is *panem et circenses*, bread and circuses, the art of plying citizens with pleasures to distract them from pain. Today, low prices are the circus.

In the postwar boom years of 1947 to 1973, real median family income doubled, as did the value of what the typical worker produced. Fully one-third of Americans belonged to labor unions that secured jobs, benefits, and wages, and those who didn't benefited as well because non-union employers strove to keep workers happy to dissuade them from organizing. A middle-class family was usually supported by one earner, typically a skilled or semiskilled factory worker, clerk, or manager. Income distribution leveled thanks to a progressive tax structure—top earners paid a marginal 91 percent under Republican president Dwight D. Eisenhower, and 78 percent under Democrat John F. Kennedy—and a shuffling of the corporate hierarchy that raised the wages of low-level workers.

FROM THE 1970S through 2008, the national product tripled and Americans were treated to a vast array of nifty new gizmos: computers, cell phones, Hummers, hybrids, big-screen high-definition television, MP3 players, digital cameras. The list goes on and on. Prices for many of these and other goodies dropped, in some cases dramatically. Yet at the same time most of us felt as though we were losing ground, not gaining it. Here is why: All that productivity did not benefit *us*. The medium family income had been flat for years, and the youngest earners in particular were hurting. It is well known that even before the crash of 2008, Americans born in the 1990s were in danger of becoming the first generation in history to do less well than their parents, and that families of workers born in the 1980s were already in a bind. Except for women with college degrees, the earnings of workers age twenty-five to thirty-four were lower then than they had been a generation previous. Young men without a college degree had lost the most with an almost incredible real-income decline of 29 percent since 1975. Meanwhile, the rich got richer and the super rich got richer still: Eighty percent of net income gains went to the top 1 percent of earners, boosting their share of total income to levels not seen since the Great Depression. It's an old, familiar story and one that left the vast majority of Americans holding the bag—and holding the door for the uberwealthy. In this "new gilded age," CEOs earned on average eight times as much per dollar of corporate profits as they did in the 1980s. To cite one not entirely random example, before retiring in February, 2009, Wal-Mart CEO Lee Scott Jr. took home in his biweekly paycheck what his average employee earned in a lifetime. The Wal-Mart board of directors was confidant Lee was worth every penny. Some economists agreed, arguing that the low prices at Wal-Mart and other discounters benefited poor and low-income consumers. A Wal-Mart–commissioned study by independent think tank Global Insight pronounced that Wal-Mart saved American families $2,500 a year in 2006, a figure widely reported by the news media and touted by the company. There were quibbles that the report was built on faulty statistics and self-interested analysis, but there was no question that it had a profound impact on public perceptions of the company, which in 2007 changed its slogan from "Always low prices" to "Save money. Live better."

The waning years of the last millennium brought profligate spending in a time of reduced means. There were more tempting outlets for disposable income than ever before, and more payment schemes and forms of credit with which to buy them. President George W. Bush's stirring call to spend after the fall of the Twin Towers in New York City on 9/11 seemed surreal to those Americans who recalled President Carter's 1979 "sweater speech," in which he donned a cardigan and asked Americans to turn down their thermostats to conserve energy for the sake of national prosperity and security. National leaders cranked up mass consumption through tax cuts and other spending stimulants, while taunting countries such as Japan where the culture promoted saving over spending. With the real price of many consumer goods only half of what they were a century ago, Americans worried less about accumulating debt than about the lost opportunity of not buying. Obsessed with "getting ours," we sometimes failed to notice or acknowledge the real price we paid for all those marvelous bargains.

In a carefully constructed consideration of Wal-Mart's impact on the retail sector, Arindrajit Dube and his colleagues at the Institute for Research on Labor and Employment at the University of California at Berkeley focused on 1992 to 2000, the years when the chain expanded outside the South and into major metropolitan areas across the nation, growing from 1,800 to 2,500 stores. By the end of the 1990s more than half the counties in the country had at least one Wal-Mart, with three-quarters of the newly built stores located in urban counties. Dube found that the opening of a Wal-Mart store lowered wages and benefits in the surrounding region by up to 1 percent, with grocery store workers losing about 1.5 percent of their income. At a national level, the study found that thanks to Wal-Mart the total earnings of retail workers declined by $4.5 billion, with most of these losses concentrated in metropolitan areas. Dube acknowledged that Wal-Mart made low-priced goods available to these workers and to their neighbors, but pointed out that since wage and benefit savings are not the main part of the cost advantage for the company it could (conceivably) "continue to pass on most of these savings while paying higher wages and benefits."

Lee Scott did not agree. Wal-Mart, the nation's largest employer with 1.8 million employees worldwide, is not in the business, he said, of providing secure jobs on which to build a life or necessarily a career. "Some well-meaning critics believe that Wal-Mart stores today, because of our size, should, in fact, play the role that it is believed General Motors played after World War II. And this is to establish this post–world war middle class that the country is so proud of. The facts are that retail does not perform that role in this economy."

That's a stark assessment and an honest one. Each year *Fortune* magazine ranks companies by size, profitability, and a number of other parameters. In 2008, Wal-Mart ranked number one in all but one of the relevant categories, including "high profit growth," "high revenue growth," and "high returns to investors." It did not rank number one or number two or at all under the category of "best company to work for." Wal-Mart may not be great to its employees, but it is great to its investors. In its announcement, *Fortune* explained how the company triumphed during a period of economic difficulties and looming recession: "A face lift and even lower prices kept the world's largest retailer afloat in a troubled economy. Staring down the barrel of brutal fourth-quarter retail forecasts, CEO Lee Scott dramatically cut prices on 15,000 items—including popular toys and electronics—by 20% more than usual to lure holiday shoppers. That rocked the industry, pressuring other retailers to squeeze already tight margins."

Wal-Mart and other large discounters aggregate the power of millions of individual buyers to gain leverage over their suppliers. This "consumer union," a consolidation of millions upon millions of shoppers, has largely substituted for the labor unions that once protected the nation's workers but in recent years has shrunk to less than 8 percent of the private-sector labor force. The larger the discounters grow and the larger this union of consumers grows, the greater their leverage and the tighter the squeeze. It is not Wal-Mart or Target but us, the consumers union, that is the force with which all these other forces and entities must reckon. The power to wring an extra 20 percent of cost out of bargain basement goods is what makes mega-discounters such as Wal-Mart so appealing to consumers. The leverage to do so while maintaining record profits is what makes discounters so appealing to investors.

Technology, globalization, and deregulation have made competition a death march. Many companies have had no choice but to reduce costs almost continuously. Since payrolls are the single largest expense of most businesses, jobs, benefits, and wages are the obvious places to cut. This means fewer jobs and even fewer secure, well-paying jobs with benefits, the sort of jobs that Americans once built their lives on and now seem to believe the country can no longer sustain. And there are other places to cut as well: quality, safety, environmental responsibility, and human dignity. As citizens we recognize this "collateral damage," deplore it, and frequently decry it. But as consumers we habitually downplay and ignore it. We rail against exploitation of low-paid workers in Asia as we drive twenty minutes to the Big Box to save three bucks on tube socks and a dollar on underpants. We fume over the mistreatment of animals by agribusiness but freak out at an uptick in food prices. We lecture our kids on social responsibility and then buy them toys assembled by destitute child workers on some far flung foreign shore. Maintaining cognitive dissonance is one way to navigate a world of contradictions, and on an individual basis there's much to be said for this. But somehow the Age of Cheap has raised cognitive dissonance to a societal norm.

On May 1, 2008, the *New York Times* ran a cover story in its Styles section headlined "Is This the World's Cheapest Dress?: How Steve & Barry's Became a $1 Billion Company Selling Celebrity Style for $8.98." Reporter Eric Wilson reveals the secret of the store's success with a quote from co-owner Steve Shore: "'To be great, you have to have these ridiculous, insane prices, and not sacrifice quality,' [Steve] 'The question we constantly ask ourselves is how to hit the price point that even Wal-Mart is not hitting.'" How, indeed? Shore and his co-owner Barry Prevor claim to have kept prices low by flying economy class, staying in cheap hotels, maintaining a rundown office in New York City, hiring mostly twenty somethings, and cutting out the middleman. Careful consumers know this begs the question. We know that $8.98 will barely cover the cost of two large cappuccinos at Starbucks. How then can it be the purchase price of a fully formed dress? Interestingly, this question was anticipated. As Wilson reported, "Though the prices will raise concerns that the clothes are made in sweatshop factories that underpay or otherwise exploit workers, Mr. Shore and Mr. Prevor said absolutely not."

How is it possible that without exploitation, criminality, or deception, a $8.98 dress could be designed, sewn from real cloth in India or China, packed in a shipping container, shipped thousands of miles, unloaded into a truck powered by diesel fuel, driven smack across the country, unpacked by human hands, hung on a hanger, and displayed for at least a day or two on a Manhattan shop floor? The answer to this question is that it is not possible or, for that matter, sustainable. Shore and Prevor kept their operation afloat by locating stores in struggling malls and charging them an up-front fee for the favor of attracting foot traffic. Since these mall fees were essential to its survival, the company was required to expand continuously. In a sense, the company relied for its existence on a fully legal variation of a Ponzi scheme. Business plans like this are not built on a foundation of frugality. They are built on a platform of cognitive dissonance. Three months after boasting of their great success to the *New York Times*, Steve and Barry filed for bankruptcy.

THRIFT MAY BE a bedrock American virtue, but it is no more branded into our DNA than it is branded into the DNA of any other culture. Benjamin Franklin, whose most famous homily translates roughly into "A penny saved is a penny earned," confessed that thrift would elude even him were it not for Deborah, his frugal and hardworking wife. In a letter to a friend he wrote that "frugality is an enriching virtue, a virtue I could never acquire in myself." Thrift connotes some level of sacrifice and self-discipline, of patiently weighing one's options and forgoing the immediate for deeper satisfactions. A thrifty person digs in for the long haul. But in the era of cheap, the long haul is hard to see, let alone plan for. The view of thrift has been obstructed for some time now. Writing in 1938, William L. Nunn, chairman of the Newark Labor Relations Board, observed that as Americans moved from farm to crowded urban centers, the place of thrift in society shifted, too.

> *Such persons are exposed to types of economic and social insecurity considerably different from those prevailing in an agricultural economy, and therefore make different demands on the thrift notion. For example, they have shown themselves without too much sales resistance, and as such are peculiarly susceptible to all gadgets and commodities—both good and bad—with which the enterprising producer attempts to appease their insatiable appetites. . . . In the urbanization of America, the successful application of the simple Puritan virtues of*

*individual frugality and thrift has been lost or sidetracked, to a certain extent,*
*in the bewildering maze of urban streets and city blocks.*

A thrifty person does not drive miles to save three bucks on tube socks. A cheap person might. Every schoolchild knows that cheap thrills are not thrilling, and cheap talk not worth listening to. In books and theater and movies, the cheapskate is either the bad guy or a figure of fun. Yet we are all drawn to Cheap. Cheap is about scratching the itch, about making real the impossible dream of having one's cake and eating it, too. While it goes too far to suggest that Americans are addicted to Cheap, it is certainly a national preoccupation and a priority. We demand and expect it, and miss it terribly when, as with rising gas and food prices, it lets us down. At the same time we revile it.

What to make of this seeming paradox, this dysfunctional relationship we have with low prices? There is no easy answer. America's pursuit of and dependence on Cheap goes beyond public policy to something far more fundamental. It is etched deeply into the national psyche but also into each of us, part of who we are not only as a culture but as individuals. The psychology of Cheap is both fascinating and frightening. And it all begins with price.

## CHAPTER THREE

# WINNER TAKE NOTHING

What happens is fact, not truth. Truth is what we think
about what happens.

> ROBERT MCKEE, *STORY: SUBSTANCE, STRUCTURE,*
> *STYLE AND THE PRINCIPLES OF SCREENWRITING*

The Behavioral Pricing Conference at Fordham University did not fulfill
the glamorous promise of its Lincoln Center address. Passing through the
security gate and into the dingy lobby only deepened the gloomy prospect of spending two sparkling autumn days cooped up in a darkened
lecture hall with a pack of pricing geeks. Still, my fellow attendees were
chipper and surprisingly colorful. Among them, two spike-haired economists jet-lagged from their long flight from Finland and clutching cans of
Red Bull settled in behind a puckish Turkish academic. That afternoon
the Turk told me sagely, "Unlike you Americans, Turks know the price
of everything."

Pricing theory respects no boundaries, and this conference, organized
each year by two Fordham University marketing professors, brings together the top experts from around the globe. It is a tightly knit group,
which makes for some startlingly frank conversations. Over coffee the first
morning a marketing professor boasts of his consulting gig with McDonald's, where he is reconfiguring the menu board to make it easier to
navigate. I find it hard to imagine how McDonald's could possibly make
its menu navigation any simpler—and mutter something about my daughters picking out a Kid's Meal from ten paces before they could read. Hear-
ing this, the marketing professor, an expert on pricing in the hospitality

industry, leaped to clarify. "Don't you see there is a long distance between the burger and the price on the menu?" he said, pulling out a pen to draw a diagram on a napkin streaked with muffin residue. "That great distance causes people to lose their place, and it takes them a long time—wasted time—to find it again. My idea is to bring the price and the item closer together so that customers see instantly that a burger costs this much, French fries that much. The savings in time add up to about eighty thousand dollars per restaurant per year."

So repositioning a list of digits on a menu board can really save a restaurant eighty grand a year. One might think there would be objection to this supposition, and there was: Drexel University marketing expert Rajneesh Suri said that the cost savings could be even higher. Suri's research shows that positioning prices on the left side of a menu rather than on the right allows people to access and process the price point more quickly. "The same price in different visual fields will be processed differently," he said. Apparently the left side of the brain is better equipped than the right to decode numbers and letters. Placing prices far to the left allows customers more opportunity to decode quickly, helping franchisers shave still more fractions of a second off each customer's purchasing decision and thereby greatly increasing efficiency and saving millions.

Corporations spend billions of dollars for such insights every year, but not all of them are golden. For example, other experts I spoke to had doubts about Suri's theory. Apparently the human eye scans so quickly that the difference in response time between right and left price placement is inconsequential. Yet the very fact that such exacting research is under way—and bankrolled by major corporations—is evidence that price, or more precisely the way in which consumers perceive price, is a central business obsession. History reveals it is a human obsession as well.

The medieval philosopher Saint Thomas Aquinas noted the irony that in God's eyes, living things are of greater worth than are inanimate objects, but in the marketplace we pay more for a slice of bread than for a mouse. There is a difference, Aquinas held, between "natural value" and "economic value." Natural value is based on inherent worth, while market value is based on supply and demand. Considerations of market worth dating back to the Romans affirmed quite sensibly that the "value of a thing was the price for which it could be sold." But Aquinas took a more nuanced view, observing that what people were willing to pay depended a good deal on what they were able to know. As illustration he told a story (borrowed from Cicero) of a merchant driving a wagon piled high with wheat into a town sunk deep in famine. The merchant knew that there were other wheat sellers behind him on the road and that the price of wheat would drop when they arrived. Is he morally obligated to tell the starving townsfolk that more wheat is on the way? Aquinas reluctantly concedes that he is not, writing that "disclosure or reduction in price would spell more abounding virtues, yet is not required by strict justice." Strict justice, then, allows sellers to keep buyers in the dark, and it is that darkness that makes it difficult—and sometimes even impossible—to ferret out value even today.

If, as pundits say, Americans are intimidated by numbers, prices are a notable exception. We encounter prices so often that we feel comfortable with them, but maybe we shouldn't. As Aquinas hinted, prices are devilishly slippery things, open to interpretation and manipulation. When I told Harvard Business School sociologist Gerald Zaltman that I was trying to pin down the meaning of price, he laughed. "There is nothing more subjective," he said. "Price is a convenient, necessary proxy for a lot of other things. But where does the meaning of price reside? What are the things that influence its meaning? By this I mean you get away from price as a "given" to price as an interpretation. Price in and of itself has no meaning at all. Price is so vexing because the meaning of price resides not on the sticker but in people's heads."

All prices come down to a number, of course, and numbers are absolute, or at least seem to be. But numbers carry meaning that goes beyond their numerical value. For instance, the numbers one, two, and three are used far more commonly than are all other numbers except when they happen to be the final digit of a price. Very few prices end in the numbers one, two, three, or, for that matter, seven or eight. How often have you bought an item priced at $4.32 or $100.07? Those prices seem odd and even suspicious. Generally, prices are rounded to make them easier for our number-phobic minds to grasp. In his seminal and lively *The Number Sense*, Stanislas Dehaene, a mathematician and cognitive scientist at the Institut National de la Santé et de la Recherche Médicale in Paris, explains why "sharp" prices—such as $96.08—might make us nervous: Numerals we call "round" can refer to an approximate quantity, while all other numerals have a precise meaning. It is simply not credible to price every item to the penny. How could the seller possibly arrive at precisely $96.08? Why not 2 cents more or 8 cents less? We expect and prefer our prices rounded off because, thanks to a quirk of evolution that gave us five fingers on each hand and five toes on each foot, we tend to think in multiples of five and ten. The metric system is built on powers of ten, as is our monetary system. This system, Dehaene writes, "fits our number sense because it approaches an exponential series while comprising only small, round numbers."

Children learn to count automatically by five and ten almost as soon as they learn to count. (Counting by four or seven or eight seems far more difficult. Even most adults find it challenging.) Roman numerals clump by five and ten. We prefer multiples of five—twenty-five, fifty, and seventy-five—to other multiples. This seems to be a universal quality, for according to Dehaene, "All the languages of the world have selected a set of round numbers." Hence, setting prices to this predilection is only natural—what Robert Schindler, a professor of marketing at Rutgers School of Business, calls the "pull of the salient."

Schindler was the keynote speaker at the Fordham University pricing conference. Slightly built and tonsorially challenged, Schindler has the bland, distracted look of a backroom accountant. But he is a rock star in this circle, and his presentation, provocatively titled "What Prices Reveal About the Mind," brought down the house. Price promotions, Schindler began, are designed to evoke excitement by mimicking play and bringing out the customer's inner child. For example, "nine for the price of ten" loyalty cards at Starbucks and other retail emporia seduce customers to buy more just to "score" free product. Buying more overpriced coffee than you need or want makes no rational sense, of course, but that's the point. "We buy with our emotions, but that only describes the behavior; it doesn't explain it," Schindler told me. "We don't know the first thing about our emotions; in fact, we're in darkest Africa when it comes to understanding our emotions. What we do know—and what's amazing—is how effective price has become at raising emotions and recruiting our mental energy. We pay attention to prices in a way we attend to nothing else. Price points have magical properties."

Schindler bases this view on theory, and also on experience. Price is not only his job, it is his obsession. He is fascinated by people who classify themselves as "deal prone"; that is, who actively seek out and enjoy good deals. We may all believe we fit this category, but for psychologists like Schindler it is a matter of degree. He recalls speaking with a middle-aged woman who insisted that he take a look at the bargains she had accumulated in her living room. "She showed me this frayed and sagging sofa from 1986 or 1987," Schindler said. "She bought it on sale and was still getting pleasure from it because buying it, owning it, validated her. Being a smart shopper, getting a good deal was central to her self-esteem. This may not have been logical and may not have made sense to someone else, but it was very real for her."

Pricing doesn't defy reason, but sometimes it does skirt around it. For example, beginning in 1880 or so the magical number nine started creeping into prices. Before then most numbers were round, but the nine seemed to get customers' attention. Since then, nine has become the most common number found on a price tag and is especially popular when pitching low-price appeal. "This is a worldwide phenomenon," Schindler said—except in Japan where the more auspicious number is eight. Nines are especially potent, of course, when they make the left-most digit on a price tag drop down a notch—$30.00 to $29.99, say, or $200.00 to $199.99. Even though we all "know" this trick, that $9.99 is essentially $10.00, not $9.00, the penny reduction lures by conveying the "cheaper" message subliminally. And, sorry to say, we are fooled every time. "There is a processing system within the brain that is not so smart," Schindler explained, "a primitive mentality intuited by Freud and now being detected by scientists."

Nearly a century ago, long before the development of scanning technologies, Freud postulated a two-stage processing system in the brain: the primary process and the secondary process. The primary process is impulsive and childlike, the devil on your shoulder. The secondary is more cautious, the "angel" on your other shoulder. As Freud's daughter, psychoanalyst Anna Freud, later elaborated, "When the primary process prevails, there is no synthesis of ideas, affects are liable to displacement, opposites are not mutually exclusive and may even coincide, and condensation occurs as a matter of course." The primary process is the primitive, unconscious element of the mind; it doesn't fret about the past or speculate about the future. Like a small child, the primary process can't see beyond the "now." The more staid secondary process can conceptualize both the past and the future, and ittests reality by applying rules of logic and evidence. It is the patient, sensible, grown-up part of the brain. The primary process leads you to grab the last piece of cake on the plate, the secondary process forces you to weigh that action, to consider how much you've already eaten and how many other people are vying for the slice. The primary system appears early in life and peaks at about age seven, when the secondary process kicks in. Freud contended that these two states coexisted, that the primary process remains active throughout life in the unconscious and even the conscious mind, sneaking out especially during times of stress or conflict. Recent experiments indicate that the primary process can be evoked even by minor distractions.

When setting discounts, marketers aim to activate the primary process in the brain, the emotional, impulsive side. In technical terms, their goal is to "spike the affective response to block the cognitive assessment." In layperson's terms, their goal is to distract customers from thinking hard about a purchase or, for that matter, thinking hard about anything at all. None of us—no matter how rational—is totally immune to this strategy. "The nine price ending thing is small, but it is real, and it serves as an illustration of a larger point," Schindler told me. "Illusions guide our buying behavior."

FOR SOME TIME illusions also guided economists who predicted buying behavior. Chief among these illusions was that we humans always act in our own best interest. This fantasy, although losing currency in recent years, had prevailed in one form or another in American political and economic thought for over a century.

It was not always that way. Like psychology, economics was once a branch of "moral science," concerned with the mind but also the heart. Adam Smith, the crusty Scottish philosopher generally credited as the founder of modern economics, began his *Moral Sentiments*: "How selfish soever man may be supposed, there are evidently some principles in his nature which interest him in the fortune of others and render their happiness necessary to him, though he derives nothing from it except the pleasure of seeing it. . . . The greatest ruffian, the most hardened violator of the laws of society, is not altogether without it."

Smith and his followers were moral philosophers who regarded emotions as key to human decision making. But twentieth-century economists increasingly positioned themselves not as philosophers but as "hard scientists" who focused on the quantifiable and the absolute. They wanted nothing to do with psychology, which they considered a "soft science" and therefore subjective. In order to depict economic decisions mathematically, this "neoclassical school" discarded ephemeral variables such as guilt, fairness, justice, and regret, and made the hard-nosed assumption that human behavior was always built on a certain self-serving logic. They created as their model an economically "perfect" being called *Homo economicus*, a purely hypothetical creature who knows what he wants and strives to get it unperturbed by emotion and driven almost entirely by calculating self-interest. Homo economicus was considered a stand-in for Homo sapiens, who economists by definition were pressed to assume in their modeling to be purely rational, self-interested beings striving methodically to get as much for themselves as possible. This reasoning led to the theory of "utility maximization," the idea that when normal humans do something—no matter how weird or stupid it seems—it is rational because they wouldn't have done it if it did not maximize their personal gain.

This theory has significant predictive power: Humans do strive much of the time to maximize personal gain. But it also has its limits. Saying consumers act in a certain way because they believe it will benefit them restates the circumstance rather than explaining it, a tautology that simply does not hold up under scrutiny or in real life. It doesn't explain why people wait in line for half an hour at the gas station to save 4 cents a gallon on gasoline or why they drive 5 miles out of their way to use a 50-cent coupon to buy a carton of eggs. It doesn't explain why people decline to pay more than $200 for a ticket to a football game and yet refuse to sell that same ticket for $300. (If they won't pay more than $200 for the ticket, then $300 should in theory be *worth* more to them than the ticket.) In fact, utility maximization doesn't explain many ways in which real people relate to money.

In their seminal "Prospect Theory: An Analysis of Decision Under Risk," published in the journal *Econometrica* in 1979, Israel-born psychologists Daniel Kahneman and Amos Tversky challenged the homo economicus orthodoxy. They argued that human decision making is less a matter of weighing evidence and calculating probabilities than it is of reconciling new information with old familiar patterns branded into the brain from as early as birth. These patterns of mind, or what psychologists call "heuristics," allow us to make judgments quickly. Much like Freud's primary system, they require very little if any conscious thought, and that is as it should be. Our brains were forged in the crucible of evolution, when a slow reaction time could be fatal. Confronted with a scowling enemy or a growling beast, those who hesitated were almost certainly lost. But in the modern world these cognitive shortcuts sometimes lead us astray. When it comes to money, focusing too hard on scowls and growls can cause us to act in a way that seems irrational and can ultimately harm rather than help us.

As illustration of this, Kahneman and Tversky evoked the universal phenomenon of loss aversion, the tendency of most people to strongly prefer avoiding losses rather than acquiring gains. At first blush this sounds counterintuitive. Doesn't everyone want to win? The answer, of course, is yes, but not as much as we don't want to lose. If you don't play, you can't win, but you also can't lose. And that's the reason so many of us decline to play when we should. Not playing results in lost opportunities, but scientists have shown that humans are not wired to spontaneously factor in missed opportunities, particularly when those opportunities are projected far into the future. We are wired, however, to worry a good deal about losing. And when it comes to feelings of loss, it is not necessarily the actual loss but the perception of loss that keeps us from acting in what would seem to be a rational manner.

Loss aversion is what spurs a scorned lover to cling to a bad relationship, an unhappy worker to cling to a bad job, and unhappy stockholders to cling to a plummeting stock rather than sell the loser and invest the proceeds in something more promising. In the latter case, the only logical reason to hold a stock is that you believe it is likely to grow in value. But because of our reluctance to admit mistakes and to cleave to what we already own, many of us prefer to avoid facing that central issue. This allows us to persist in the illusion that buying the stock in the first place was the right decision rather than an unfortunate and costly error. Following the thread of this distorted "logic" we convince ourselves that holding on to the stock is reasonable, because if we were right to buy it in the first place, we are right to hold on to it now. This is not the sort of thinking *Homo economicus* would engage in, but it is the sort of thinking real people engage in all the time—including those "brilliant" dot-com paper millionaires who were reduced to paper pauperhood when their star took a tumble.

We humans place an inordinate value on our own experiences and are highly influenced by context or what psychologists call "priming." Sometimes this is fairly obvious and understandable. For example, we are more likely to worry about getting killed in a car accident if we have recently witnessed a fatal crash. But some priming influences are so indirect as to seem outlandish. Kahneman cited one experiment in which students were asked to estimate the distance on a map between themselves and various cities. The smaller the typeface on the map, the larger the distance estimated by the students. There is a twisted logic to this: The smaller font made the cities appear to be farther away. But it is not a logic that makes sense in the real world. Experiments like this underline the critical role that subjective variables play in cognition, especially when people are pressed to make decisions based on imperfect information. And in economics, information is rarely perfect.

In 2002, Kahneman was awarded a Nobel Prize (tragically, Tversky died prematurely in 1996) for having "integrated insights from psychology into economics, thereby laying the foundation for a new field of research." Speaking at the annual meeting of the American Association for the Advancement of Science in February 2008, he explained the foundations of his insights. He said that as a rule humans tend to push aside difficult questions in favor of simpler questions that they can answer easily. This is why so many of us have such difficulty with investments. All of us want to regain our losses, naturally, but how to regain a loss is a very difficult question, far more difficult than simply hanging on to a particular stock. So rather than ask ourselves that question, we ask whether our current strategy is a good one. Of course this question does not address the larger and more important question of how best to make money, but how best to make money is a question we are reluctant to face, in particular when we are currently not making any. "If the question is difficult and an answer doesn't immediately come to mind, we ask ourselves a related question that is easy to answer," Kahneman said. "Generally speaking, the easy question is the wrong question."

Tversky and Kahneman may have made less practical sense of such psychological insights had they not teamed up with the promising young economist Richard Thaler. Today a professor of behavioral science and economics in the Graduate School of Business at the University of Chicago, Thaler was, when they met in the late 1970s, a newly minted visiting professor at the National Bureau of Economic Research at Stanford University. Tversky and Kahneman were fellows at the Stanford Institute of Advanced Studies in Behavioral Sciences, and Thaler translated their psychological research into a hardheaded consideration of consumer behavior. His article, "Toward a Positive Theory of Consumer Choice," published in 1980 in the *Journal of Economic Behavior and Organization,* is a guiding text in what was to become the field of behavioral economics. In it Thaler pointed out that economic theories based on a "rational maximizing model" describe how consumers *should* choose but not how they *do* choose. He argued that in certain well-defined situations many consumers act in a manner that is inconsistent with prevailing economic theory, concluding that "in these situations economic theory will make systematic errors in predicting behavior." Thaler proposed an alternative descriptive theory built on Kahneman and Tversky's work, making the case that price was not merely a number but a relationship between buyer and seller in which context is extremely important. In a series of influential papers he described a variety of apparently irrational behaviors that humans engage in when making financial transactions. A common theme in what Thaler called these "anomalies" was the resistance to deal rationally with ambiguity. Humans simply cannot cope with too many unknowns.

Consider the Ultimatum Game, first described by three German economists in 1982. The game is between two players who interact only once, so reciprocation—or "payback"—is not at stake. The first player is given a sum of money—for simplicity let's call it $10—and asked to divide it between himself and the other player. He can divvy it up any way he chooses, but if the second player rejects the division, neither player gets anything. If the second player accepts the deal, the first player takes his self-determined cut and the second player gets the rest. Both players know the rules: The first player knows that if he takes more than his share, the second player will either lose out or reject the offer outright; the second player knows that if he declines the first player's offer, neither player will get any money at all. If the second player were *Homo economicus*, he would accept any offer above zero dollars for the excellent reason that some money is better than no money. But Homo sapiens behave differently: Most players decline to take an offer below $3 and some refuse anything less than a fifty/fifty split. Why anyone would leave empty-handed rather than accept less than half the pot has very little to do with reason and very much to do with perceptions of fairness.

The inclination for people to play fair and demand fairness from others has baffled economists for decades. Many people when confronted with what they consider an unfair deal—even one that benefits them—prefer no deal at all. In this context, humans are not acting in their own best financial interest: They willingly sacrifice their own share to ensure that the other player does not get more.

Sarah Maxwell, an associate professor at Fordham University and codirector of the Fordham Pricing Center, is an expert on fair pricing. A fair price, she told me, is one that is "emotionally okay" with the person doing the buying. This is hardly a precise assessment, but it is an eminently sensible one. Scientists have contended for some time that emotions are critical to economic decision making, far more important than economists once thought. This is not mere speculation, it is provable fact. For example, patients with brain injuries that impair their emotions find it almost impossible to make economic decisions. University of Southern California neurologist Antonio Damasio refined this observation in a series of experiments that he described in his book *Descartes' Error: Emotion, Reason, and the Human Brain*. He outlines in fascinating detail how patients with prefrontal cortical damage can no longer generate the emotions necessary to make the simplest choices, such as the date and time of their next doctor's appointment. Damasio describes one particular patient as he pondered various possibilities, never settling on a course of action: "For the better part of a half hour, the patient enumerated reasons for and against each of the two dates: previous engagements, proximity to other engagements, possible meteorological conditions, virtually anything that one could reasonably think about concerning a simple date." This patient and others in the study showed no sign of intellectual or psychological impairment and could think perfectly rationally. But their inability to raise their own emotional temperature made it impossible for them to make a decision.

Damasio argued that both logic and emotion are required for decision making, and that systems that control these functions, while separate, communicate with one another to jointly affect our behavior. That said, the emotional system—the older of the two in evolutionary terms—typically exerts the first and more powerful force on our thinking and behavior. If we sense we are getting the short end of the stick, we balk, even if not grabbing the short end makes us tumble back into the lake.

SCIENTISTS AGREE that an aversion to inequity is innate and probably inescapable. This is true not only for humans but for other primates. At Emory University researchers trained female capuchin monkeys to trade a plastic token for a piece of cucumber. The monkeys appeared quite pleased with the deal until they spotted other monkeys in nearby cages getting the more favored grapes in exchange for their token. Seeing this, the monkeys grew furious and in a fit of rage began throwing their cucumber bits out of their cages. A cucumber may not be as good as a grape, but it is edible, so tossing out chunks of the stuff appears self defeating and irrational. This behavior is consistent with the way monkeys and humans deal with what we perceive to be unfairness. At least some monkeys prefer nothing to less than the next monkey. The Ultimatum Game suggests that the same is often true for humans.

Mathematician and evolutionary biologist Martin Nowak, now director of the Program for Evolutionary Dynamics at Harvard University, has studied the evolutionary underpinnings of fairness. Nowak designed a virtual version of the Ultimatum Game in which players who collected the most money were also the fastest to reproduce. (One of the central tenets of evolutionary theory is that the fitter one is, the more likely one is to pass on one's genes to the next generation.) Under this scenario, players who accepted any fraction of the total offered by the first player—even if it were far less than half—ultimately won more money, had more offspring, and were thereby "fitter" by natural selection standards. But when Nowak included one additional variable in his simulation—player reputation—everything changed. Under this new scenario, players could obtain information about an opponent's previous behavior and therefore know which players would accept amounts of less than half. This resulted in the first players offering less and less to the second players, who they now knew would take any offer above zero. When reputation was factored in, a player who accepted any amount had less money and fewer offspring. Under this more realistic "natural selection" scenario, then, the demand for and pursuit of fairness contributed to fitness. People who pursued and demanded fairness were more likely than others to pass down their genes to the next generation and therefore had an "evolutionary advantage."

Of course, evolutionary theory does not seem to explain why we sometimes subvert our own best economic interests, a thorny problem that has dogged economic psychologists for decades. Notable among those grappling with this mystery is behavioral economist Daniel Ariely, author of the best-selling *Predictably Irrational*. As a professor at Duke University as well as director of the e-rationality group at MIT's famous media laboratory, Ariely has a lofty vantage point from which to observe and analyze the perplexing vagaries of human economic behavior. Ariely is an intensely intelligent but lighthearted fellow, and among his favorite crowd warmers is a joke that, told in his charming Israeli accent, goes something like this: "Two economists are walking on the street. One of them is noticing a hundred-dollar bill. He says, 'Hey, look, a hundred-dollar bill!' The other guy says, 'That can't be. If it was a real hundred-dollar bill, somebody else would have picked it up already.' "

Ariely has said, "People have two masters: cognition and emotion." And the two don't talk to each other much." Ironically, Ariely said, this communication gap is at least partially the result of evolution or perhaps the lack thereof. The survival strategies of our ancient ancestors did not include learning the art of assigning monetary values to things. Before the onset of agriculture ten thousand years ago, commerce was likely a simple matter of trading one scarce resource, such as meat after a kill, for another, such as roots and berries to complement the meal. When we needed berries and had extra meat, or needed meat and had extra berries, we made the swap, plain and simple. But people don't barter much anymore. They deal with money, which we can neither eat nor wear. Monetary values are abstract, highly variable, and vulnerable to the power of suggestion and manipulation: People will pay more or less for the same thing depending on the context of the transaction. As example, Ariely described an experiment in which he offered to recite Walt Whitman's *Leaves of Grass* to a classroom full of students. Half the students were asked whether they would pay $2 for the pleasure of hearing him read the poem, while the other half were asked if they would be willing to listen if they were paid $2. Then both sets of students were asked whether they would attend the recitation if it were free.

Only 8 percent of the students who were offered money to listen to the recitation were willing to attend the performance without pay, compared with 35 percent of the students who were originally asked to pay to hear it. Clearly, the "framing" of the event—the context from which the proposal emerged—influenced its perceived value, a perception that trumped whatever inherent value it might have held for the students (unlikely to be much).

"Economics is a religion," Ariely said. "It assumes rational behavior and that people will do what is best for them. But like religion, this is only a belief; there is no proof." I did not ask Ariely about his own religious leanings, but there is little doubt that his faith has been brutally tested. Born in New York City, he moved to Israel with his family, where at age eighteen he enlisted in the army. His military service was cut short by an exploding magnesium flare that left him with third-degree burns over 70 percent of his body. He spent three years in a hospital bed and his first year of college wrapped head to toe in an elastic stocking designed to create pressure on his recovering tissue. There were holes for his eyes, ears, and mouth, and it was through this tormented vantage point that Ariely witnessed the world. Notable among his observations was that people made judgments based on emotions, not evidence. "I had a strong feeling that when others observed me, they not only saw my injury but were also making inferences that my appearance and my intelligence were highly correlated," he said. "It was very important to me to show my peers that this correlation did not exist."

Ariely was quite successful in that regard; in the United States he earned doctorates in both business and psychology. It is from this dual perspective that he came to study human behavior, a quest that has led from the banal to the bizarre. One of his more controversial experiments involved dressing up as a bartender to investigate the impact of peer pressure on customer selection and the enjoyment of beer. Another entailed asking thirty-five male college students a series of sexually charged questions as they masturbated. The purpose of the latter exercise, Ariely told me, was to show how sexual arousal can influence judgment, producing insight that could be used, for example, to encourage men to don condoms before becoming overly aroused. Studies of this sort make colleagues wonder whether Ariely is as much provocateur as scientist: That sexual arousal has the power to sway judgment is not exactly breaking news, but a professor who asks college students to masturbate most certainly is. No doubt Ariely's sometimes impish tactics serve a pulsing ambition, but this irreverence does nothing to diminish the significance of his work, which is focused on getting us to think much harder than we do now about what drives our financial decisions.

Shopping, Ariely said, is not a rational exercise but a process fraught with emotions ranging from guilt to jubilation. Shopping forces us to extrapolate future needs from current evidence, a surprisingly difficult task. How do we really know what we will want or need tomorrow, let alone a month from now? "The main problem is that shopping is for later, but for humans the here and now is always more important," he said. Thanks to what psychologists call "hyperbolic time discounting," humans are able to deal rationally when a reward is significantly delayed. But as the reward gets closer, our passions lead us to fits of impulsiveness. This is not a terribly deep insight: Everyone knows that it's easy to make resolutions for the future but far harder to put those resolutions into immediate practice. That's why so many of us pledge to stop overeating or smoking or gambling . . . next week. Still, hyperbolic time discounting can have far more subtle and surprising effects, especially when it comes to discounting.

"If I ask you whether you would prefer half a box of chocolates now or a full box in a week, you'll take the half box," Ariely said. "But if I ask you whether you'd prefer a half box of chocolates in a year or a full box in a year and a week, you'll take the full box." The difference in time—one week—is the same, whether next week or a week and a year from now. But the prospect of consuming something now versus later shades the calculation and the decision. Retailers can take advantage of this by offering "exploding discounts," price reductions rigged like an arbitrary time bomb. "Exploding discounts work by really heightening the emotions," Ariely said. "Whether you need it or not, whether you want it or not, the time limit itself gives you a reason to act now. The emotional response is 'Buy it now, or it will be gone.' The benefit of the buy is the discount itself; it's what makes you feel good, smart, savvy, right now. You are focusing on the present, not the future, and that's where they want you to focus, because we are all much more emotional about the present and more rational about the future."

Discounting plays many tricks on the human mind, and among the more intriguing is the influence of discounting on our relationship to the purchase itself. Although almost everyone seeks bargains, most of us make the tacit and often unconscious assumption that doing so involves a trade-off of quality for price: Regardless of what the tag or brand claims, we perceive things bought on sale or at a discount as less desirable or efficacious or durable than things for which we paid full price. The less we pay for something, the less we value it and the less likely we are to take care of it, with the result that cheaper things—even if well made—seem to wear out and break more quickly. For most of us the fact that we paid less than full price actually discounts in our minds the value of what we bought, and that impression, in turn, can have a profound impact on our expectations of the worth and power of the product.

In a series of elegant experiments, Ariely and colleague Baba Shiv, a professor at the Graduate School of Business at Stanford University, have demonstrated just how powerful these expectations can be. In one of these experiments, 125 college students were asked to drink SoBe Adrenaline Rush, an energy drink that claims to sharpen mental acuity. (Being college students, almost all the subjects were well acquainted with this product.) The cost of the drink was billed against their college accounts; half of the students were charged the full price of $1.89, the other half only 89 cents, thanks to what they were told was a bulk purchase price reduction. After drinking their pick-me-ups and watching a film on its benefits, the subjects were then asked to complete a series of word jumble puzzles. Students who drank what they were told was the full-price drink scored the same on the tests as did a control group that had no drink. But students who drank the discounted drinks performed poorly on the test; remarkably, drinking the discounted product actually impaired their performance. Hence, price not only had a significant impact on the perceived potency of the drink but even, it seemed, on the students' physiological response to it.

Ariely learned from his experience as a burn victim that expectations are powerful mediators of perception, and he says these expectations are easily manipulated by price. In one extraordinary experiment, he tested this theory on painkillers. He began the study by measuring pain thresholds in a large group of subjects; then he broke the subjects into two groups and offered one group a painkiller at full price and the other group the same painkiller at a 25 percent discount. The discounted pain-killers had a far less powerful effect on pain. "The cheap price seemed to reduce the secretion of opioids in the brain," Ariely said. "This is very worrying, because what does that tell us about the effectiveness of generic drugs? The only way to eliminate this effect is to remind people before they take the pill that the price should have no effect—but this, of course, is impossible for a doctor to do." Airely, who endured as a young man more pain than most of us could bear in a lifetime, said that generic painkillers may be no bargain.

THE IMPACT of price, then, goes far deeper than the pocketbook. How deep is growing increasingly clear as scientists use new tools to get be-neath what people say they think and into the brain structures that do that thinking. Chief among these is functional magnetic resonance imag-ing, or fMRI, which uses a powerful magnet and radio signals to monitor and map fleeting fluxuations in oxygen levels in the brain. It has been known for over a century that blood flows to certain areas of the brain when those areas are active. The more active the brain cell, the more oxygen it consumes and stores in hemoglobin, which is oxygenated with air from the lungs. Oxygenated and deoxygenated hemoglobin have dif-ferent magnetic properties, and by measuring these differences, the fMRI determines which part of the brain is involved in various modes of thought. Among the more interesting things fMRI has taught us is that what sometimes appears to be irrational behavior reflects an entirely predictable brain response.

Brian Knutson, a neuroscientist at Stanford University, is an expert on the neural basis of emotion. His focus is not on the "thinking" part of the brain but on the more primitive structures that operate just beneath our conscious control. Among these is the nucleus accumbens, a tiny organ buried deep behind the eyes. The nucleus accumbens plays a cen-tral role in the brain's reward pathways by regulating the ebb and flow of two well-known neurotransmitters: dopamine, which promotes desire, and serotonin, which promotes satiety and inhibition. The thrill of most pleasurable human experiences—getting high on psychoactive drugs or luxuriating in a great cigar—has at its core the nucleus accumbens. Within that nucleus the dopamine system motivates us to eat, drink, and have sex while we can. Evolution created the dopamine system for a very good reason: Given the short, brutish lives of our early human ancestors, delaying gratification raised the probability that there would be no gratification at all. When confronted with matters that were dangerous, edible, or sexual, primitive man knew instinctively that it was safer to act now and think later. Today, those of us more genetically inclined than others to react impulsively are likely to have particularly sensitive dopamine pathways: The more impulsive we are, the more we are driven to action by a danger or incentive—or perhaps more accurately, by the *prospect* of a danger or incentive.

Filmmaker Alfred Hitchcock once wryly observed that "there is no terror in the bang, only in the anticipation of it." Hitchcock was a maestro of suspense and built his masterpieces on the underlying presumption that pleasure and pain are most keenly felt in their expectation, not their execution. In a 1939 lecture he delivered at Columbia University, he explained how he used expectation to raise suspense: "We have a name in the studio, and we call it the 'MacGuffin.' It is the mechanical element that usually crops up in any story. In crook stories it is most always the necklace, and in spy stories it is most always the papers." The MacGuffin—the necklace and secret papers—were proxies; their pursuit provided the real drama.

Hitchcock was a fabulist, a maker of entertainments, but he was also prescient. Scientists now know that anticipation is an incredibly powerful driver of human behavior. Hard evidence of this surfaced not long ago when Knutson and other researchers used fMRI to map the brains of volunteers engaged in games of chance. For most subjects the *possibility* of winning or losing even $5 set off frantic activity in the brain, but *actually* winning or losing this amount had almost no effect. It was the anticipation of the payoff that excited: the moment the $5 was won or lost, the nucleus accumbens went quiet. As Hitchcock knew intuitively, the reflexive, primitive area of the brain responds more powerfully when confronted with what *may* happen than with what *does* happen.

The flip side of anticipation is dread, the sickening feeling when confronted with future dangers or disappointments. Parents sitting vigil in their bathrobe at 4 a.m. on a Saturday morning waiting for a tardy teenager to walk through the door know the psychic torture of dread. Scientists do, too. In one study, volunteers were put into an fMRI machine and given a series of electric shocks to the foot. The shocks varied in intensity from barely detectable to the pain of a needle jab. Prior to being shocked, subjects were told how strong the feeling would be and how long the wait for it would be, from one to twenty-seven seconds. Later, participants were given a series of choices: Would they prefer their medium jolt in five seconds or in twenty-seven seconds? What about a mild jolt in twenty seconds versus a sharp one in three seconds? Surprisingly, volunteers almost always chose to have the shock as quickly as possible, and a significant number—fully 28 percent—chose to endure a shock at the highest voltage in exchange for getting it over quickly.

This seems to make no rational sense. More pain is more pain, whether administered now or later. Why should dread even enter into this calculation? Scientists believe the answer is that dread of pain *is* a sort of pain. fMRI scans of the subjects showed activity in brain areas governing pain *before* the subjects were shocked. "Anticipation of pain seems to be a source of misery," Carnegie Mellon psychologist George Lowenstein wrote in an accompanying review of the study.

The brain's chemical response to the prospect of good and bad, called by Antonio Damasio and other neuroscientists the "beacon of incentive," is part of our evolutionary endowment, designed to motivate us to do whatever is necessary to stay alive and reproduce. In prehistoric times the actual taste of fruits and berries was not what got early man out of his cave and foraging. It was the anticipation of that taste. Actually being eaten by a saber-toothed tiger was not what got early man running; it was the dread of being eaten by that tiger. Modern humans benefit from this legacy because it is not failure per se but the fear of failure, not success per se but the prospect of success, that gets us out of bed in the morning. And when it comes to discounts, it is not necessarily the object per se but the anticipation of getting a good deal on that object that motivates us to make a purchase.

Some of us more than others are susceptible to the allure of discounts, but none of us is immune. It is for this reason that retailers work hard to frame prices as a good deal even when they are an ordinary deal—or no deal at all. The thrill of anticipation is often all it takes to block out any negative feelings about the transaction. No matter that the color is off, the pattern peevish, the fit less than perfect; the prospect of getting a good deal sets our nucleus accumbens aquiver. And scientists have found the evidence to prove it.

Knutson peered into the brains of people as they contemplated making a purchase and found distinct brain circuits anticipating gain and loss. Twenty-six adults participated, each given $20 to spend on a series of products. If no purchase was made, subjects were allowed to keep the money. The products and their prices appeared on a computer screen that the participants viewed while under fMRI. Knutson and his coauthors found that merely viewing the products activated the nucleus accumbens. When the subjects were presented with prices the subjects considered excessive, however, the insula, a brain region associated with social emotions such as empathy, guilt, humiliation, and pride, lit up while the prefrontal cortex, a part of the brain associated with weighing gains and losses, went silent. Knutson said he could predict whether the study participants would decide to purchase each item by looking at how their brains reacted: When the nucleus accumbens and prefrontal cortex lit up, they would buy; when the insula lit up, they would pass. Confronted with discounts, the accumbens lights up like a Christmas tree.

"People treat money as a good," Knutson said. "Having to give it up is a bad. A sale sign reframes the loss as a gain. You aren't just saving money, you are turning a loss into a positive. What I find amazing is that you can scan the brain and find an activator that will actually predict what you will do and that this is predicted by phylogenetics—chemical changes in ancient brain structures. If you want to predict what people are going to do or what they would be willing to pay, look at what they anticipate doing, not how they feel after they've done it."

Those of us without ready access to a brain-scanning machine know that anticipating buyer reactions is a delicate and frustrating exercise, especially if we have something to sell. Setting too high a price is obviously a bad tactic, but setting too low a price can be equally counterproductive. Like many of you, I learned this tenet through personal experience. My lesson involved a 2004 Honda CRV. I enjoyed but no longer needed the car, and it was sitting idle in the driveway consuming money in insurance and depreciation, like a taxi stalled in traffic with the meter running. I decided to sell it and advertised in all the usual outlets. Because I wanted the sale to be quick and painless, and because I hate to haggle, I cunningly priced the car below other Hondas of similar make, mileage, and vintage. To my surprise I received few calls, and the handful of potential buyers who came to look at the car were hypercritical. One actually drove nearly 75 miles to my home, got out of his car, took a quick look, and spotting superficial scratches on the front side door, returned to his car and drove 75 miles back home. This was all very disconcerting. The Honda was *mine,* a great car in great mechanical condition and at a price with which no one could—or did—quibble. Like so many sellers of unloved merchandise, I was beginning to regard this experience as a personal rejection. Did people think I was trying to rip them off, or what? I lowered the price further, figuring I'd get deluged with calls. But, if anything, inquiries grew fewer, no-shows increased, and the only potential customer was a shady guy who left with a shrug after I declined to let him test-drive the car without me in it. Winter was coming, and I began to wonder whether it was "'til death do us part" with this car and me. I consulted a number of friends and colleagues and also a neighbor who by odd coincidence had sold her daughter's Honda CRV earlier that year. She suggested I raise the price. I told her she was nuts: who would pay more for a car no one seemed to want? But after a couple more weeks of no-shows and crank calls, I figured I had nothing to lose and raised the price by nearly a thousand dollars. Within a week the car—scratches and all—was sold to a young architect.

Pricing is rife with paradoxes of this sort. We all believe we want low prices, but when actually confronted with them, how we respond depends largely on the context.

Most of us like to think of ourselves as unbiased, rational consumers who make decisions based on evidence. Psychologists call this belief the "illusion of objectivity." Lowenstein once observed, "The conscious mind plays a less active role in controlling behavior than it does in making sense of that behavior after it occurs. In other words, post hoc rationalization is a vibrant and ubiquitous component of the human psychological repertoire. We believe what we want to believe. After the age of three or so, though, we don't like to admit this to ourselves and attempt to rationalize our decisions by unconsciously adjusting our attitudes to justify our actions.

Behavioral psychologists say that discounted prices provoke two diametrically opposed responses depending on the expectations of the buyer. From what is called an "attribution perspective," a low price signals low quality, because the buyer attributes the steep discount to some deficiency in the product. Assessing the object through this lens, the buyer takes particular notice of every flaw, both real and imagined, and tends to overlook most virtues. The guy who drove 75 miles—wasting all that time and burning all that gas!—to view my perfectly good car, only to turn around and drive 75 miles back home—probably believed he was justified in this action. The low price predisposed him to suspect the car was a lemon, and the scratches merely confirmed this belief. The architect, by contrast, was motivated to buy the car even before he saw it. A new father who could no longer rely on public transportation to get to work, he needed a safe, reliable vehicle, and he needed it fast. When I pointed out the scratches, he seemed impatient, as though he didn't want to be persuaded that the car was not a good buy. If he had asked, I would gladly have lowered the price, but predisposed to want the car, he didn't haggle. Like all highly motivated buyers, his inclination was to overvalue virtues and overlook defects. Motivated buyers are far less likely to be suspicious of low price. If I had offered the architect a "deal" by, say, throwing a roof rack or child seat into the bargain, chances are he would have been all the happier. But because he was so motivated, he probably preferred not to tip the deal by asking.

Erica Dawson, a psychologist at Yale School of Management, is an expert on motivated reasoning, which she roughly defines as how people sift through evidence that bears on things they care about. Our desires, she said, shape the way in which we access and consume information. Most of us are motivated to hang on to existing self-enhancing beliefs, and willing to exert significant cognitive effort to maintain these beliefs. We are also willing to accept flawed information and flawed evidence if it supports our beliefs. We all rely on cues to make decisions—signals that tell us how to respond. A discount is often interpreted as a negative signal unless it is countered by a signal of quality, such as a celebrity endorsement or a designer label or an expert opinion. Note that the operative phrase is "signal of quality," not quality per se. The trick for retailers—and certainly low-price retailers—is not necessarily to ensure that their products are the best they can be but to associate the product with quality in consumers' minds. Once quality is assumed—as it is for many branded products—a lower price is a plus. When quality is in dispute, as it is when we buy things we know nothing about at flea markets or eBay, low price can be a negative.

Dawson has not only observed this phenomenon but has quantified it in a series of experiments. In one she enlisted 227 undergraduate volunteers to log on to a Web page and check out a photograph of a hip-looking stainless steel study lamp. The test subjects agreed that the lamp was pretty cool and well worth the price of $99.95 plus $3.95 for shipping and handling. They were then asked to imagine that another well-known Web site wholesaler was offering the lamp at a discount. The subjects were split into six groups, and each group was offered a different level of discount: 8 percent, 25 percent, 45 percent, 65 percent, 85 percent, and 100 percent (that is, free). In the 8 percent case, participants were told the lamp was being offered for $91.95 plus shipping and handling. In the free case, participants were told they need pay nothing except shipping and handling. The test subjects were then told to use three different 100-point scales to rate the lamp's aesthetic value, quality, and usefulness, as well as the likelihood that they would buy it.

Dawson theorized that participants offered a large discount would find this desired object even more desirable, and as it turned out, she was correct. The students judged the usefulness and aesthetic value of the lamp in precise proportion to its price: the cheaper the lamp, the better their opinion of it. Meanwhile, no level of discount—not even 100 percent—diminished the students' assessment of the lamp's quality. "Positive prior attitudes combined with a large discount will fuel a process of motivated perception resulting in a more favorable product assess-ment," Dawson and her coauthor, Yale colleague On Amir, concluded in their assessment.

Since this study tested subjects who had an intrinsic attraction to the product, it says nothing about the allure of discounts for consumers who are neutral or negative about a product. So Dawson and Amir ran another experiment in which 537 men and women subjects were asked to give their impressions of a pricy eye cream. Not surprisingly, the male subjects were far less enthused about the eye cream than were the female subjects, and said so in a pretest. The volunteers were again divided into six groups, and discounts of the eye cream assigned at 7 percent, 20 percent, 40 percent, 60 percent, 80 percent, and, yes, 100 percent. As in the previ-ous experiment, the subjects were asked to rate the products on a scale of 1 to 100 for aesthetic value, quality, and usefulness. Once again, the larger discounts prompted an overall greater desire to purchase the eye cream. But when the results were broken down by gender, it became clear that the women were more likely to purchase the cream at a greater discount, and the men were somewhat less likely to purchase the cream at a greater discount. As predicted, participants were motivated by the higher discounts to purchase the eye cream only when it held intrinsic appeal for them. When the product lacked intrinsic appeal, the discount seemed only to confirm what the male subjects already believed: that the product was not for them.

"When products have great appeal, retailers can get by with moderate or even very small reductions in price," Dawson told me. "And when consumers have no idea as to the quality of a product, or feel neutral or negative about it, deep discounts can actually discourage them from mak-ing a buy."

It is not very surprising that preconceived ideas skew our response to price. A Rodeo Drive or Madison Avenue address predisposes us to anticipate that a shop will be expensive and to be grateful for any price break it offers. Deep discounts at Big Box stores may prompt the op-posite reaction: When something is cheap, making it cheaper still might push us to question its value. But behavioral scientists are learning that consumer reactions go beyond this predictable pattern; they are rooted in something deeper than simple preconceptions. It is hard to know what customers are willing to pay for any given item at any given time, and even harder to balance that knowledge with considerations of cost and profit margins. Price is burdened by memory and guilt. Our reaction to it is personal, particular, and almost impossible to predict.

Consider for a moment that you have a family heirloom, perhaps a quilt lovingly stitched by a beloved ancestor. You cherish the quilt but no longer have a need for it, and have decided, albeit reluctantly, to let it go. You've seen what looked like similar quilts selling for $150 at flea markets, and you've also seen what looked like similar quilts appraised at thousands or even tens of thousands of dollars on *Antiques Roadshow*. You're no fool, but you're no expert, either. Which quilts do you decide will appropriately "anchor" the price of your quilt? How you "frame" it—whether as a precious heirloom or as a funky castoff—has everything to do with what price you and your potential customers will consider fair. In this case, as in many cases, price is not about the object per se. It's about context.

Ariely conducted an ingenious experiment that demonstrates the remarkable power of "anchoring" to prime the mind for price. He gathered a group of students and asked each one to recite his or her Social Security number. Then he asked each to guess the price of a bottle of 1998 Côtes du Rhône. (He used Côtes du Rhône rather than beer because he assumed college students were unlikely to know its price.) Students whose Social Security numbers contained low numbers in the last two digits estimated the bottle at an average of $8.64 (not far from the actual price).Students whose Social Security numbers contained high numbers in the last two digits priced the same bottle at an average of $27.91. What did their Social Security numbers have to do with the price of a French wine? Not a thing. How much influence did the recitation of their Social Security numbers have on what they thought was the price of a bottle of French wine? Enormous.

Findings like these offer clues as to why pricing is so difficult. We all rely on external cues when we estimate the value of things, and it's almost impossible to know in advance what those external clues might be.

This is especially true of things with which we've had little or no experience. It is for this reason that works of art and antique cars are so often sold at auction. No one really knows in advance how much these items are worth to buyers. The price is quite literally what the highest bidder is willing to pay. The price of auctioned goods starts low and then rises to the precise point where supply meets demand. The amazing success of eBay is testament to the psychological appeal of auctions, which seem to satisfy buyer and seller alike.

But perhaps this satisfaction is built on illusion. For decades economists agreed that auctions offered the perfect compromise, that they were immune to the passions inflamed by factors such as rabid discounting. But recently Ulrike Malmendier, an economist at the University of California, Berkeley, put that assumption to the test. She tracked 166 eBay auctions of CashFlow 101, a personal-finance-themed board game retailing for $195. eBay sellers generally offered an opening price of $45 and set a one-click "buy-it-now" price of roughly $125. That is, if a buyer was willing to bid $125, he or she got the CashFlow 101 immediately, without further bidding. This was a terrific deal, allowing bidders to end the auction and pay less than the going price; or, if they preferred to take a gamble, they could bid an even lower price. Astonishingly, 43 percent of CashFlow 101 buyers blew right past the "buy-it-now" price and paid more. Some even exceeded the $195 retail price. Why didn't they just click in at $125? Malmendier and her team wondered if there might be something special about CashFlow 101 buyers and decided to test other goods. They observed thousands of auctions for iPods, and, again, 45 to 50 percent of eBay users paid more than the "buy-it-now" price. Malmendier's team then expanded their investigation, to include auctions of men's cologne, perfume, and autobiographies of both Barack Obama and Bill O'Reilly (presumably to catch both Democratic and Republican eBayers.) Incredibly, they found that, again, between 40 and 50 percent of buyers paid more than the "buy-it-now" price. Buyers seem to derive significant pleasure from bidding—even more pleasure, it seemed, than they did from getting the desired item at the lower price. The Romans had a term for this weird phenomenon: They called it *calor licitantis*, bidder's heat or auction fever. In Rome, bidders afflicted with *calor licitantis* were sometimes forgiven their lapse and had their money returned. Unfortunately, eBay makes no such provision.

LEGIONS OF PH.D.'S have for decades studied the intricacies of why people are willing to pay what they do, yet pricing remains a most imperfect "science." In the words of one economist, "For most businesses, pricing is a profit-leaking paradox." Blame this on Wanamaker's scrappy invention, the price tag. Virtually the opposite of auctions, price tags fix the price and discourage bargaining, thereby de-skilling the salesclerk's job. Lower-skilled jobs are lower-paying jobs, so this saves retailers money. But fixed prices also carry a significant cost: By reducing or even eliminating the possibility of price negotiation, they create gaps between supply and demand, leaving stores holding too much of what customers aren't willing to pay for and selling too cheaply merchandise for which customers would be willing to pay more.

At the Fordham pricing conference, I met Bidisha Burman, a young professor of marketing from Appalachian State University in North Carolina. Burman studies the relation of price to a response with which most of us are familiar: regret. Regret is a much maligned emotion, but it is not necessarily irrational. According to University of Michigan psychologist Janet Landsman, regret is "a defensible response to a world that inevitably presents decision makers with irreducible conflicts that at times require acting in opposition to one of their various judgments." Having regret implies that we believe we have done something bad or foolish, or neglected to do something good or wise. We regret because no matter how logical and carefully made our decisions, we wish we had not made them. People who pride themselves on their decisiveness often claim to never feel regret, but they are likely lying. Were such a "decider" presented with making the choice of submitting a beloved pet to surgery for a broken leg, scheduling the operation would be a perfectly logical choice. But if the pet dies on the operating table, whatever satisfaction this decider might get from having made this logical choice would probably be overwhelmed by regret. Yes, the decision was rational, but it is also regrettable. Humans regret because we have the ability to compare real outcomes with possible alternative outcomes. We can extrapolate beyond what is and imagine what could have been.

Regret cannot change the past, but it can influence the future. It can teach us not to repeat mistakes or overlook opportunities. And like all emotions it influences us to act or not. Burman told me that regret comes in two flavors: regret of decision and regret of outcome. The first form, regret of decision, is rather surprising. Who would regret a decision if its outcome was neutral or favorable? If I cheat on a test, get an A, and no one is the wiser, do I regret it? Well, yes, I do. But why? Burman responded to this question with an example. Imagine waking up early on a Saturday morning to the realization that you had driven rip-roaring drunk the previous night. The outcome of this decision is not the problem. You found your way home and safely to bed. But thinking back on this reckless action, you may well be horror-stricken. You may regret the *decision* to drive drunk despite the fortunate outcome. Then again, you may not. Regret, Burman points out, is a cognitive response; you have to think to experience it. Thinking about driving while under the influence may flood you with remorse and fill you with determination not to repeat the folly. But not all of us are so introspective, and not all of us experience the same level of decision regret. In fact, some of us experience almost no decision regret at all. That is why some people feel triumphant when they wake up alive and well the morning after a drinking spree. They don't regret their bad judgment. They believe their decision to drive drunk was rational ("I know my limits; I wasn't that drunk") and convince themselves that the fortunate outcome—no fatal car accident—is proof of their own good sense.

Those of us with what psychologists call "high cognition" tend to experience high levels of decision regret. These folks take a long time to make decisions and are more likely to respond negatively if they later perceive a decision to be a poor one. People classified as "low cognition" are more impulsive, less thoughtful, and less likely to suffer decision regret. They tend to worry less about making a bad decision and therefore seem more decisive and less likely to blame themselves if the decision turns out to be disappointing. Burman told me that high-cognition types

are not necessarily more intelligent, just more introspective. Highly introspective people are not always the most successful, particularly when
their introspection leads to indecision. "Deciders" such as Donald Trump
and President George W. Bush are not known for their introspection,
and there is no evidence that they suffer greatly from decision regret.
They don't seem to suffer from much outcome regret, either, although
this is mere inference.

Burman is fascinated by the concept of regret and, in particular, by
the impact of this noisome emotion on our everyday lives. She told me
that the power of regret to shape consumer decisions is profound, particularly in the case of discounting. In an elegantly simple experiment,
she offered three groups of research subjects a chance to buy a digital
camera "on sale" for $249. One group was told the retail value of the
camera was $799, the next group that it was $499, and the third group
that it was $299. Burman asked each group how they felt about their
deals. Interestingly, while few subjects in the first group actually believed
that the camera was worth $799, they reported the highest overall satisfac-
tion with their hypothetical "purchase." For some reason just being told
that the price was more than three times what they paid for it gave them
great pleasure. Members of the other two groups believed what they were
told about the real value of the cameras and were pleased with their
purchase, but not to the same degree.

After recording her subjects' responses, Burman sorted them into two
groups based on what she determined to be their "need for cognition,"
the personality variable that reflects the extent to which people engage
in and enjoy thinking. People with a high need for cognition (HNFC)
are more likely to form opinions and make decisions by paying close
attention to evidence and relevant arguments, while people with low
need for cognition (LNFC) are more likely to form opinions built on
peripheral cues, such as how attractive or credible they find the salesperson. After sorting them into these categories, Burman informed the members of each group that their camera's actual retail price was only $249,
precisely what they had paid for it. Given that few of us like to be fooled,
it was no surprise that members of all groups were disappointed that
their $249 "bargain price" was actually full retail. But HNFC subjects

experienced much higher levels of disappointment than did the LNFC subjects. HNFC types regretted not only "buying" a camera that was less valuable than they were led to believe but also regretted making the decision that led to that outcome. The higher the bogus "reference price," the worse HNFC subjects felt about their decision and the greater their regret. The HNFC subjects told that the camera was worth $799 felt downright miserable. They deeply regretted their decision despite the fact that making it had actually cost them nothing.

Discount retailers rely heavily on psychological manipulation to set customers up for the buy, but as Burman demonstrated, this tactic can backfire if customers get wise to it. "High-cognition customers will feel cheated, and this negative feeling will be transferred onto the product," she said. "The value perception of the product itself may be reduced."

Again, most of us are highly sensitive to what we perceive as the fairness of transactions. Daniel Kahneman once surveyed randomly selected adults, asking them whether they thought it was okay for a hardware store to raise the price of snow shovels during a snowstorm, and the response was a resounding no. Years later another team of social scientists asked the same question of a large group of executives and got pretty much the same response. Yet whether it is truly unfair to raise the price of a snow shovel during a storm is debatable. After all, this system might serve to discourage customers from buying multiple shovels, thereby diminishing the available supply. No matter, Americans abhor price "rationing" and are highly resistant to it. Such "dynamic" pricing, in which some customers pay more than others do for the same thing, is considered by most people to be patently unfair. When a customer discovered that Amazon was charging new customers less for books than old customers, he broadcast it over the Internet to universal outrage. Such pricing is not illegal, but it is dangerous. If customers discover it, they rebel. As one industry insider told the *Wall Street Journal,* "Amazon.com's biggest mistake was getting caught." The same was true for Apple when it sharply reduced the price of its iPhone just a couple of months after putting it on the market. Customers complained that this was simply not fair and that it made them lose faith in the company.

A close cousin to price rationing is the equally familiar "yield management," whereby airlines and hotels moderate prices depending on demand. This practice is widespread and largely (if grumpily) tolerated. We have come to accept the idea that the guy sitting next to us in the back of the plane might have paid far less than we did for the seat. "Price discrimination is considered fair if it takes place for a socially acceptable reason," Sarah Maxwell told me. Of course, "socially acceptable" is determined by context. If we all agree that airlines have a right to charge someone double for a ticket because he or she happens to purchase it outside a certain time frame, so be it.

Ultimately, most of us consider "fair" almost any price that benefits ourselves. On its face this seems a self-serving assessment, and it is: In most transactions our focus is not on the general public but on ourselves. Imagine this: What if, rather than offering a discount, retailers offered you the opportunity to pay a bit more so that others could pay a bit less? Would you take this offer or assume it was wacky and demand the lower price? Given that you have little or no control over what happens to the next customer—who, after all might be far richer than you—you are likely to fight for the best possible deal for yourself, hoping that whatever bargain you make does not adversely affect the next guy.

Humans are adept at rationalizing whatever conditions benefit them directly, and that includes discounts. As I've said, early adapters of the iPhone were furious when the price dropped by 40 percent sixty-six days after the rollout. But less impulsive customers who bought the iPhone after the price drop reasoned that the early birds *deserved* to pay more. Among the rationales stated for this gloating behavior was that early buyers should be punished for trying to be "too cool." Such reasoning constitutes not a reasonable explanation but a sort of post hoc "Just-So Story" that justifies the good luck of the slow adapter.

When you think about it, any true discount by definition means that some people will pay a higher price for an item than others will. All of us like discounts and consider them fair, but most of us want to be on the winning end of the deal. That sets us up for promotional tricks that lure us into buying more and spending more for the pure satisfaction of scoring a "bargain" which—it is implied—is not available to just anybody.

"Price promotions are designed around the psychology of game playing," Robert Schindler told me as he packed up to leave the Fordham meeting. "The key elements of a game are action with some intrinsic appeal, a goal that is attainable, and clear feedback on how you're doing. Discounts have all of these. Some people play the waiting game, waiting for the price of something to drop. Some people play the radar game, in which they scope out bargains throughout a store, often following the same path every time. Some people play the "guess what I paid for it" game, when they buy something just to brag about how little they paid for it. And some people play the Santa Claus game in which they stock up on cheap stuff just to give it away. All these games are terrific at recruiting mental energy. All are great at inducing people to buy. These games, like all games, are about winning. And with discounts everyone feels like a winner no matter how much they lose."

# CHAPTER FOUR

# THE OUTLET GAMBIT

**HOMER:** Look at these low, low prices on famous brand-
name electronics!

**BART:** Don't be a sap, Dad. These are just crappy knockoffs.

**HOMER:** Pfft. I know a genuine Panaphonics when I see it.
And look, there's a Magnetbox and Sorny.

**SALESMAN:** Listen, I'm not going to lie to you. Those are all
superior machines. But if you like to watch TV, and I
mean *really* watch it, you want the Carnivale. It features a
two-pronged wall plug, a pre-molded hand grip well,
durable outer casing to prevent fallapart . . .

**HOMER:** Sold. You wrap it up, I'll start bringing in the
pennies.

| THE SIMPSONS, "SCENES FROM A CLASS STRUGGLE IN SPRINGFIELD,"

FIRST AIRED FEBRUARY 4, 1996

The "deluxe" room at the Excalibur was a bargain. There were even cheaper options available in Las Vegas that week, but not with Exacali-bur's Knights of the Round Table meets Six Flags décor and its prime location just steps from the Strip. For $69 plus tax I got the full-throttle Sin City experience: a lobby thick with slot jockeys in track suits and sneakers plugging their Social Security checks quarter by quarter into electronic slot machines; billboards flashing round-the-clock neon teasers for bare-breasted "exotic" entertainment; and round tables of low rollers drinking scotch at 9 a.m., hope draining from their faces like transfusing blood. The baby stroller cavalry and the cavalcade of wheelchairs surprised me: "What happens in Vegas stays in Vegas" for sure, but it never occurred to me that it was happening to infants and their barely ambulatory great-grandparents.

To be fair, not much about Vegas had occurred to me. I was a naïf—not quite a Vegas virgin but close enough to be confused by a place where scoring a fair price on a decent cup of coffee was as unlikely as rolling a string of sevens at the craps table. Vegas is disorienting, but you have to squint hard to notice. The casinos are dimly lit and famously devoid of clocks, so night and day bleed together in a blur. Dropping a fistful of coins down the rabbit hole of a slot machine, I felt like every other sitting duck, but so what? Primary process appears to be the only brain function on call here, with heroic attempts at self-control and resolve utterly beside the point.

I was in Vegas to gamble, though in truth the casino was only a detour. My mission was to check out the retail gambit, which in Vegas seemed just as dicey as the slots. Scores of stores circle the hotel lobbies, and hundreds more line the Strip, hawking everything from tattoos ("Fresh needles for every new customer!") to Corum Golden Bridge or Chopard Haute Joaillerie watches with an optional diamond wrist strap. It is terra incognita for a bargain hunter, but fortunately I had a guide: Gillian Naylor, a professor of marketing at the University of Nevada, Las Vegas.

Naylor's paper, "Price and Brand Name as Indicators of Quality Dimensions for Consumer Durables," in the *Journal of the Academy of Marketing Science,* had alerted me to her expertise in connecting the dots of brand name, price, and consumer perception. Her standards were high, and when I shuffled into her modest office, her appraisal of my stated mission was, to put it kindly, dubious. "The mall you've picked," she said evenly, "is pretty bad. They have Catherine Plus Sizes and Dress Barn Woman." Naylor is tall and elegant and no plus size. I felt a little foolish to have come all this way with no fashion sense. Sensing my discomfort (and panic), Naylor gently suggested that we aim a tad higher. She named a glamorous-sounding venue featuring discount versions of Coach, Dolce & Gabbana, A/X Armani Exchange, and 120 other stores. Ashamed to admit that my budget was more Dress Barn than Gabbana, I agreed, and minutes later we were off in her Acura TL, windows up, air-conditioning steady, destination Las Vegas Premium Fashion Outlets.

Outlet malls are big in Europe, Japan, and Hong Kong. They exist in Turkey, Dubai, and South Africa. If there is one deep in the Amazon rain forest, and another just south of the North Pole, it would not surprise me. But no matter where you find them, outlet malls are a deeply American institution. Like cowboys and football, no one builds them or loves them quite like we do.

The *New York Times* once reported that outlet malls were not only the fastest growing segment of the retail industry but one of the fastest growing segments of the *travel* industry. Franklin Mills Outlets in northeast Philadelphia rings in four times the visitors of the Liberty Bell. A pair of outlet malls near San Marcos, Texas, outdraw the Alamo. Colonial Williamsburg can't hold a candle to mega-outlet mall Potomac Mills. This is not to suggest that Americans don't take pride in our national heritage; we surely do. We revere the Liberty Bell and Colonial Williamsburg. We salute the Alamo. It's just that most of us prefer to spend our time where we believe our dollar will go further.

About 55 million Americans shop in at least one of the nation's roughly three hundred outlet centers every year. Stretched over five years, that number adds up to nearly every man, woman, and child in the country. Even more astonishing is the number of miles chalked up in this annual pilgrimage. The total distance that Americans travel to outlet malls each year equals 440,000 circumnavigations of the globe. If that number seems a little abstract, consider this: The distance to the moon is roughly equal to 10 trips around the globe. That is, we make 44,000 moon launches' worth of outlet visits each year.

People travel celestial distances to outlet malls because until recently outlet malls were located celestial distances from people. On the surface this makes no sense; full-price "regional" malls are always situated with regard to demographics gauging the buying power and density of surrounding communities. And as a rule investors won't put money into malls without the requisite "threshold population densities" that all but ensure sales. Nor will builders build them. But outlet malls are different. Resolute in their remoteness, they stand secure that, like Muhammad and the mountain, the customers will come to them. Freed from the need to offer convenience, outlet malls are plopped down with what appears to be wild abandon. Of course that is an illusion: They are almost always located off a busy byway and, whenever possible, between two or more population centers. Generally this is a long drive from any particular population center—25 to 100 miles outside the metropolitan shadows, where real estate is cheap and the tax incentives sweet. In fact, until recently manufacturers preferred and sometimes even required outlet malls to locate far enough away from their department store rivals to avoid angering full-price retailers. But the remote location of outlets is not merely a defensive, cost-saving maneuver. It is also a deliberate *strategy*. In the public mind, convenience is a trade-off for price, and price is traded off for convenience. Inconvenience connotes cheap, while convenience connotes pricy. This is why restaurant valets can get away with charging $20 to park your Honda on the street and why "convenience" stores can charge $3 for a can of condensed chicken noodle soup. In a very real sense, outlets are the anticonvenience store. Visiting the outlets demands an investment in time, deliberation, and energy beyond what we invest in most other leisure activities. And because the effort required to reach and shop at them is substantial, even extraordinary, the experience of going to the outlet is elevated in our minds to "special occasion" status. A trip to the outlet mall is not passive, not simply a matter of popping in to pick up a few things. We have to work to get there, piling up hefty "sunk costs." All that time! All that gas! "I gave up my entire Sunday afternoon and even missed the game to come here!" Psychologically speaking, all this and more must be repaid in the form of purchases made. In making that long trip we are actually engaged in a transfer of power away from ourselves to the outlet itself. The mall has extracted a price, and in demanding repayment, we are in fact taxing ourselves. Our expectations are raised at the same time that our guard is lowered, and in making this bargain we are willing to forgo many things that we once demanded from a satisfying shopping experience: variety, serendipity, aspiration—and fun.

IN HIS NOVEL *Au Bonheur des Dames*, detailing the rise of a fictional department store in nineteenth-century Paris, Emile Zola painstakingly describes the mostly female clientele swooning over the store's luxurious settings: "all the velvets, black, white, colored, interwoven with silk or satin, scooping out with their shifting marks a motionless lake on which reflections of sky and landscape seemed to dance." Few if any shopping centers today can boast of velvet lakes, but many strive to offer at least the impression of luxury: soaring atriums, fashion shows, valet parking, a jazz band or high school choir performing on Sunday afternoon. The purpose of this embellishment is to seduce clients, to lure them in and set them up for the sale. Similar efforts stretch back half a century to the work of Victor Gruen, the undisputed father of the modern shopping mall.

Gruen's mark on America's shopping landscape is as indelible as it was unexpected. Born and bred in the fabled elegance of turn-of-the-century Vienna, Gruen was a talented student destined for a life in the arts. An intellectual and aesthetic, he graduated from the Vienna Academy of Fine Arts, the venerable institution that rejected fledgling painter Adolf Hitler twice. Gruen, whose real name was Grunbaum, wisely fled Austria in 1938, chauffeured to the airport by an actor friend disguised as a Nazi storm trooper. He stopped briefly in Switzerland and the United Kingdom before boarding a ship for New York. With his partner and second wife, Elsie Krummeck, he founded an architectural and design firm that developed a reputation for, among other things, fitting Fifth Avenue boutiques with lavish marble-covered entrance vestibules. This may seem a trivial matter to us today, but at the time it was a revelation. In the words of culture critic Lewis Mumford, Gruen's lobbies lured customers like "a pitcher plant captures flies" and eliminated what he called the "phobia of entering a store." Anyone who has paced nervously outside the entrance of a swanky boutique waiting to be "buzzed in" knows that this is not always true, but it was true enough at the time to make Gruen a star in the cloistered world of retail architecture.

Gruen's ambitions went well beyond designing dashing entrances. A visionary and social theorist, for him shopping was but one thread in the rich fabric of human experience, and he argued that merchants would achieve greater success if they integrated commercial activities more seamlessly into cultural and community life. To that end he envisioned what he called "shopping towns," where both retail and nonretail functions would coexist symbiotically. In 1954 he was able to manifest this vision with Northland, an open-air center situated just outside of Detroit, with nearly a hundred shops and ten thousand parking spaces. Northland was indeed a triumph, featuring a post office, "club rooms," auditoriums, and lavishly landscaped plazas, all sprawled over an astonishing sixty-three acres. Critics raved, and throngs strolled the manicured grounds even on Sundays when all the stores were closed. Northland was every bit the community resource Gruen envisioned, and it was also a commercial juggernaut: Sales figures soared well beyond projections to an unheard-of $10 million over five years.

Gruen was at the top of his game when he began work on his second shopping center, Southdale, near Minneapolis. This project was even more ambitious, a feat no one had ever attempted. Faced with broiling summers and frigid winters, Gruen calculated that in Minneapolis an open mall could realistically sustain only 126 shopping days a year. So he built the world's first fully enclosed shopping center: a $20-million retail Xanadu. American shopping centers of the time were what architects call "extroverted"; their store windows and entrances faced outward, toward the parking lot and exterior pedestrian walkways, in an effort to make them expansive, to bring the exterior in. Southdale, by contrast, was introverted and cocoon-like; its sight lines lead to the interior, climate-controlled to a comfortable 72 degrees thanks to air-conditioning and an elaborate heating system. To lessen the distance that customers had to walk, Gruen arranged seventy-two stores on two levels serviced by zigzagging escalators, plunging elevators, and a two-tier parking lot. The centerpiece was what Gruen called "town square," a sky-lit atrium with balconies, flower arrangements, fountains, trees, and a twenty-one-foot cage alive with brightly colored birds. More than a wonder of its time, Southdale was the archetype upon which future malls would be modeled and are still.

Gruen was at heart a socialist, a utopian who envisioned his shopping centers as idealized European-style villages, with schools, offices, hospitals, housing: a "crystallization point(s) for suburbia's community life." He hoped the shopping center would become a lively and lovely alternative to urban squalor and suburban sprawl, the perfect balance of community and commerce. But between Gruen's first triumph in Detroit and the shopping mall boom of the 1960s, consumer attitudes had shifted; consumerism was no longer just one among many forces driving change; it was *the* driving force. Gruen's rosy optimism gradually soured as he watched his dream towns co-opted into symbols of suburban isolation and commercial manipulation. He returned to Austria in 1967, not heartbroken, exactly, but chastened and eager to redeem his legacy. He founded the Victor Gruen Foundation for Environmental Planning, based in Los Angeles, and its sister organization, Zentrum für Umweltplanung, in Vienna to promote environmental education for the improvement and protection of natural resources in urban areas.

Gruen's mark on the retail landscape was indelible. With their soaring atriums and sculpted gardens and cafés, his generous spaces tempted visitors to linger, and that was the point. A psychological state known as the "Gruen transfer" has come to signify when a "destination buyer" shopping for a specific purchase loses focus and starts wandering in a sort of daze, aimless and vulnerable to the siren call of come-ons of every sort. Developers today strive to motivate this state by doing everything possible to anticipate and stimulate desire. How they do this varies, but as one prominent mall developer observed, "The more needs you fulfill, the longer people will stay." It is unlikely that many mall prowlers would claim they need to be entertained, but they may sense that need when a fashion show or promotion is announced through the mall's loudspeaker system. The show captures attention and entices shoppers to forget their promise to themselves not to linger or, worse yet, overspend. Thanks in part to such innovations, the typical visit to a mall extended from twenty minutes in 1960 to nearly three hours in 1979.

A TEAM OF business scholars recently observed that "making efforts to improve patron satisfaction with mall attributes will improve the hedonic shopping value patrons believe they get from a mall visit and will increase the likelihood that they will visit again in the future." Plainly put: Build it nice, treat them nice, and customers will stay longer and return more often. No quibbles there. But what these scholars failed to recognize—and what discounters know—is that customers staying longer or coming more frequently does not necessarily translate into their spending more money. The zombies in *Dawn of the Dead* wandered the mall for days in numb fascination, never once pulling out a credit card. The same is often true of real-life patrons for whom the mall has become a point of congregation but not necessarily commerce. You'll recall that people flocked to Gruen's Detroit mall on Sunday afternoons when the stores were closed. Today the stores are open on Sundays and most other days, but that doesn't mean every visitor intends to spend money in them. Senior citizen "mall walkers" come for a brisk mid-morning stroll and then commune for hours over a cup of coffee in the food court. Teenage "mall rats" spend entire weekends roaming in packs. (Mall managers complain of becoming a "babysitting service" for too-young-to drive teens who are all but abandoned by their parents.) Stay-at-home parents use the mall as an escape hatch for restless toddlers.

The more enchanting, the more inviting, and the more comfortable the mall, the more powerful its draw as one giant living/play room. For this reason not all outlet malls subscribe to the Gruen doctrine and not all are overly concerned with the "hedonic impact" of their environments. Rather, many outlet developers follow what might be called the "Golden Arches" approach to social engineering. At McDonald's and many other fast-food restaurants, the lighting tends to be unflattering fluorescents, and the seats are bolted to the floor at an awkward distance from the tables. The purpose of this is not to prevent theft of the chairs, as many think, but to discourage elders, teenagers, and other undesirables from getting comfortable and congregating for hours over a small coffee, or an order of fries. Discomfort does seem to keep the customers churning; on average, fast-food patrons spend only eleven minutes at their tables. (The optimal fast-food customer—as defined by the fast-food industry—takes no table time at all but does a quickie through the drive-through.)

Outlet malls, too, minimize amenities to discourage wasteful lingering.

You are not likely to stumble on a fashion show, listen to a chamber orchestra, or enjoy a gourmet meal at an outlet center. But that doesn't mean you won't spend a lot of time dispersing your paycheck. On average, shoppers spend nearly 80 percent more money at a bare bones outlet mall than they would at a fully loaded regional mall. A popular rationale for this seeming paradox, in addition to the inconvenience hypothesis, is that outlet shoppers spend more to save more on things they really need. This theory certainly makes sense. What better place to stockpile staples such as underwear, T-shirts, sheets, and other basics than the outlets? Unfortunately, there is no actual evidence for this—no evidence, for example, that outlet mall shoppers are more likely than other shoppers to buy in bulk or to have a specific purchase in mind before getting in their cars to drive an average of 50 miles round trip. Outlet shoppers are pretty much like all shoppers, which is to say that while they might have an idea of what they are looking for, they are also very much open to suggestion. But unlike other shoppers and very much like gamblers, outlet shoppers believe they can "beat the house" by scoring great deals on expensive brand-name products. What these shoppers too often forget is that, just as in Vegas, the house almost always wins.

*Outlet* is a mnemonic for *value;* the very word loosens inhibitions and purse strings. You will recall that the original factory outlet concept was defined by slightly defective but perfectly usable goods sold directly to consumers straight from the factory store. Today this is a rarity. Factory outlets now offer mostly what they claim are first-quality brand-name products, and this claim reduces worries that the merchandise at outlets might be second rate. The brand-name distinction is critically important, because many consumers perceive any discounted goods as less desirable unless given a reason to believe otherwise.

If a penny saved is truly a penny earned, outlet shoppers feel that they are "earning" plenty. As literary scholar Marianne Conroy wrote, "The lure and the rationale that draw customers to the factory outlet mall is price, not escape. . . . [The factory outlet] secures a pragmatic and instrumental vision of shopping over and against the recreational model of consumption." For this reason we forgive the outlet mall many things. We don't expect the service there to be fluid or the products necessarily top-notch. At the outlet mall, shopping is severed from its mooring in frivolity and might even be described as a Calvinistic enterprise; spending money is not play but work, sometimes very hard work. So, psychologically at least, the bargains aren't gifts; they are earned.

Navigating Las Vegas Premium Outlets felt very much like work: 435,000 square feet of brand-name storefronts lined up in standard mall formation like so many dominos. The mall was of the open-air variety, scattered with scraggly palm trees and cooled with an astonishingly primitive system of what appeared to be canvas canopies and humidifiers. There were no fountains, no music, and no place to sit. Most customers looked exhausted and not what you'd call fashion forward. Though not all were wearing T-shirts emblazoned with slogans, enough were to make Prof. Naylor a true standout. She wore a Diane Von Furstenberg–style wrap dress accented with a stunning Plino Visona handbag. Probed for details, she described the bag as "high quality without the risk of dilution of the brand from knockoffs."

A single mother of three, Naylor knows a thing or two about value. On our twenty-minute drive to the mall she mentioned that her youngest daughter, a high school senior, was mulling over her college choices. Naylor was less concerned about the status or emotional fit of the prospective colleges (just the right size, just the right mix of students, just the right location) than with the fiscal fit. She had constructed a spreadsheet of public universities offering the best value for the money and had given her daughter a choice of the top three.

Given this assiduous attention to value, Naylor's opinion of outlets is worth noting: She uses them, but sparingly. She prefers department stores, which she said generally carry better quality merchandise at prices that are frequently lower than outlet levels. Apparently this view differed from that of the half-dozen friendly British Columbians sitting cross-legged on the walkway, comparing their purchases. One of these, a lively blonde with the robust look of a field hockey midfielder, proffered for our inspection a hooded sweatshirt of the sort commonly sported in police lineups. "This would cost at least $75 at home," she said. "I got it for $45.95." The "sunk" costs of airfare, hotel, restaurant meals, and cabs apparently did not diminish the thrill. We bid the Canadians happy hunting and window-shopped our way down the long row of store-fronts—Crabtree and Evelyn, Journeys, and Samsonite. We detoured at Naylor's suggestion to have a look inside Crescent Jewelers, part of a West Coast chain that occupied a spacious corner across the mall from a K. B. Toy Outlet. (This placement seemed strategic. Harried dads could haggle over Mother's Day earrings at Crescent while across the way their kids haggled over Hannah Montana dolls and Lightning McQueen remote-control vehicles.)

Naylor's interest in discount jewelry stems in part from the work of one of her graduate students; she had recently completed a study of the jewelry department of J. C. Penney, the no-frills department store chain where Sam Walton got his start. The student concluded that Penney's and other discount jewelers lure customers with drastic reductions off the manufacturer's suggested retail prices, but the manufacturer's suggested price is not even intended to reflect the real price. More accurately, Naylor said, it is a mythical price, a *reference price* with which to manipulate customers' willingness to buy. She was almost certain that Crescent would offer some vivid examples.

Crescent was as dimly lit as the casino had been that morning, and spookily devoid of customers. A matronly "associate" with the helpful look of an elementary school librarian greeted us the moment we crossed the threshold, and we asked her to show us the store's best-selling item. She unlocked a glass case displaying "circle of life" pendants; dainty rounds of white gold or other precious metals encrusted with diamonds. She reached in, pulled out a pendant, and turned it over to reveal the manufacturer's suggested retail price: $3,329. She quickly assured us that this was not the Crescent price. What was the Crescent price? She smiled. It was $832, one-quarter of the original price. This seemed an astonishing discount. But was it worth $3,329 or, for that matter, $832? The embedded diamonds seemed to be of industrial quality, tiny specks that barely twinkled. The 14-carat white gold setting had the look of stamped tin. The clerk pulled a calculator out from behind the counter. "I can get you a better price," she said, "if you are willing to buy today." We asked who designed the pendant and where it was made. The clerk admitted cheerily to having not a clue and called over the manager, a man at least two decades her junior who looked less like a jeweler than a counterman at Johnny Rocket. The manager didn't know who designed the pendant or where it was made, but he did express some certainty that the diamonds "probably come from someplace in Africa." He assured us that if we truly desired this item, he would give us the "best possible price." Just how good a price we never learned because our desire was less than true. A quick check on the Internet a few days later revealed that the diamonds in the circle of life were in fact just one step north of industrial grade, and what appeared to be identical pendants were selling on eBay for prices ranging upward of $299.

Discounters like Crescent succeed by offering the perception of value using two signals: one, being situated in an outlet mall associated with so-called premium brands, and two, setting very high reference prices. Had we wanted the pendant but were uncertain of its value, the $3,329 reference price would almost certainly have swayed us, regardless of whether we knew it to be inflated. Most of us are suckers for this "high/low retailing," particularly when we are shopping for what we think of as luxury goods: leather gloves and wallets, silk jackets and ties, linen shirts, high-end stereo equipment, and designer anything. A designer label can make us believe that a flimsy T-shirt is worth the $150 manufacturer's suggested price (MSP) or at least close enough to it to make it a steal at $25. Rummaging through a pile of boxy, ill-fitting cashmere sweaters reliably discounted to $75.99 at basement stores each holiday season, we suspend disbelief that the $250 MSP might actually mean something.

Donald Lichtenstein, a professor of marketing at the University of Colorado, has devoted much of his career to the link between cost and value. Lichtenstein is known among his colleagues as a fastidious and thrifty shopper, and his basement is stacked with entire pallets of discounted running shoes, pasta sauce, and sports drinks. A dedicated marathon runner, he is confident that he knows the true value of these things and is therefore resistant if not immune to high/low pricing come-ons. But he is leery of buying less familiar products at a deep discount. Scams, he said, are ubiquitous and nearly unavoidable.

"The biggest misconception is that consumers believe that if something is not true, the store is somehow not allowed to say it," he said.

"Whatever the legal considerations, in reality the whole consumer protection thing is very limited. You have to be your own policeman. The variance in price is enormous. You have to check prices online or elsewhere before you shop. But consumers tend not to check prices. That's a huge mistake. When it comes to prices, background knowledge is absolutely critical."

Most of us think we know a lot about prices, and we do. We know the price of things we buy every week: gas, soft drinks, lunch at our favorite sandwich shop. We know what it costs to ride the subway, the price of the Sunday paper, and the cost of the cup of coffee that goes with it. Things we pay for less frequently—furniture, rugs, jewelry, mattresses, computers, digital cameras, used cars—are things we tend to know less about, including price. Kent Monroe, a pricing expert and professor of marketing at the University of Illinois, said that some states have laws mandating that retailers sell items at full price for a certain period of time before discounting them, but these laws are rarely enforced. As many of us suspect, sale prices are often full prices dressed up in discount drag.

Monroe served as an expert witness in a particularly egregious case in which a mattress manufacturer sued the (now-defunct) May Department Stores for wildly overstating the reference price of mattresses. The case raged on for three years and was finally settled, but this did little to dissuade mattress retailers from inflating reference prices to increase the apparent value of their wares. The tactic has become so common that department stores typically rotate discount offers through a number of mattress brands so that at least one brand appears to be on sale at any given time. (In reality, no mattress is significantly discounted; rather, the brands not on sale carry inflated prices.) Given that most of us buy mattresses very rarely and have little or no knowledge of or preference for a particular brand, we are likely to purchase whatever brand is on sale, none the wiser that the sale price is actually the real price.

This may seem benign, but from a business perspective, it is not. Monroe and other marketing experts agree that inflated reference prices are a serious problem. Although savvy consumers tend to discount high reference prices, they don't discount them enough to be unmoved by them. We are more likely to buy a mattress—or any number of items—with a high reference price than an item with a lower, more accurate reference price, regardless of its quality or even our real preferences. And as a result of these very high reference prices, our concept of prices of all kinds remains skewed, biasing our thinking on future purchases. We may actually believe that a $250 mattress should be priced at the original manufacturer's suggested price of $1,000 or at least $500, making it difficult for an honest broker to sell a $250 mattress tagged as such. We want a $1,000 mattress for our $250, not a $250 one! This leads to a cycle of inflated reference prices, more deception, and more consumer confusion about the meaning of price.

Sleight-of-hand reference pricing is especially common when retailers demand and get unique names for the various models of items they sell, making it all but impossible to compare features across stores or even across brands within a store. In the case of mattresses, selling points such as the number of coils or the thickness of "memoryfoam" are meaningless to consumers and, for that matter, to most salespeople. If we are going to check on quality, we need a number or name by which to compare a given model to others in its category. But when these numbers and names vary from store to store, they are useless as a reference point. As one industry insider told *Consumer Reports,* "It's difficult to compare mattresses unless you cut them open. The retailers demand exclusivity of the cover and label. They don't want their product shopped."

Reference prices and selective discounting direct our everyday buying behavior in ways most of us don't notice and would never suspect. At the grocery store we are far more likely to buy an item at a reduced price even if the sale price is higher than the regular price at another store. Just seeing the difference between the full and reduced price motivates the purchases. It is as though, rather than *spending* the cost of the product, we're actually *earning* the savings. Lichtenstein has done surveys of shoppers exiting supermarkets, asking them the prices of various items in their shopping cart. "Usually they burst out laughing because they have no idea how much they've spent," he said. "But they usually do know how much money they've saved." Reference pricing is so powerful, Lichtenstein said, because it seems to confound the consumer paradox of wanting more but wanting to spend less. An inflated price makes a product more desirable and makes the actual price seem low by comparison. So whether or not you were actually looking for that product or can even use it, you now desire it. This phenomenon holds an almost irresistible psychological allure. "No one—not even me—is not influenced by reference prices," Lichtenstein said. "Once you see them, you can't get them out of your head."

FACTORY OUTLETS AND Las Vegas both play into this natural human desire to "beat the house." And like the house, outlets are nearly impossible to beat, at least consistently. This is doubly true in "premium" luxury outlets where fantasy is a key marketing tool. While luxury is not apparent in these places, the very word instills the impression that it is hovering invisibly over the proceedings like a benevolent fairy godmother waving her magic wand.

Luxury has always been with us, but until recently luxury goods were by definition attainable only by the few. In her riveting book *Deluxe: How Luxury Lost its Luster,* reporter Dana Thomas traces the luxury market back to eighteenth-century France where Marie Antoinette "overran her annual clothing budget of $3.6 million by buying gowns encrusted with sapphires, diamonds, silver and gold . . . " Clothing designed and made for royalty and its retinue was in those days so fabulous and fragile that packing it for travel was a job in itself. Louis Vuitton, a farmer's son, walked from his home in the Jura mountains in eastern France to Paris to apprentice himself to a trunk maker, where he learned to build and pack trunks for the world's most discriminating clientele. Eventually, Vuitton had his own business, for which his son Georges designed the distinctive interlocking *LV* logo, thereby launching the phenomenon of luxury brands.

As related by Thomas, the rise of Louis Vuitton is similar to that of many luxury brands such as Dior (which Vuitton now owns) and Gucci. All of these began as family-owned workshops specializing in one or two items and serving a small and exclusive clientele. This pattern changed in the 1960s when Yves Saint Laurent, a Dior assistant at the time, introduced a lower-priced ready-to-wear line and a selection of fragrances and accessories affordable to a wide range of consumers. "From then on," Thomas wrote, "luxury was no longer simply about creating the finest things money could buy. It was about making money, a lot of money."

Coach was at the cutting edge of this trend. Founded in 1941, the company started as a small leather workshop where craftsmen tooled wallets and belts for sale by major retailers. In 1946, Miles Cahn, son of one of the firm's investors, joined the company fresh out of the army. Cahn didn't know much about leather goods, but he was a natural businessman. Among his innovations was using leather treated in the manner commonly used in the making of baseball gloves to develop softness and patina with wear. Eventually he bought the company and, at his wife Lillian's suggestion, began making a variety of women's handbags to supplement the factory's low-margin wallet business. Sold under the brand name Coach, the bags were fashioned from sturdy cowhide, the grain and seams of which were deliberately kept visible, a notable improvement on the leather-pasted-over-cardboard technique used by most mass-market manufacturers of the time. Cahn built his bag business into a $20 million company and sold it to the Sara Lee Corporation in 1985.

Cheesecake giant Sara Lee repositioned Coach as "affordable luxury," an increasingly popular marketing slogan as brands took on a significance that eclipsed the stores selling them. In 2000, Coach broke away from Sara Lee and developed a collection of wallets, purses, and bags in both leather and canvas. These "signature" items were branded with the distinctive C logo set in a checkerboard print, and many were hot sellers. The company opened new stores in North America and Asia (the European market was considered too competitive), and outsourced most of its manufacturing to China and other developing countries. Today, Coach is a $2 billion operation. And according to Cahn, most of the company's profits stem from its seventy-five-plus factory outlet stores.

The first Coach bag discount outlet was in East Hampton, Long Island, a side project Cahn concocted to unload bags with slight defects. Run by Cahn's children, the outlet was incredibly successful, with inventory frequently selling out within hours after the store opened. "We wanted to be fair to our customers, and we figured that selling slightly defective goods at half price was a reasonable thing," Cahn said. "The customers agreed."

Some brands continue to stick to this formula, offering deep discounts on damaged or slightly blemished goods. Others sell last year's line or, in the case of electronics, refurbished or floor models or returned goods. But Coach, the Gap, Brooks Brothers, Ann Taylor, and Donna Karan, among others, add to their mix items made explicitly for the outlets. Generally these items are cheaper to produce, have fewer details, and are of lesser quality. Still, they carry the brand name, and therefore seem to be worth if not the reference price, then certainly more than the asking price. Lichtenstein put it this way: "Outlet malls today are the absolute epitome of the reference pricing scam."

When Naylor and I visited the Coach store at the Las Vegas Premium Outlet Mall, no shoppers seemed interested in the $85 shapeless brown canvas sacks heaped on a table in the center of the store. Neither of us recalled seeing bags like this in Coach's regular store, but a salesclerk assured us that every item here was also available in the full-price Coach stores. Naylor raised an eyebrow and then took me on a tour. The tags on the brown bags and on most of the other merchandise was branded with an F for "factory outlet." (The one exception was a display of green and pink summer canvas purses, four months out of season.) Naylor pulled from the shelf a large slouchy leather bag. It didn't take a magnifying glass to see it lacked the finish, feel, and details of a luxury brand. Good quality, yes, with the heft and look of a department store private label, but not luxury. Roughly 80 percent of the goods sold at Coach outlets are lower-end pieces manufactured specifically for these stores. Connoisseurs would take a pass on this stuff, Naylor said, but very few shoppers are connoisseurs. "Generally speaking, Americans who shop at Coach outlets are *Sex and the City* types, younger single women or housewives who want the brand but can't afford it," she said.

Economists Anne J. Coughlan of the Kellogg School of Management at Northwestern University and David A. Soberman of INSEAD (originally an acronym for Institut Européen d'Administration des Affaires, one of the world's leading business schools) are editors of the definitive "A

Survey of Outlet Mall Retailing: Past, Present, and Future." In it they trace the history of outlet malls more than a century to when clothing and shoe manufacturers sold overstocked and damaged goods to their workers out of spartan "factory stores" on the company grounds. These goods, whether stained, mismatched, dirty, or just out of season, were deeply discounted and were at first regarded as "perks" of employment. Gradually, factory stores proved so profitable that they were opened to nonemployees and the selection expanded to include a variety of off-price merchandise. In 1936, New England men's clothes maker Anderson-Little opened the first set of freestanding "factory direct" outlets, all of them in remote locations so as not to compete with the regular stores. More factory outlets followed, and until the early 1970s, Coughlan and Soberman wrote, "outlet stores served primarily to dispose of excess or damaged merchandise, in isolated single-store locations."

As the outlet was physically liberated from the actual factory it represented, new retail possibilities unfolded. In 1974 lingerie maker Vanity Fair Clothing Company opened the first multistore outlet sixty-five miles northwest of Philadelphia in an old knitting mill and warehouse in Reading, Pennsylvania. The outlet sold panty hose, underwear, jeans, and socks out of mammoth bins. Some of these clothes were defective, and all had labels roughly chopped off to ensure the integrity of the brand. The Vanity Fair operation was so successful that other manufacturers followed suit, and by the end of the decade, Reading had so many outlets that it acquired the nickname Outlet City.

Outlets rose as a product of their time. The fall in discretionary income and the rise in visibility of private-label merchandise contributed to the outlet boom of the 1970s. Individual outlet stores clustered in large outlet malls that popped up around the country. Gradually the stores in these malls came to offer not only "seconds" with missing labels but first-quality, in-season goods. This led to another burst of growth, with the number of outlet malls in the United States more than tripling from 113 in 1988 to a peak of 325 in 1997. Since then the field has thinned out a bit as the size of each individual outlet ballooned to as large as 600,000 square feet.

In *Discount Dreams,* cultural historian Marianne Conroy links the rise of outlet malls to "larger structural transformations in U.S. production away from mass manufacturing and Ford-style economies of scope." Outlets, she writes, function as "safety valves," a way for manufacturers and retailers to vent their overheated engines of production and exert control over their costs, distribution, and inventory. Outlets draw customers with brands, thereby diminishing the importance of the reputation of the store that sells the brands. Ultimately, then, it was the rise of brand names that made possible the outlet juggernaut. A philosopher might question whether a Coach bag of questionable quality hawked by clerks who do not know the provenance of their merchandise is the Coach bag of our dreams. Shoppers might ask that, too, but mostly we seem not to. Many other popular brands offer down-market sub-brands: The Gap has Old Navy, Anne Klein has Anne Klein II, and Armani has the Armani Exchange. Others—such as uber-popular outdoor-wear maker The North Face—sell merchandise at their outlets that they decline to guarantee and will not exchange. Once again this leads to a philosophical question: Is a North Face outlet product really a North Face at all?

Discount outlets depend on brands for their survival, for without them they would be nothing but a collection of cut-rate stores. Branding was born with civilization, an age-old technique to conspicuously display ownership or value. The association of quality with brands extends back to ancient Roman craftsmen and, even before that, to ancient Egyptian seals.

In modern marketing, brand equity refers to the extent to which a brand's characteristics exceed expectations among other products in its category. A branded suit implies to the consumer a higher quality than an unbranded suit. In the early days of outlets, manufacturers ripped labels from items because they were reluctant to link their brand with the cut-rate price. But today many discounters do just the opposite, trumpeting goods under brand names to give the impression of quality while not necessarily backing that claim in a meaningful way. Online marketer eBay has tested the outer limits of this tactic by auctioning off brand-name merchandise at absurdly low prices. In 2004 high-end jeweler Tiffany sued eBay in New York's federal court, claiming that 80 percent of goods sold on the site under the Tiffany label were fakes. In 2006, luxury purveyor LVMH filed a similar suit in Paris, claiming that up to

90 percent of Vuitton and Dior items peddled on the site were counterfeit. Four years later a Paris judge fined eBay almost 40 million euros ($63 million), arguing that the Internet auctioneer didn't do enough to stop the sale of counterfeit goods. The French court also ruled that eBay was not qualified to sell LVMH perfumes, which it said should be distributed only through selected retailers with trained staff. In New York a couple of weeks later, the Tiffany case was decided in eBay's favor; the judge made clear that in the United States it is the manufacturer's responsibility to protect its own brand, something that in the face of cutthroat price competition fewer and fewer manufacturers appear willing to do.

Do we shop at factory outlets and dollar stores and price clubs and eBay because we believe we are getting the genuine article, or is there something deeper involved? This question, Naylor said, has no sure answer, but she personally believes that most discount shoppers get something close enough to name brands to give them lasting pleasure. Apparently it is the brand, not necessarily authenticity, that discount shoppers are after. But when paying $250 for a briefcase or a handbag at an outlet, the question "When is a Coach not a Coach?" is more than a philosophical quibble. The uncoupling of brand name and product can't help but confuse us and, over time, even undermine our trust.

DISCOUNTING dilutes brands, making it less certain that they are a mark of quality. This diluting effect has forced some producers to up the ante with premium versions of their brand-name products. For example, The North Face "Summit Series," designed for what the company describes as "the most demanding athletes and the most extreme conditions," is rarely if ever discounted, thereby maintaining its status. Hundreds of other brands from Levi Strauss to Mercedes-Benz slice and dice their offerings for various markets, selling different products in different types of stores for different prices under the same brand. This practice is pervasive at discount retailers. Chains such as Wal-Mart, Best Buy, Target, and Home Depot have items manufactured "to their specifications," meaning that the brand name is almost devoid of meaning. A television with a model number available only at Best Buy or Wal-Mart is—no matter its apparent brand—a Best Buy or Wal-Mart television. A lawn mower made to be sold only at Home Depot is—for all intents and purposes—a Home Depot lawn mower.

Brand dilution occurs in all the obvious places but also in the less obvious—for example, in higher education. Harvard University flaunts its brand to draw students to Harvard University Extension School, a program with no threshold to entry and a much smaller price tag than the institution to which it is tethered. Harvard University officials insist that extension school graduates receive an authentic Harvard degree, yet the education they have experienced, though presumably of high quality, is not really a Harvard education. By running a second-tier program under its name, Harvard is diluting its brand and in a sense counterfeiting itself.

Brands have become an end in themselves. Many of us who seek them have little if any idea of what's behind the name. But it is not the brand alone that entices discount shoppers; it is the high value we link to that brand versus the low price we pay that is so seductive. Spinning the wheel of low price is at best a gamble, but it is a gamble few of us can resist taking. The pull of markdowns, always seductive, has in recent years become an unstoppable force.

# CHAPTER FIVE

# MARKDOWN MADNESS

Having a sale every day is a bad idea, but retailers are afraid
to stop.

| RAMA RAMAKRISHNAN, FORMER CHIEF SCIENTIST OF ORACLE RETAIL

It is often said that New Englanders talk more about the weather than
about all other topics combined. There is scant hard evidence for this,
but I'm inclined to believe it. Temperatures here can sink from balmy to
arctic overnight, icing streets into axle-twisting slicks that melt into moats
in the next day's sun. But even weather-hardened Bostonians found December 2006 puzzling. As Christmas closed in, it looked as if Donner and
Blitzen would be swapping the sled for a cigarette boat. Daytime highs
hovered at 15 degrees above normal. There was not even a whiff of snow.
The heat spelled sweet relief for the thin-blooded endless summer enthusiasts. But it was very bad for retail.

Sales of woolly hats, boots, snow blowers, and rock salt plummeted.
No one, it seemed, needed fleece. Down jackets twisted on department
store racks like hungry ghosts. As haberdashers and furriers prayed for
cold, the weather gods scoffed and threw another log on the fire. In a
last-ditch effort to reclaim the season, merchants closed their eyes, held
their breath, and kicked off the "post-holiday" markdown fest three days
*before* Christmas.

Bloomingdale's slashed the price of designer overcoats by 30 percent.
Saks slapped a 40 percent discount on its entire cold weather line. The
Gap went straight for the jugular, "repositioning" its fabulous faux fur
parka from $169 to $68. These measures were every bit as desperate as

they seemed. One analyst wailed to the *New York Times*: "Retailers are getting caught with their pants down—and their coats off." Those pants have been hanging low ever since. Markdown madness is turning even luxury emporia into something closer to the "everyday low price" model. Watching numbly as shoppers pawed through a pile of handbags, a salesclerk at once-tony Bergdorf Goodman put it bluntly: The world, he said, is "off its axis."

There is nothing new, of course, about holiday sales. But today draconian price reductions are a retail imperative pre-holiday, post-holiday, and most days in between. Radical price cutting has turned the swankiest outposts—Neiman Marcus, Barneys, Bergdorf Goodman—into upscale versions of discount outlets, hustling merchandise out of the store in the largest volume possible as quickly as possible. "Runway clothes next year will arrive in the store in April, and we will have three weeks to sell them at full price before the department stores put them on sale," moaned one boutique owner to the *New York Times*. "What I'm worried about is the creativity." By which she meant the loss thereof.

The rise of markdowns has given customers unprecedented purchasing power. It has also given merchandisers unprecedented power over manufacturers and suppliers—the power to demand and get extraordinary concessions. Those of us who merely shop are blissfully unaware of what vendors go through to get their merchandise on the store floor. For some it is merely a trial, for others a travesty. As that boutique owner worried, creativity and innovation can get lost in the stampede toward ever lower prices. But the problem cuts even deeper: When consumer goods are marked down to a pittance, those of us who can least afford it end up paying the difference in the form of low wages, lost opportunity, and crushing debt.

The story begins with a radical change in the way Americans do business. When the retail industry was made up of thousands of players—when there were more independent stores, more regional chains, and fewer mega-conglomerates—vendors and manufacturers had the leverage to insist that retailers share in the financial risk of marketing their goods. This is not to say that vendors held all the cards; if a delivery was damaged or just wrong, a refund from the vendor was definitely in order.

And if merchandise was daring or dodgy and didn't sell well—such as a particularly edgy line from an innovative young fashion designer— vendors helped buffer the full financial blow by sharing the loss with the retailers. But a retailer did not expect to have to pay the difference when a store found itself forced to mark down its wares, a practice called pay-ing "markdown money." Stores could, of course, mark down Ralph Lauren at season's end, but Ralph Lauren was not about to pony up to bolster the retailer's margin. The art of department store merchandizing, after all, was selling products at a fair price. Fire sales were for bargain basements, something department stores decidedly were not.

In the 1970s and 1980s, the climate changed. One after another, depart-ment stores merged into one another, as did pharmacies, toy stores, and hardware stores. As each of these conglomerates grew in size, they also grew in clout. Vendors and manufacturers could no longer afford to make demands, because losing even one conglomerate meant losing big. Even iconic designers like Ralph Lauren began cutting deals with retailers, promising to pick up the slack if and when sales went south.

From the 1990s onward Lord & Taylor, Kaufman's, Famous-Barr, Mar-shall Field's, Bloomingdale's, and Macy's, among others, were absorbed into even larger chains. In 1993 the top five retail organizations held 48 percent of the apparel market, and by 2000, ten retail chains sold 72 percent of American clothing. Meanwhile, untold numbers of indepen-dent book, audio, appliance, and other specialty stores closed their doors. Today the surviving behemoths have the power to squeeze vendors even harder, especially in volatile retail sectors such as toys, electronics, appli-ances, and fashion. Markdown money has become commonplace and expected. One clothing retail executive put it this way: "The pressure goes right down the line. Pricing starts from the retailer and moves down. It doesn't start from the bottom, from the real costs of making the gar-ment. The retailer can always go down to the street and find someone to make it for less. The manufacturers and contractors are stuck." Retail-ers call markdown money good business. Critics call it extortion, and sometimes it is.

In 2005, Saks Fifth Avenue settled federal charges that it improperly collected more than $30 million in markdown money from a dozen designers, including Oscar de La Renta and Michael Kors. Thanks to pressure from a Security and Exchange Commission investigation, Saks was forced to repay the vendors but admitted no wrongdoing and paid no fine. While this was an extreme case, markdown money has grown so pervasive over the past few years that in some industries it has all but paralyzed smaller vendors and manufacturers. Certainly it has made it far more difficult than it once was to innovate, to create something new and unexpected for which there is no guaranteed market.

MARKDOWNS have been with us for some time, of course, but until half a century ago, most stores cut prices on merchandise at preordained intervals and for predictable reasons generally involving seasonal change. In that precomputer era, retailing was as much art as science, and merchants built their inventory around what they knew or thought they knew of their clients. Buyers for stores prided themselves on anticipating the needs and desires of customers and quickly adjusted selection to accommodate preferences and anticipate or even create trends. Intuition honed by experience told them what to stock. That intuition was rarely perfect, but it was good enough to avoid rabid discounting: In 1955 the dollar value of total markdowns as a percentage of department store sales was a paltry 5.2 percent.

The advent of computers and "lean retailing" methods designed to thicken profit margins correlated with a powerful surge in mainstream discounting. Department store markdowns grew to 6.1 percent of all dollar sales in 1965, to 8.9 percent in 1975, and to a startling 18 percent in 1984. Business scholars point to the onslaught of new products and to the growing importance of fashion in America, especially among professionals no longer limited to a uniform of three-button suits and white button-down shirts. There is certainly truth to this: Office workers in the 1980s were awash in options, making it increasingly difficult for retailers to anticipate fashion trends. Whether a powder blue shirt with barrel cuffs would be the season's big seller over, say, a pink pinstripe with French cuffs was nearly impossible to guess, and many merchants ended up eating their bad calls.

At the same time the United States was, in the words of Harvard economist Richard Freeman, using its "overvalued dollar" to "import—suck in—goods from other countries." Globalization, a key component of which was to outsource manufacturing to the world's poorest nations, resulted in a huge surge of imports—from $265.1 billion in 1990 to more than $1.2 trillion in 2000. For reasons that I will soon explain, imported goods are more likely than American made goods to be marked down. By the mid-1990s only 20 percent of all department store merchandise sold at full price, and in 2001 the dollar percentage of marked-down goods across all sectors—toys, electronics, clothing—had grown to an astonishing 33 percent.

Markdowns happen for many reasons, the most common being to clear out "slow-selling" merchandise to make room for new stuff and to free up a bit of cash with which to buy it. The operative words are *slow selling*. Historically, small shopkeepers kept unsold goods on their shelves for months or even years. Today an item that doesn't sell in four or five weeks—or even sooner—may be relegated to the markdown bin. As a result, retailers have come to count on markdowns and plan for them when setting prices. Sometimes the initial price seems so tentative as to be experimental. If the product takes off at the original price, then markdowns are unlikely. Not even Wal-Mart was in a position to discount the hugely popular Apple iPod in 2001. But when sales stall, markdowns can come fast and deep, as was the case of the $599 Apple 8 GB iPhone marked down to $399 within two months of its launch.

As we have seen, setting prices of all kinds is very difficult, as much science as art. Setting markdowns is equally complex. Very small discounts tend not to move merchandise, while extremely large or sudden discounts tend to make customers suspicious. And the proliferation of variables is daunting. Owners of small stores can use a sort of trial-and-error system and begin by making educated guesses. When they guess wrong, they sometimes have room to maneuver. I recently selected a belt at a small consignment shop. At the checkout counter I realized I had misunderstood the price, which was higher than anticipated. I must have winced, for the store owner took note of my discomfort and offered an instant 20 percent discount. It was clear to her that I was either going to decline to buy the belt or buy it reluctantly and leave feeling bad about my decision. She made a quick judgment based on a mix of intuition and experience, and it worked: By reducing the price by an amount I deemed significant, she personalized the experience, clinched the deal, and gained a very satisfied customer.

Unfortunately, this trial-and-error approach does not work on a large scale. Not many department store managers have the discretion to lower prices when a customer winces, and fewer still have the training to use that discretion if they had it. They may have amassed data on the average income, gender, and age of their customers and created bar charts and graphs, but they know relatively little about individual preferences or limits. There are too many customers, too many items, and too many variables. But there are also clues. For example, imported goods are more likely than domestic goods to sell slowly or not at all, and therefore need to be marked down. Marketers call ths (not too creatively) the "staleness factor." Lead times for procuring foreign goods are generally substantial; it takes much longer for a shipment of pajamas or tennis rackets to arrive in Scranton from Shanghai than from, say, Chicago. The result is that some imports go out of fashion in transport. This is not true of all imports; it takes less time to ship an item to the United States from Mexico than it does from China, where goods must be ordered in February to be ready for the next Christmas season. So category by category, the Mexican items tend to be fresher, easier to sell, and less likely to be marked down than the Asian imports.

Regardless of origin, more expensive items are more likely to either sell fairly quickly at full price or linger on store shelves and be heavily discounted. Price experts say the reason for this is that expensive goods generally have more features—more buttons to push on the electric mixer, more beadwork on the dress, more options to deal with on the digital camera or cell phone. Hence they carry with them more price uncertainty. Customers either love them and lap them up, or they don't. This is particularly true of fashion, and the racks of pricy yet strange designer duds reduced to a whisper of their original price at Filene's Basement are testament to this phenomenon.

Seasonal variations also play an important role. At one time there were two seasons: "spring-summer" from March through August and "fall-winter" from September to February, each with its own end-of-season sale. Seasonal boundaries are now so blurred as to be meaningless. As one marketing expert told the *Wall Street Journal*, "They can't even name sales anymore because it would have to be called the June 13 sale followed by the June 14 sale." Consumer goods are expected to sell fast and if they don't, many are quickly discounted. If discounted items don't sell, the price is lowered repeatedly until they do. But markdowns are no longer a simple matter of overlaying price tags with new stickers. Knowing what, when, and by how much to mark down is a monumentally complex task.

AS THE FOUNDER and CEO of two successful high-technology companies, Rama Ramakrishnan is no stranger to complexity. When we met, he was chief scientist and vice president of Oracle Retail, heading up a brain trust of mathematicians, computer scientists, and economists working to solve the thorny markdown problem. A steady gaze and practiced handshake underscored his "most likely tech guy to succeed" affect. He looked fit, well pressed, self-assured, and unmistakably affluent. Still, settling into a beige-on-beige conference room to chat, he admitted to being slightly frustrated. Too many retailers, he said, are slow to change, and when setting markdowns they rely not on Oracle's excellent software but on their own imperfect intuition.

"We compete with gut instincts," he said. "But the question is: How do you make bets on merchandise before you have a clue as to trends? The answer is that you really can't. When merchandise hits the stores, some is hot and some is clearly bad. The bad stuff goes to the outlets. But then there is that middle sixty percent, and as time goes by, some of that merchandise becomes stars, some dogs. You can't just wait it out for the dogs to come to life. By January you have to clear your store for the spring. How do you get rid of the dogs? You use markdown pricing as a lever to stimulate demand."

Ramakrishnan went to the white board and started layering on the equations. Soon the board was nearly black. Surely he sensed that most of what he scribbled was lost on me, but he was too gracious to say so and too caught up to cut the lecture short. "Some customers don't care about price, but most do, and price-sensitive customers anticipate markdowns," he said. "They wait for markdowns. So effectively retailers are playing a game with consumers, a cat-and-mouse game. If you lower the price by thirty percent, you are training the customer to anticipate markdowns by casting a spotlight on price. Usually, that's not good."

By cutting prices radically, as they did in the winter of 2008, retailers plant doubts in consumers' minds about their motives. If reductions of this magnitude are possible, does the normal price mean stratospheric profits? Given the depths to which retailers were willing to sink to lure us, we customers wonder whether we have been ripped off in the past and, if so, whether we should hold out for even deeper discounts in the future.

Ramakrishnan explained that building a business model on a foundation of low price is best for "cost leaders," large discount chains that claim the absolute bottom price on every item in stock. "Wal-Mart's costs are so low because their economies of scale are so large," he said. "If Wal-Mart sneezes, everyone catches a cold. But if you aren't Wal-Mart, you need a more nuanced pricing strategy than 'everyday low prices.' " Tracking all the variables and boiling them down into such a "nuanced" strategy is as tough as predicting New England weather.

Mathematically-based price optimization is not new. Airlines and hotels have relied on it for decades. When a flight starts to fill or a hotel runs short of rooms, yield management ensures that prices go up. Likewise, when rooms or seats aren't filling fast enough, prices go down. This phenomenon is not reliably linear; many of us have had the experience of booking a flight or hotel room and watching it become cheaper over time. Yield management requires anticipating trends before they happen and discounting or raising prices well ahead of the actual events.

Like hotel rooms and seats on an airplane, many consumer goods and services are in demand for a limited time period, so the timing of discounts is crucial. Too early, and money is left on the table. Too late, and the goods or services don't move. The technology to manage markdowns mathematically has been available since at least the mid-1980s, but was priced out of reach of most retailers. The computer power required to analyze the data collected from hundreds of stores on hundreds of thousands of products involved in millions of transactions was huge and prohibitively expensive. But when the cost of computer power plummeted in the mid-1990s, many retailers were poised to take advantage. Enter Oracle and a handful of other software makers.

Experts customize markdown optimization software with the understanding that retailers and consumers are necessarily at odds: The customer's goal is to buy at the lowest possible price while the store owner struggles to keep the price high enough to clear a profit. Balancing these opposing goals requires a continuous gathering of information: past and current sales figures, holiday schedules, and store locations. Weather patterns are also important, but not as important as many of us think. "Retailers blame weather for everything, but other things can matter much more," Ramakrishnan said; "For example, the level of inventory of a particular item a store has in stock."

If a store has one hundred of the same style of sweater, the sheer gravity of the display will promote sales. But as the inventory dwindles, sales decrease. All things being equal, it is easier to sell fifty of one hundred sweaters than one of two sweaters, Ramakrishnan said. The fifty sweaters may fly out of the store at full price, but an isolated pair of sweaters of the same style, color, and size may well languish indefinitely unless the price is marked down significantly. This makes the paying of markdown money all the more painful. Merchants may well know a particular item won't sell out but they order it in large numbers to build a plentiful display, only half of which will be sold at full price. This leaves the other half to be marked down repeatedly, generally at the retailer's discretion and the vendor's expense. One marketing scholar wrote: "The pyramid of power puts the giant retail chains, significant manufacturers themselves, in the most concentrated position. They are the price makers, not the price takers."

Markdown optimization software helps retailers avoid "leaving money on the table" by aligning price reductions with customer demand and automatically lowering prices on individual items when they cease to move. The software is sophisticated enough to allow for variations among individual stores and tells retailers when to move merchandise from one store to another to maximize sales. This means that in many chains the markdown on at least some items will vary from store to store, a phenomenon that few consumers are aware of since retailers are loath to make public that the same item might be available at another store in the same chain at a lower price.

Markdowns come in several varieties, each designed to elicit a different consumer response. "A coupon is less dangerous than a straight promotion," Ramakrishnan said. "Someone has to physically cut it out and bring it to the store, and not everyone is willing to do that. Coupons are a way of having two prices: A price-sensitive person will use the coupon and get a lower price, while a less-price-sensitive person might be willing to pay the full price." Essentially, coupons are an attempt to solve the fixed price dilemma by offering different customers different price options. And we seem to love them: A 2005 study found that 83 percent of us redeem coupons, for a total of roughly 5 billion and a combined savings of $3 billion.

Rebates do something similar, using a very different strategy and offering a rich source of insight into both discounting and human frailty. Like coupons, they are an enormously popular form of discounting, especially in the high-technology sector where in 2004 roughly 25 percent of all purchases—and nearly half of all computer sales—involved them. The catch is that no matter how much we enjoy the idea of rebates and account for them in our buying calculus, few of us enjoy filing for rebates—and for very sound psychological reasons. Filing for a rebate is anticlimactic, an afterthought demanded of us after the thrill of the hunt is long behind us. It makes perfect sense to seek a rebate and deduct that amount from the mental price of the purchase: A $150 printer with a $100 rebate becomes a $50 purchase in our minds. The rise of rebates offers evidence that the thrill of the now can easily trump the prospect of a long-term payoff. "We play a game of funny math with rebates," Daniel Ariely told me. "If we buy a fifty-dollar item that promises a thirty-dollar rebate, in our minds we have paid only twenty dollars, and we forget to grab the rebate. We are pleased with ourselves because we account for the money we save, not for the money we spent." Supermarkets capitalize on this phenomenon by printing more prominently on their cash register receipts the amount shoppers have saved than the amount they have spent, conveying the impression that we are somehow *earning* money in the transaction. "This is motivated reasoning. We want to believe things are a certain way, and so we do," Ariely said. "We want to believe we got a good deal because it makes us feel richer."

Rebates come in two varieties, instant and mail-in. Mail-in rebates are by far the more common option, and they are also the more psychologically satisfying for those who use them: Cutting out, filling out, and filing the required paperwork makes us feel that we have earned our reward. For retailers and manufacturers, though, the special beauty of the mail-in rebate is that relatively few of us actually cut out, fill out, and file it. Tracking down reliable rebate redemption rate data is difficult because industry insiders are understandably reluctant to make public this side of their business. But there are hints. As one retailer put it, "Manufacturers love rebates because redemption rates are close to none. They get people into the stores, but when it comes time to collect, few people follow through. And this is just what the manufacturer had in mind."

This is not always true: Larger rebates for such things as big-screen TVs are more likely than smaller ones to be redeemed. But, as a rule, rebate redemption rates are very low, hovering in the 5 to 10 percent range for many items. Interestingly, some people apparently do not even intend to redeem their rebates when they make a purchase, either because they just don't care about saving the money or because they consider their time too valuable. This certainly makes sense, but most of us are less rational: We plan to redeem but do not. Marketing scholars refer to this phenomenon as "breakage," an apt phrase but one that begs the question of precisely what is being broken. Tim Silk, a professor of marketing at the University of British Columbia, is probably better prepared than anyone to answer that question. He has studied rebates for over half a decade and told me that consumer reaction to them is predictable, though counterintuitive.

Manufacturers often affix a deadline to rebates in what they assume is an effort to minimize redemption rates. But Silk's research gives evidence that the longer we are given to redeem a rebate, the less likely we are to do so, thanks to the normal human inclination to procrastinate in the face of prolonged deadlines. He also found that the more difficult a rebate is to redeem, the more likely it is that it will be redeemed. "There's a backlash," he said. "When you cross the threshold of what people believe is a reasonable effort, they get angry and become more determined to get their refund . . . up to a point. Naturally, if you make the process extremely difficult, you'll probably find fewer takers."

Rebate breakage plays a critical role in marketing strategy by allowing merchants to have it both ways; they can lure customers with the promise of discounts without having to make them. And as Daniel Ariely explained, while most of us do not redeem our rebates, we *believe* that we will. Hence, in our mental calculus we perceive the slimmed-down rebated price—not the bloated sticker price—as our cost. And we tend to say and even believe we paid the lower price whether or not we redeemed the rebate. This twist of internal accounting is the primary reason that rebates have become so common and so popular.

Our response to rebates is typical of our responses to what psychologists call "intertemporal decisions," the outcomes of which don't affect us until well after we make them. Often an action that seems right for now—risking a month's pay at the races or quaffing three martinis at lunch—will feel terribly wrong tomorrow. As Ariely and others have shown, most of us prefer to grab rewards quickly and delay thinking about the consequences, especially monetary consequences. In the case of a rebate, once we've made the purchase and gotten enjoyment from the transaction, an act of will is required to summon the energy and interest to move it forward. The rebate fulfillment industry depends on our not mustering that will since rebate schemes are considered successful only if most purchasers do *not* take advantage of them. Promotions that generate redemption rates greater than 35 percent are considered marginal by manufacturers and retailers; and a 50 percent redemption rate is considered an abject failure. As Tim Silk observed, "From the perspective of the issuing firm, successful rebate programs should increase the number of rebate-dependent purchases (i.e., incremental sales) without encouraging redemptions."

THE COST OF rebates goes even beyond that incurred by self-delusion. Too often a rebate steers us to make purchases with little forethought, tainting our decision. This is particularly true of items offered with rebates that refund the total price of the purchase. That is, rebates that make things free.

Free is a category unto itself. It can rob us of our reason. Razor blade maker King Camp Gillette took full advantage of this temporary insanity. Gillette grew rich handing out free safety razors to generate demand for his pricy disposable blades. A hundred or so years later a similar business model informs the workings of entire product segments: computer printers and cell phones, to name but two. Rebate the full price of a printer and gain a buyer for your overpriced printer cartridges. Rebate the full price of a cell phone and freeze the customer for two years into your service plan. Most of us respond to free offers by assuming that they are better than other options; it is very difficult to pass up a free printer for one that costs real money. But at the same time most of us know instinctively that freebies must come with a catch. For this reason we have developed some unconscious but fairly consistent internal rules for free.

Consider the free sample in the local supermarket, perhaps a selection of tempting cheddar cheese bits impaled on toothpicks. Studies show that most of us will take only one, perhaps because taking more would appear discourteous or greedy. But when we are charged a penny for each nibble of cheese, more of us take more than one, perhaps because the penny payment psychologically liberates us from the guilt of freeloading. Daniel Ariely has tested this phenomenon using candy as a lure. He found that when offered a Starburst for a penny, the average subject bought four, but when offered free Starbursts, the average subject took only one. Free, he said, elicits a response like no other: It is the point on the mental money meter at which reaching the lowest possible price (zero) both increases and reduces demand. Free is unique among price points because it jettisons market-based values and the question of whether the object or service is worth the cost, in favor of social-based values and the question of whether we are worthy of the object or service. It also softens us up for the sell: Research shows that samplers are much more likely than nonsamplers to buy the product.

Ariely was so intrigued by the paradoxical power of zero to both stimulate and stifle demand that he conducted another empirical study to test it. He offered sixty subjects three choices: a Hershey's Kiss for one cent, a Ferrero Rocher hazelnut chocolate for twenty-six cents, or nothing at all for zero cents. Twenty percent of subjects chose nothing at all, 40 percent chose the Kiss, and 40 percent went for the more luxurious Ferrero Rocher candy. Ariely then offered the same subjects the same choice on different terms: nothing for no money, twenty-five cents for the Ferrero Rocher, or a chocolate Kiss for free. This time every subject took something, but only 10 percent took the Ferrero Rocher and 90 percent went for the Hershey's Kiss. "When something is free, it has no down side and becomes elevated in our minds," Ariely said. Those who chose the free chocolate forfeited the opportunity to get a more valuable chocolate at a much reduced price, but as merchandisers well know, the average shopper does not worry much about such "opportunity loss."

One of the mysteries of free is why we so often pursue it when it is against our interests to do so. I once attended a street fair in Cambridge, Massachusetts, and noticed an extremely long line of people snaking toward an open serving window of a Ben & Jerry's ice cream truck. On closer inspection it became clear that the ice cream was free. "Free ice cream," it occurred to me, was not the same thing as ice cream. "Ice cream" did not explain why at least two-dozen teenagers—iPod's firmly in place—were waiting with uncharacteristic patience. "Free ice cream" explained this perfectly. But "free" did not entirely account for the twenty or so middle-aged patrons shuffling slowly toward their single scoop. From the well-dressed look of them, most of these boomers earned something more than minimum wage. An ice cream cone costs about $3 and is worth maybe ten minutes of their time, but certainly not the thirty-plus minutes it was taking them to get served. At least some of these people were bound to be highly paid professionals who were effectively shelling out $50 or even $100 in billables for a scoop of Chunky Monkey. But was

Chunky Monkey even available? As it turned out, it was not. Only chocolate, vanilla, and chocolate chip cookie dough were on board the truck that afternoon. Ben & Jerry's Cambridge Scoop Shop, just four blocks away, had many, many more choices, and when I strolled over to take a look, had no line at all. The people waiting in line were willing to invest their time—and forgo their freedom of choice—for free. Very low prices—especially zero—tend to make us overvalue the deal itself in relation to the object of the deal. This is a boon for merchants who know that as their price approaches zero, consumers tend to lower their expectations and become more willing to endure significant costs, generally the highest cost being their time.

Benjamin Franklin wrote, "Remember, time is money. He that can earn ten shillings a day by his labor, and goes abroad or sits idle one half of that day, though he spends but six pence during his diversion or idleness, ought not to reckon that the only expense; he has really spent, or rather thrown away, five shillings besides." Economists, too, consider time in monetary terms, often represented in their calculations as "an opportunity cost." While this makes sound theoretical sense—we say we "spend" both money and time, after all—in practice it does not always apply. Research shows that most of us fail to calculate the opportunity cost of time, and when reminded of it, we tend to underestimate its value.

As consumers our reaction to the passage of time tends to be inconsistent, sometimes even schizophrenic. The same person willing to wait thirty minutes in line for a free ice cream cone might a few hours later be willing to pay double the supermarket price for a half-gallon of ice cream at a convenience store. Waiting in line at an ice cream truck to score a deal seems worth the time, while standing in line at the supermarket simply to save money may not.

Markdowns may be calibrated mathematically, but their impact is felt viscerally—and deeply. As do sex, alcohol, and drugs, markdowns tap into our brain's pleasure center and sap our reason. Distracted, we make mistakes. We overvalue what we say matters very little, such as saving a few pennies, and undervalue what we say matters very much, variety, quality and—most important—our time. Our preoccupation with low prices makes it easy to forget that every penny we save on mark-downs must be taken from someone else or, failing that, extracted from the value of the object of our desire. In discount nation, what once was solid, permanent, and dependable has become disposable, ephemeral, and dicey.

# CHAPTER SIX

# DEATH OF A CRAFTSMAN

> Despite his resolute belief in progress, des Pereires had
> always detested standardization. . . . From the very start he
> was bitterly opposed to it. . . . He foresaw that the death of
> craftsmanship would inevitably shrink the human
> personality.
>
> | LOUIS FERDINAND CELINE, *DEATH ON THE INSTALLMENT PLAN*

> No One Will Bother You.
>
> | SIGN AT THE ENTRANCE TO AN IKEA STORE

Gillis Lundgren was an industrious man, and determined. A skilled carpenter working out of his home in the remote farming village of Almhult,
Sweden, he had been hired by a local furniture dealer to build and deliver
a table. Lundgren was comfortable with his tools, and crafting the piece
was simple enough. But delivery was another matter: Try as he might,
he couldn't cram the thing into the trunk of his Volvo PV445 Duet Station
Wagon. After several failed efforts and some thought, he attacked the
problem in a manner familiar to young boys the world over: "Oh, God,
then," he was said to mutter, "let's pull the legs off."

Lundgren's client that day in 1956 was Ingvar Kamprad, the farmer's
son who years later would be among the world's richest men. A preco-
cious and prescient entrepreneur, young Kamprad instinctively recognized the auspicious implications of Lundgren's desperate fling at furniture
dismemberment. "Flat packing," as he came to call it, not only allowed
large tables to be crammed into small vehicles, but it also squeezed the

air out of the packaging process, thereby eliminating the cost of shipping vast quantities of empty space. In one stroke, two noisome problems were solved.

Kamprad hired Lundgren into the company he called IKEA, where flat packing soon became an informing concept. In addition to minimizing shipping costs, flat packing deftly unloaded the time-consuming and expensive chores of delivering and assembling furniture onto the one person reliably willing to do it for free: the customer. Without knowing it, Lundgren had laid the groundwork for one of the great marketing gambits of the twentieth century: the discreet transfer of costs from seller to buyer.

Flat packing and all that went with it not only saved money, it liberated tables and chairs and bookshelves from historical reference. Rather than being passed down from generation to generation, accumulating nostalgic heft, furniture was cut loose from its history. For scores of millions of IKEA customers the world over, heirlooms gradually became obsolete. Why settle for dusty hand-me-downs when the stylish and new cost a pittance?

Half a century after Lundgren's groundbreaking epiphany, Spike Jonze, the quirky director of *Being John Malkovich*, *Adaptation*, and a slew of terrific music videos, produced a commercial for IKEA. The spot opens on a blandly furnished urban apartment. A young woman walks into view, unplugs a red reading lamp, hauls it out to the curb with the garbage, and returns to her sofa and the glow of a sleek new replacement model. The camera pans back to the street. The lamp, shivering in the bluster and cringing like a beaten dog, seems almost to weep. We know this is only a lamp, but this wind and this cringing makes us want to weep, too. Suddenly, a man with thinning hair and what sounds like a fake Swedish accent appears out of nowhere and addresses the camera. "Many of you feel bad for dis lamp," he deadpans, rain pelting his face. "Dat is because you are crazy. Duh lamp has no feelings. And the new one is much bedder." The ad is funny, hip, irreverent, and a tad embarrassing. Why cry for an inanimate object? It's a lamp, not a lover, for God's sake, and a new one *is* so much better. The ad provokes an uncomfortable thought: If objects have no feelings, does that mean we really are crazy to care about them?

IKEA itself seems to be of two minds on the matter. On one hand, the company denigrates nostalgia. On the other, it creates pet names for everything it sells, from sofas to ice cream scoops. There are Lack coffee tables and Rusig rugs and Kura loft beds. There is the Galant drawer unit and the Bomull twin fitted sheet. There is a method of sorts to this madness. Bathrooms, for example, rely heavily on Norwegian lakes for their names. This has nothing to do with retail convention. It is hard to imagine Home Depot christening a kitchen sink "Sweet Pea" or Wal-Mart naming lightbulbs of various wattages after small towns in upstate New York. If IKEA thinks it's crazy to care deeply about objects, why does it sell a wok named after a girl?

Answering this question requires a bit of self-reflection. What is IKEA to us? With its focus on sharp design and Scandinavian élan, its sly, ironic commercials, its conspicuously progressive outlook, IKEA appears to be the anti–Wal-Mart: a classy, high-minded company where value and good values coexist. Image may not be everything, but sometimes it's enough. Cognitive scientist Kathryn Fitzgerald of FKF Applied Research Neuroscience in Los Angeles has made a study of retail strategies and how customers respond to them. Wal-Mart can't escape its downscale connotations, she told me, but IKEA has artfully decoupled low price from its unsavory side. "IKEA is an example of using youth, friendliness, and other brand personality traits along with design innovation to make the notion of buying low-priced furnishings socially acceptable," she said. "Retailers of this sort use style and other cues to make sure their low prices don't come along with heavy low-status baggage." Target takes a similar approach, as does H & M and a number of other low-price purveyors. "They are all trying to establish trust that the low prices aren't merely a signal of poor products," Fitzgerald said.

Price is a vital consideration for any business, the bottom line being the bottom line after all. But for IKEA, price is no mere variable or signal; it is the starting point. Wal-Mart, Target, Lowe's, and other Big Box discounters scour the globe for low-price suppliers from which to buy their low-priced goods. IKEA takes matters one step further: It *designs* to price, commissioning its suppliers to build not a mug, per se, but a custom-designed 50-cent mug; not a kitchen table and two chairs, but a custom-designed kitchen table and two chairs for less than one hundred euros. Every year IKEA challenges its suppliers to lower their prices, and every year it challenges its designers to dream up still cheaper objects to sell, whether new ones or updated versions of classics. A facsimile of the very table Lundgren deconstructed so many years ago retails at this writing for an astonishing $69. I asked a master furniture maker what he thought of this, and he responded with awe. "It's mind-boggling," he said. "I couldn't buy the wood for that price, let alone build the thing." He wondered how IKEA could manage it. I figured the best way to find out was to go straight to the source.

IKEA HAS CARVED its corporate headquarters out of a converted sugar factory in Helsingborg, Sweden, a historic coastal city with a fine view of Denmark over the strait of Oresund. The company is one of the city's largest employers but maintains such a low profile that a cab driver circled the building several times before reluctantly stopping at what we both knew had to be the correct address. Given IKEA's knack for playful design, the faceless, stumpy brick structure was disappointing. But inside all was brightly lit exposed brick, lofty and frenetic. The sleek open cafeteria echoed with the babble of multilingual employees cradling signature blue and white mugs. I had arrived smack in the middle of *fika*, the obligatory communal coffee break that is a charming hallmark of Swedish life. I later learned that Swedes, Danes, and Finns drink more coffee per capita than any other nationality, perhaps to keep roused through the short, dark winter days. I accepted a cup gratefully and went off to meet IKEA president and CEO Anders Dahlvig.

Dahlvig wasn't drinking coffee and didn't appear to need any. Focused and deliberate, he is a plainspoken MBA with what appears to be a deep inner calm. Dahlvig explained that IKEA is legally not Swedish at all but a holding of Ingka Holding, a Dutch company that itself is owned by the tax-exempt Stichting Ingka Foundation. In 1982 founder Kamprad donated all his shares to Stichting Ingka, thereby creating the world's flushest charitable foundation. In 2007, Stichting Ingka Foundation had a net worth of at least $36 billion, devoted to "innovation in the field of architectural and interior design." Architectural and interior design is not the usual target for philanthropy, and Dutch foundations are subject to very little oversight or regulation, so it's hard to know where all the money goes. One observer thought he knew, telling *The Economist*: "Clearly, the Kamprad family pays the same meticulous attention to tax avoidance as IKEA does to low prices in its stores." That Kamprad is a tax refugee living in Switzerland gives some level of credence to this speculation.

IKEA's core mission, Dahlvig said, is fundamentally philanthropic: "to create a better everyday life for people by being cost conscious and working within small means." To that end IKEA positions itself as the great equalizer, a force for spreading Scandinavian levels of comfort around the globe one Lack table or Kura bed at a time. Dahlvig is aware of the trade-offs involved, but IKEA, he says, is no Wal-Mart. "Cost is a big concern, the main concern," he said. "But there is no evidence that the cost goes up when you make a cleaner, more orderly factory or buy wood not from virgin forests but from well-managed forests only."

Dahlvig's abrupt segue from price to trees was not random. IKEA is the third largest consumer of wood in the world, just a step or two behind discounters Home Depot and Lowe's, and just a step or two ahead of Wal-Mart. The timber used in the wood products sold by these chains comes mostly from Eastern Europe and the Russian Far East, where wages are low, large wooded regions remote, and according to the World Bank, half of all logging is illegal. Forests in this region are on the decline, especially forests of high-demand varieties such as oak, ash, birch, and Korean pine. In pursuit of these and other valuable species, illegal loggers cut in restricted riverbanks, fish-spawning sites, and other conservation areas, and they bribe officials in exchange for documentation that the timber they poached was acquired legally. In 2007, the *Washington Post* published a penetrating and exhaustive investigation of illicit forestry practices that focused on Vostok, Russia, where villagers earned roughly a hundred dollars a month felling trees and hauling logs. The Russian logs were milled into planks by low-wage Chinese workers and shipped to border towns in low-wage China. More wood, much of it illegally harvested, poured into China every day from timber depots in Indonesia, Malaysia, the Mekong Delta, central Africa, and the Amazon. Most of this wood goes to make cheap tables, chairs, bookcases, and other wood products sold by discounters, especially in the United States.

Wood is in theory a renewable resource, but environmentalists warn that the demand for cheap Chinese-made furniture—half of all timber in the world is traded there—has stoked a "cut and consume" cycle that is destroying the world's forests at a rate unprecedented in human history. This harvest is not sustainable, and what is being taken—and what is being lost in the largest sense—is not renewable. Illegal logging operations generally locate in remote areas that are difficult to oversee, including wildlife habitats and conservation land. Over the long haul, deforestation contributes mightily to climate change, accounting for over 18 percent of global carbon dioxide emissions—more than the entire global transport system or the whole of the industrial manufacturing sectors. Despite knowing this, few players on the global scene, be they factory owners, wholesalers, retailers, or customers, are motivated to question seriously the provenance of their wood products. Questions would only raise the price.

DAHLVIG assured me that IKEA was asking questions and demanding answers. The company's timber, he said, is harvested legally, a claim often made by other discount retailers as well. But unlike most other companies, IKEA has gone beyond lip service to take the extraordinary step of hiring a team of forestry experts to monitor its suppliers. Dahlvig graciously introduced Yale-educated forestry coordinator Sofie Beckham. Beckham supervises IKEA's international forestry interests and seems deeply knowledgeable on all things arboreal. Her lecture on tree anatomy, complete with diagrams, was informed and fascinating. Just as Native Americans once used every part of the buffalo, from the snout to the hoofs, IKEA suppliers use every part of the tree, including the twiggy, knotty, and prickly bits disdained by traditional furniture makers. IKEA, Beckham said, is very mindful of sustainability, aiming to be "as close as possible to our suppliers, to keep an eye on them as well as to keep our prices low. It's very clear to IKEA that if we don't satisfy the environmental side, [eventually] we aren't going to have any wood to work with." She said IKEA has fired suppliers for using illegally harvested wood. Unfortunately, this approach is unlikely to prevent all or even most infractions because the suppliers are too many and too dispersed to ensure adequate monitoring. "As IKEA has grown, the challenge of monitoring tree harvesting has grown," Beckham said, adding that the number of monitors and enforcement officers has not grown with it. Her team consists of eleven forestry monitors worldwide—five in all of vast China and Russia combined, certainly not enough eyes and ears to closely monitor such a massive enterprise. Dahlvig said that he regretted this but could do nothing about it. Hiring more inspectors would be costly, adding to the price of his company's products. This, he said, was unacceptable.

I thanked Dahlvig for his time and that afternoon drove to Almhult in the charming company of IKEA spokeswoman Charlotte Lindgren. On the two-hour drive through the stark Swedish countryside we passed acre after acre of spruce trees, most of them uprooted and mangled, trunks splintered, branches twisted—a pitiful sight. Two years earlier, Lindgren told me, a nightmare of a storm flattened 75 million cubic meters of timber. It was a tragic loss and costly. To prevent forest fires the logs must be watered down regularly, at great fiscal and environmental expense. I asked Lindberg whether IKEA was making use of the fallen trees. She said she didn't think so. But shouldn't the company capture and capitalize on this tragic bonanza scattered across its own backyard? She smiled patiently. The furniture factories were too far away to make that idea practical.

Many of us think of IKEA as the world's largest furniture maker, but that's wrong. It's the world's largest furniture *retailer*. IKEA's vaunted "made in Sweden" quality is hammered out by tens of thousands of workers mostly in the employ of other companies—1,300 vendors in fifty-two countries. China is the company's largest supplier, but that's just for now. If Chinese workers demand better wages, protections, and benefits, as they have in the past, IKEA is likely to move on to India or Vietnam, where the company already has a strong foothold. Or it might expand in Africa or even the United States where to great fanfare it recently installed a factory in Danville, Virginia.

Lindgren and I reached Almhult in time for a lunch of Swedish meatballs with lingonberries at Hotel IKEA, where we were booked for two nights. The food was plentiful, but the rooms were Spartan; thin mattresses and Lilliputian bathrooms equipped with industrial-size vials of soap and the tan woody toilet paper found in Boy Scout latrines. If Hotel IKEA was not the most elegant hostelry in town, name recognition seemed to have made it the most popular one: The place was packed.

Almhult boasts of being home to "two of the world's best ideas." The first was botanist Carl Linnaeus's systemization of the animal and plant kingdoms into the coherent taxonomy that made modern ecology possible. The second was Ingvar Kamprad's application of "shrewd logistics to offer home furnishings products at such low prices that the masses could afford to buy them." These feats get roughly equal billing in the town's tourist brochures, although IKEA is by far the more prominent icon in town, and no wonder. With over 2,500 of its 15,000 citizens on the IKEA payroll, Almhult is the largest stable agglomeration of IKEA employees on the planet.

"Making the impossible possible is what we do" was a refrain I heard again and again in Almhult while touring the IKEA facilities—the IKEA museum, the original IKEA showroom, and the IKEA cafeteria, sauna room, and recreation area. Asked to elaborate, an IKEA product manager in charge of kitchen supplies offered this cryptic example: "When you meet a supplier who has not worked for IKEA, that is a challenge. Every supplier is unique, and each one has the opportunity to find more cost-efficient solutions." Loosely interpreted, this seemed to mean make the cheap cheaper. The manager had been to China, to a factory that specialized in the production of pine products. "We told them they could help us if they made the right choices," she said. "We briefed them on the challenge." The challenge was to meet IKEA's price demands.

The manager escorted us on a tour of a model kitchen and pointed proudly to what she called a dining table. It was unpainted wood and very small, barely containing the two chairs tucked beneath it. It looked just the right size to host a child's tea party. The manager said it had been designed to fit precisely on a pallet for easy transport in shipping containers from China.

For IKEA, designing a table to fit snugly into a shipping container—as opposed to, say, fitting snugly under a Thanksgiving dinner for twelve—makes good business sense. In the IKEA catalog, the table looks sturdy and inviting, and since more than 200 million copies of this catalog get circulated each year—more copies than the Bible!—it is perhaps beside the point that up close in the showroom the table looks like firewood. It is made of pine and pocked with what I was told were "healthy knots." Pine is not the optimal choice for furniture, especially chairs, because like all softwood it tends to compress under pressure. And knots, healthy or not, weaken wood and tend to splinter when stressed. The good news is that when the table starts to wobble or buckle or splinter, it can be recycled. Everything IKEA sells is built with the endgame in mind.

IKEA environmental manager Jens Lindell is an endgame specialist. A twenty-plus-year veteran of the company, he dreams of recycled tables and especially of flat pack sofas, sofas being the one category that has so far resisted the two-dimensional condition. Several of his coworkers had earlier mentioned the same fantasy. Lindell likes flat packing because it uses less packing material, and he's borderline obsessed with saving packing material. "If I could, I would ship things with no packing material," he said. Packing material costs money, and Lindell, like all IKEA coworkers, are charged with minimizing costs. I ask him if he had given any thought to the environmental benefits of longevity, of building products that last for decades or even a lifetime. He told me he hadn't but added that he'd been environmental manager for just a year and a half. Most of his two decades at IKEA had been spent selling children's goods.

Lindell offered to show me around the IKEA compound. We strolled past the IKEA function room, which is sometimes leased out for weddings. "We love it so much, we even get married here!" From there we walked to the product testing facility, which he described as "the world's largest furniture testing laboratory." It seemed about the size of a tennis court. A lonely technician manned a number of punishing contraptions—machines repeatedly rotating swivel chairs, pummeling sofas, or opening and slamming disembodied file drawers. I asked the technician why he was testing older designs that had been on the market for years. "Because sometimes greedy people cheat by using less material or changing products in other ways," he said brightly. By "greedy people" he meant the company's suppliers. Lindell glared. The technician winced and, in a weak attempt to recover, muttered strangely: "Thanks to our great suppliers, all our materials are flame retardant." Lindell stiffened, clearly perturbed that the specter of toxic chemical flame retardants had been raised. The technician literally hung his head. "It's within us to use less material, more recyclables, and no hazardous substances," Lindell intoned, leading me briskly out the door.

From his manner it occurred to me that Lindell had committed to memory Kamprad's *The Testament of a Furniture Dealer*. Kamprad refers to the testament as his "sacred concept" but credits its authorship to no higher power than his own. In it he promises to lead employees to a "glorious future," writing: "Those who cannot or will not join us are to be pitied."

Kamprad may not be much of a philosopher, but he is a folkloric figure—an intrepid farm lad who sold matches at age five and peddled goods from a milk truck at age twelve. He is a CEO who calls staff members by their first names and gives them mountain bikes for Christmas. He is also a billionaire who flies coach and barters for day-old vegetables at farm stands.

That the seventh richest man on earth haggles with a dirt farmer over the price of lettuce is a cruel irony that should give us pause, and for some it does. But IKEA soothes its few fitful critics by acknowledging flaws and forming alliances with not-for-profits. In response to complaints from environmental groups over its wood policy, the company partnered with the World Wildlife Fund and Greenpeace. When human rights activists accused IKEA of child labor violations in India, Pakistan, Vietnam, and the Philippines, it partnered with Save the Children and

UNICEF. What these partnerships have produced in terms of societal betterment is unclear since IKEA offers no guarantees and few specifics. Yet in the minds of consumers these alliances apparently offset any nagging negatives. At this writing a Google search of "I Love IKEA" revealed 36,380 distinct Web entries, and that's not counting the 1,850 "I Heart IKEA" sites. More important, 1.1 million customers visit an IKEA store every single day.

Wal-Mart's relentless march toward world retail domination provokes scathing exposés in books, articles, and documentaries. But most media responses to IKEA verge on the hagiographic, swallowing whole the well-polished rags-to-riches story the company wrote for itself. Wal-Mart's mascot is a bouncing price tag, while IKEA goes straight for the heart. Consider a recent advertising campaign, "Home is the Most Important Place in the World." An IKEA home is not about bricks and mortar. It's about beauty, joy, and security. "We don't just sell a chair or a table," an IKEA employee once publicly declared. "We sell a philosophy and a mission."

The much vaunted "Miracle of Almhult" was not designing chairs composed of recycled plastic bottles mixed with sawdust. The Miracle of Almhult was convincing millions of people around the world that mass-manufactured furniture that looks, feels, and smells like extruded Lego blocks is not only affordable and stylish but *soulful*.

IKEA's designers work directly with suppliers to ensure that whatever object they dream up can be built for less money than customers have any right to expect. The company works with scores of freelance designers but relies for the basics on a small in-house team. Chief designer Anna Efverlund is a legend and looks the part. Large and billowy, she frames her impish eyes in black shadow and tints her hair something beyond blond. The day we met she wore a black caftan and trailed a whiff of mystery—mentioning in passing a youthful stint designing bicycles in Brazil and a grown son but never a husband. At IKEA, her employer since 1980, she is best known for her whimsical children's accessories—a heart-shaped pillow sprouting arms and a ladybug lamp. These are hits, but not her biggest. "The first product I designed for

IKEA was the Bagis," a plastic children's clothes hanger in neon colors, $2.95 for a flatpack of eight. "If I got royalties, this would be the only product I would do. It is such a good seller. But I don't get royalties. No one here does. Only Ingmar gets rich."

The potshot was affectionate: Efverlund is a dear friend of Kamprad's and a staunch IKEA loyalist. She represents the company frequently at educational events and conferences, and has traveled to India to spotlight IKEA's much-touted campaign to market embroidered pillow covers sewn by the rural poor. In these and other efforts Efverlund is sometimes accompanied by Maria Vinka. Vinka is by blood an ethnic Sami, the reindeer-herding indigenous dwellers of northern Europe sometimes referred to (tactlessly, I was told) as Laplanders. A spiky tattoo in the style of her ancestors circles her elbow. Vinka designs fabrics for IKEA, and also cutlery, clocks, china, and furniture. Her proudest creation is a stackable "rocking chair" composed primarily of tightly woven banana leaf fibers. Vinka's chair, shaped like a cross between a spoon and a ruffed grouse, is named after the tiny Swedish fishing village of Gullholmen. It is made in Vietnam in a vast open factory. Women weave the banana fibers, and men weld the frames. Each chair takes half a day to build, and in the United States it costs $59.99. The design is intriguing, but the chair is not for everyone: Access requires lowering oneself nearly to ground level.

Vinka attributes the success of her Gullholmen chair to its "good story." "It is biodegradable, made out of stuff that was once thrown away," she told me. Apparently, furniture made of waste products is pure seduction for IKEA's target demographic. But the backstory IKEA tells is not the whole story. In Vietnam, banana leaves are used to thatch huts and to wrap food for cooking, and at last check they were selling for about $6 apiece on the Internet. It is not environmental concerns that brought IKEA to Vietnam.

In April 2008, Ingmar Kamprad met with Vietnam's prime minister, Nguyen Tan Dung, to make a deal: He wanted lower tariffs, lower docking fees for container ships, and "ensured access to wood" in exchange for employing more Vietnamese. Vietnam, itself in constant threat of deforestation, is a major Southeast Asian hub for processing illegally logged timber. While IKEA suppliers are instructed to follow the IKEA way, Vietnamese enforcement of environmental and human rights regulations is notoriously haphazard. Vietnamese factories pay workers as little as $50 a month for a forty-eight-hour, six-day workweek. As one American commentator said about doing business in Vietnam, "The effect of bringing into the global labor pool hundreds of millions of low-wage workers—people whose wages are held in check by both capital mobility and communist repression—is to hold down wages in democratic nations with advanced economies . . ." The banana leaf story may keep IKEA customers coming, but cheap labor and wood is what keeps IKEA in Vietnam and other low-wage nations.

The IKEA story is told best through its catalog, a product on which the company does not skimp. The weighty document is produced in the largest photography studio in Europe, a ten-thousand-square-meter hangar echoing with photographers, interior designers, copywriters, and product managers. Digital cameras said to "cost as much as a new Volvo" snap and snap and snap at ersatz kitchens, baths, and rumpus rooms, each meticulously arranged to exude a carefree and intimate homeyness. Plants, flowers, and watercolor brushes clumped in white mugs set off the living areas; bowls of fresh fruit, piles of leafy greens, jars of whole grains, and flasks of olive oil spice up the kitchens. Books, bought by the yard, are everywhere. IKEA carries the same merchandise in stores from China to Saudi Arabia, so the goal here is to tempt customers from every culture to bend their wants to meet IKEA's products.

I watch a photographer shoot a model living room. The space was designed to simulate a modest flat in Eastern Europe where, the designer tells, me "Mum, Dad, Gran, and children all live together in three small rooms." It's a lovely thought and a lovely room, but too small to accommodate the wide-screen TV, the opposing couch, and much of anything else. Where do the parents sleep? It turns out that the fluffy white couch is a sofa bed; after Gram and the kids turn in, the parents settle down to a "good, long snuggle." Ah, romance, but with all that gear squeezed into three small rooms, where will the kids play? Where will the family eat? And how will they open the sofa bed without busting the big-screen TV? The photographer laughed. This Swedish fairy tale may not in reality translate into a better life for a struggling Russian family, but what's my point? He's creating a fantasy.

CATALOGS are not documentaries, nor do we expect them to be. The IKEA story is one of a charmingly quirky Swedish retail chain founded by a stony but deeply caring entrepreneur who grew unimaginably rich on a diet of hard work and humble pie. But the reality is far simpler and far less romantic. IKEA succeeds the way all discounters do: by passing much of its costs on to us.

The chain has a policy of having relatively few stores—270 spread across thirty-five countries and territories. Most are enormous—in Atlanta, IKEA is nearly 366,000 square feet, about seven times the area of a football field. Like discount outlet malls, IKEA stores are positioned well outside city centers, in areas where huge spaces can be had at relatively low real estate and tax costs. This business model allows the company substantial economies of scale while at the same time compelling customers to drive very long distances—an average of 50 miles round trip in the United States. (In Europe some customers travel even farther: the northernmost IKEA outpost in Haparanda, Finland, attracts customers within a 500-kilometer radius.) Customers must drive back to the store—if need be with sofa or bed or bookcase in hand—to return malfunctioning furniture or retrieve missing parts (a surprisingly frequent occurrence). Few IKEA outlets in the United States are accessible by public transportation, and since the company does not support a home delivery service, customers willing and able to take public transport rarely do so. As a result, the traffic jams surrounding IKEA stores are so gnarly that customers are discouraged from shopping on weekends when lines of idling cars can back up for miles. IKEA touts its "green side" by lighting its stores with low-wattage bulbs and charging extra for plastic bags while its clientele burns through gallon after gallon of fuel to buy disposable tables and lamps. Asked his assessment of company practices, MIT-trained urban development expert Wig Zamore said: "IKEA is the least sustainable retailer on the planet."

IN 1939, Harvard economist Joseph Schumpeter singled out key retail organizations as causing the "big disturbance." He wrote that they "disrupt the existing system and enforce a distinct process of adaptation." Typically, these outfits were founded by what he called "new men," with "new capital." Discounters from Woolworth to Walton to Kamprad are typical of these new men. None was born into the business he would one day dominate, and perhaps as a consequence none felt bound by traditional business practices. Neither Woolworth nor Walton showed any particular allegiance to his workers or provided for them beyond the minimum level necessary to promote profit. At IKEA, workers are treated with respect and consideration (they get benefits and sometimes bonuses), but they are interchangeable and ultimately disposable. The de-skilling of labor is as critical to IKEA's business model as it is for every discount business model: Centralized capital, not craftsmanship, is where the power lies. This is no socialist screed, it is undeniable fact, and to accept it is to better understand the trade-offs.

Outsourcing to the customer critical functions—service, delivery, and assembly—keeps prices low by avoiding the cost of wages and benefits. It also avoids taxes on that labor, which means the roads leading to IKEA are not necessarily being paid for by IKEA. The *Wall Street Journal* wrote in 1994: "President Clinton's 1993 tax increase boosted IKEA's profits. IKEA likes to say that its growth has more to do with value than taxes, but in generations gone by, when lower taxes meant that Americans had more cash to spend, value meant solid oak or mahogany furniture, not veneer over particleboard or pine." The "value" of IKEA resides not in the shopping experience, which most agree tends toward the frustrating. Nor does it necessarily reside in the merchandise. The value resides in the manufactured "adventure" of hunting down, hauling home, and using one's own hands to cobble together a well-designed object. And the most fun by far is in the price itself.

Objects can be designed to low price, but they cannot be crafted to low price. Craftsmanship takes time, and time is the enemy of the discounter. A lamp, IKEA reminds us, is only a lamp. It has no feelings, and we are crazy to attach meaning to it. The logical response to this might be: Then why does IKEA name its lamps—and pillows and ice cream scoops? Doesn't a name connote intimacy? Of course it does, and IKEA knows well the power of intimacy to move us. But it is their story—not our own—that the company wants us to conjure. It is intimacy on their schedule and by their rules. Flatpacks of medium-density fiberboard hauled out of sprawling warehouses and cobbled together with IKEA's notorious L-shaped, six-sided Allen wrench are not tasteful, comfortable furniture. They are a facsimile of tasteful, comfortable furniture.

IN HIS DEEPLY considered book *The Craftsman*, New York University sociologist Richard Sennett reminds us that in old English a "job" meant "simply a lump of coal or a pile of wood that could be moved around at will." Craftsmen do not have jobs; they have careers that build over years and decades from apprenticeship to master. Acquiring skills built on experience empower workers and raise prices, so purveyors of low price must commit to the principle that almost anyone can be an employee and almost any employee can do any job. This discounting of skills leads to their further decline and a further devaluing. And because discounters hold so much sway, this means that skilled and experienced workers of all varieties—tailors, cobblers, butchers, store clerks, travel agents—are increasingly scarce.

This is not to say that craftsmanship is dead. Far from it. We cheer it on at county fairs and applaud the craftiness of those who bake their own bread or shear, dye, and weave wool and knit it into a sweater. We applaud those who go into the wilderness to build their own cabin, plant their own gardens, or build kayaks out of wood strips. But few of us expect to find craft in everyday objects.

Those who regard craft as a euphemism for elitism overlook the fact that craftsmanship need not be precious or effete; it can be practical, simple, an everyday thing: a well-made table, a sturdy chair, a butcher or tailor or travel agent who knows his or her business. A bricklayer or carpenter or teacher, a musician or salesperson, a writer of computer code—any and all can be craftsmen. Craftsmanship cements a relationship of trust between buyer and seller, worker and employer, and expects something of both. It is about caring about the work and its application. It is what distinguishes the work of humans from the work of machines, and it is everything that IKEA and other discounters are not.

Craftsmen aren't led to a "glorious future" paved with ever lower prices for "the many." They rely on their own skill, commitment, and judgment, and take pride and satisfaction in the work itself. But to raise the issue of craft in the postindustrial age is to risk scorn. Our knowledge-based service economy demands razor-sharp wits, finely tuned synapses, quick reflexes, and, most of all, drive. We are warned that workers in the developing world are rapidly outpacing us. They are smarter, more dedicated, and more focused. They can program computers, write legal briefs, and diagnose disease expertly, quickly, and at an unbeatable low price. We must work smarter and quicker, which is to say, cheaper.

MASS MANUFACTURE long ago uncoupled consumption from production. We no longer think much about who made what we buy or how they made it. In a democracy, capitalism is about making things available to as many people as possible, which means as cheaply as possible. But every hand that touches an object increases its price, thereby reducing its accessibility. So when we swap craftsmanship for price, the trade seems fair, even virtuous.

A Billy bookcase costs $59.99. Loaded with heavy books, the particleboard shelves tend to buckle. If the owner attempts to modify it—such as trying to put in a couple of supports to bolster it—the screws lose purchase. Try too hard or too often, and the particleboard crumbles. We can spray-paint the bookcase or doll it up with stickers, but in all but the most superficial sense, the bookcase is beyond our reach to modify or customize. We must embrace it or at least accept it on its own terms, with its myriad limitations.

Is this a problem? Well, again, that depends. Millions of IKEA enthusiasts around the globe contort themselves to meet the needs of the brand. Rather than burden poor Billy to the breaking point, they carefully confine their heavy books to its perimeters: Center the paperbacks in the middle of the shelf and flank them with the Shakespeare anthologies and chemistry texts. The idea of what constitutes a bookcase—a sturdy unit to reliably hold whatever number and variety of books will fit snugly in its contours—is modified to accommodate the limitations of an object that is wonderful mainly for its sleek exterior and low price. In a very real sense, a Billy is not a bookcase but a subspecies of bookcase: a cheap bookcase. The same might be said for much of IKEA's merchandise: It is not a great chair, it is a great cheap chair. It is not a great chest of drawers, it is a great cheap chest of drawers. When these objects break or buckle or otherwise disappoint, we don't ask for sympathy. We *expected* it to happen.

Cheap objects resist involvement. We tend to invest less in their purchase, care, and maintenance, and that's part of what makes them so attractive. Cheap clothing lines—sold at discounters such as Target and H & M—are like IKEA emblems of the "cheap chic" where style fills in for whatever quality goes lacking. There is nothing sinister in this, no deliberate planned obsolescence. These objects are not designed to fall apart, nor are they crafted not to fall apart. In many cases we know this and accept it, and have entered into a sort of compact. Perhaps we don't even want the object to last forever. Such voluntary obsolescence makes craftsmanship beside the point. We have grown to expect and even relish the easy birth and early death of objects.

This phenomenon has spread to things both cheap and not so cheap. We expect our cell phones, our computers, our MP3 players to be worry free, to run perfectly with minimal intervention, but only for a certain period. When they fail, we typically don't expect to be able to do much about it. The lithium-ion battery sealed inside an iPod typically loses roughly 70 percent of its functionality. Apple will replace the batteries for about $60 plus shipping and handling, but customers are discouraged from doing this themselves—the case was not designed to be opened.

We Americans once reveled in our reputation for self-sufficiency. We were tinkerers, fixers of things. Yet while many of us can recall our parents wrestling into compliance a recalcitrant toaster or washing machine, few of us today would attempt the same with a malfunctioning microwave oven, digital camera, or anything built up from a computer chip. Appliances, electronics, and automobiles are black boxes, impervious to probing and resistant to repair. Getting into the guts of things is difficult, and if we dare trespass in the innards of what we thought belonged to us, we do so at the risk of the guarantee. Even seasoned professionals are losing heart. In less than two decades, the Professional Service Association lost three-quarters of its small appliance and consumer electronics shop members. During that same period the number of electronics repair shops plummeted from twenty thousand to five thousand. Repair people of all stripes have fallen into obscurity. Sesame Street closed its "Fix-it Shop" in 1996, stating as its reason that young viewers were unlikely to encounter one.

As political philosopher Matthew B. Crawford observed, an emerging engineering culture of "hide the works" has rendered "the artifacts we use unintelligible to direct inspection." Not knowing or caring how an object is made, we are, he said, "disburdened of involvement." If the exterior is pleasing, what goes on under the hood is of no concern to us. It is only when we try to penetrate the object, to modify or fix it, that we realize what we've given up. If we do not have mastery over our objects, our objects certainly have mastery over us. There are advantages to this. "It's a sort of freedom," Crawford said. "But such freedom allows your own agency to get displaced. Having mastery over our own stuff is very satisfying, and we've traded that for convenience. So in a sense we don't really own the stuff, we lease it. And I think that haunts us."

Perhaps it haunts us because not long ago almost everyone had access to craftsmanship. This was true not only of consumer goods—clothing, toys, home goods—but of things more fundamental, such as shelter. The house I live in—a "poor man's" Victorian—was built for a blue-collar family. A carpenter, his wife, and four kids shared the place with a paying boarder in the attic. It is not large or terribly fancy, but it is well situated and solid enough to have withstood the rigors of 141 New England winters. I expect it will last at least 141 winters more. Amortizing the cost of this home over its working life, the value by today's standards becomes astonishing.

Brent Hull, a Texas-based architectural designer, told me that things are different today, that well-crafted homes are rarely built for the ordinary consumer. This is not because the price of craftsmanship is prohibitive—many poorly crafted homes cost more—but, rather, because many home buyers do not expect it, he said. Then he added something surprising: "Most of us don't think we deserve it."

We didn't always think this way. Houses built at or before the turn of the nineteenth century were built carefully. In the early 1940s this began to change. The Depression and the war had made housing stock scarce, and those studying the shortage concluded that "only by creating an industrial environment conducive alike to volume expansion and cost reduction can an approach to meeting the housing need be accomplished." Not everyone agreed, arguing that while the housing shortage was real, substantial gains could be made by simply rejuvenating old stock. Wrote one observer, "The prophylaxis of housing disease cannot be limited to the construction industry." But this view was trampled in the rush to cash in on the postwar prosperity. Builder William Levitt captured the zeitgeist perfectly: "Any damn fool can build homes. What counts is how many you can sell for how little."

William Levitt himself offered living proof that expertise was not a prerequisite to success. His father appointed him president of Levitt and Sons at the age of twenty-two. His adolescent brother Alfred was made vice president of design. Both boys were college dropouts and had no knowledge of construction. Alfred's dad, Abraham, once said of him, "Alfred loved to draw, but he didn't know what a two-by-four was."

The Levitts amassed their first fortune building luxury homes for bankers and lawyers. When that business sank in the swamp of war, they nabbed a lucrative government contract to erect 2,350 prefab housing units for defense workers in Norfolk, Virginia. It was through this project that William learned much of what he needed to know about low-cost construction. And the market was ripe. Wartime shortages of everything from wood to cement to nails had crippled the housing industry, leaving veterans stranded and living in attics and basements, doubling and tripling up with family members. Pollster Elmo Roper estimated that 19 percent of Americans were looking for a place to live and that another 13 percent would be if they thought they had any chance of finding one. In a campaign speech, President Harry Truman asked, "How can we expect to sell democracy to Europe until we prove that within the democratic system we can provide decent homes for people?" Truman backed up the rhetoric with the nation's richest-ever home-financing scheme: tens of billions of dollars in, among other things, Federal Housing Administration–guaranteed bank loans and Veterans Administration–sponsored low-interest mortgages.

Levitt cashed in, setting what was to become a new standard for low-cost single family home construction. He wangled a change in the local building code to permit his workers to pour concrete slabs directly on the ground, thereby eliminating the need for a foundation or a basement. (A sympathetic press helped make this happen by making such niceties seem obsolete. *Newsday* proclaimed in an editorial: "Maybe it was good enough for grandpappy to live in a baroque chateau, propped up over a hole in the ground, but it is not good enough for us.") Levittown homes sported no porches and no finished second stories. They had linoleum floors, minimal landscaping, and carports instead of garages. Two bedrooms, a bath, a kitchen, and a living room fit cleverly into 750 feet of living space. A washing machine was included, as was a built-in TV. Levitt built similar boxy structures one after another—seventeen thousand side by side on 1,200 acres of potato fields, 25 miles from Manhattan. Then he built two more Levittowns in Pennsylvania and New Jersey. Traditional builders of the time were lucky to finish four to five homes a year. Levitt and Sons pumped out more than thirty in a day. Soon enough, Levittown grew into the largest housing project in American history.

"Levitt was the Henry Ford of builders," Hull told me. "He broke each job down into pieces so small that it required very little skill." (One man did nothing but bolt washing machines to the floor.) Over the next twenty to thirty years a whole generation forgot how to build carefully.

The balance between craftsmanship, speed, and production costs tipped, and we have not gone back.

Levitt, who once said, "the masses are asses," aimed for high speed and low price. He created a vertical monopoly. His firm and its subsidiaries controlled every link in the supply chain, from forests to lumberyards to appliance wholesalers. Dissatisfied with the cost of nails, he built a factory to make his own. By shunning middlemen, he got great deals on appliances. By shunning craft workers, he freed himself from labor pressures. He placated the unions, cutting them out without pissing them off. Some critics complained. Lewis Mumford famously dubbed Levittown an "instant slum," but most held their collective tongues. Levittown was the future, and in the wake of the deadliest conflict in human history, the future was where people wanted to be. As cultural critic Christopher Lasch wrote in his classic *The Culture of Narcissism,* Americans "trivialized the past by equating it with outmoded styles of consumption, discarded fashions and attitudes." America was enamored with technology and immersed in the "cult of the new." Why live in an old-fashioned "used" house when you could move into a spanking new one?

Levittown was a handyman's special wrought large, a do-it-yourselfer of precut lumber, prefabricated plumbing, and fresh-from-the-factory minimalism. Almost anyone could be a carpenter at Levittown or a plumber, a landscaper, a roofer. There was so little to master; everything was ready to go, all made to fit. Levittown residents were willing to change to fit Levittown. They had no choice in the location, style, or accoutrements of their new homes. That these homes lacked even the rudiments of craftsmanship or history and that they were isolated 25 miles from Manhattan in a remote potato field seemed not to matter when the price was $7,500 with no money down—just $65 a month.

IKEA sprung fully born from this tradition: predictable uniformity in the guise of novelty; design without craftsmanship; the customer bending to accommodate the commodity. We need not save for months or even weeks to buy a Bankas coffee table for $89.99. And when its "clear-lacquered ash veneer" muddies with coffee spills, we don't despair that we cannot sand it smooth again. A coffee table, like a lamp, has no feelings and demands no feelings from us. It is simply time to buy a new one.

Whether craftsmanship even matters in our postindustrial world depends on who you ask. The knowledge economy demands smarts, drive, ambition, and speed. Craftsmanship demands skill, training, exactitude, and patience. That these two sets of qualities are not entirely compatible might imply that we should abandon one for the other—or it could mean that we need both. Many of us pride ourselves in being connoisseurs of something, be it beer or golf clubs or coffee. There are haut cheese makers and dress designers and furniture and chocolate and watch makers, but these are high-end craftspeople serving a mostly high-end clientele. As shoes and electronics and furniture become disposable, there is no need for craftsmen to craft or repair them. And as craftsmen become increasingly scarce, true craftsmanship becomes more expensive and rarefied, something for the wealthy but not for the rest of us. The combination of quality and value, once available to the many, is now affordable only to the few. For the rest of us, there is "design."

Design may be clever, amusing, and eye-catching, but if executed without craftsmanship, it does not sustain us. Like a zirconium engagement ring, poorly executed design deceives: It has glitter but no gold. How many times, caught in the rain, have we bought a fine-looking $5 umbrella from a street vendor, knowing full well that it will invert and become useless in the first serious gust? We end up holding the umbrella by its points, stretching it over our heads like an oversized handkerchief. Our relationship with this umbrella is like a one-night stand: reliably dysfunctional. We'll buy another $5 umbrella in the next unexpected downpour. Expecting little, getting little, we're making do—but barely. Without craftsmanship and the expectation of craftsmanship, our relationship to the material world breaks down into fits and starts of stopgap measures that are neither satisfying nor sustainable.

Recently, a friend mentionioned that when she moved from Washington, D.C., to New York City ten years ago, her movers refused to pack up the IKEA Billy bookcases unless she disassembled and boxed them herself. They warned her to inspect the case for cracks and to collect all the hardware; they also said that no matter how careful she was, they would not guarantee its safe arrival. Rather than go to all that trouble, my friend decided to put the Billy cases out on the front curb (like that lonely lamp) and buy new ones when she got to Manhattan. Once there, while poking around a flea market on the Upper West Side, she found a bookcase of solid oak. It was not new, but it was sturdy and distinctive, and it cost only a few dollars more than the Billy. She bought it, tied it to the roof of a friend's car, and drove it home. Ten years later it is still there, marked with age and packed to groaning with big, heavy books and memories. My friend has lots more money now and could afford a brand-new bookcase, so I asked her if she plans to put this one on the curb. She looked stricken. "Why," she asked, "would I do that?"

# CHAPTER SEVEN

# DISCOUNTING AND ITS DISCONTENTS

I'm not convinced you're going to have the same immediate desire to go back to consumption and debt. A lot of young people have learned what it's like when you're living on the edge and the bad times come. Their appetite is now towards more about living things differently.

| H. LEE SCOTT, RESPONDING TO QUESTIONS AT THE ANNUAL MEETING OF

THE NATIONAL RETAIL FEDERATION, JANUARY 12, 2009,

HAVING ANNOUNCED HIS RETIREMENT AS CEO OF WAL-MART.

Price is a number, but properly decoded, it is no abstraction. Price tells us volumes about marketing strategies, government policies, and even variations in the growing season. Economic realities, such as the efficiency of workers and factories are all reflected in price. Social and political realities—such as environmental degradation and human rights violations, are reflected as well. Discounting means that a particular good or a service is not desired at full price—or at least not designed enough to sell. The price of discounted goods is what economists call "elastic." Price elasticity is a measure of how much the demand of a good or service varies with price. A product or service is very elastic if a slight change in price leads to a sharp rise or fall in demand.

Usually, highly elastic goods and services are readily available, interchangeable with other goods and services, and not critical for daily life. If a brand of ice cream gets too pricy, we can switch brands, eat cake, or skip sweets altogether. The same can be said for many other commodities. The price of meat, for example, is fairly elastic—raise or lower the price, and consumers respond. When the price of chicken goes up, consumers can and do switch to beef or pork. An inelastic good or service, by contrast, is one in which changes in price result in no or relatively modest changes in demand. Think gasoline, cigarettes, a unique life-saving drug. Since consumers don't have a real alternative, demand for these goods is far less sensitive to changes in price; the drug, for instance, is essentially inelastic.

Successful merchants know how far to push price, and price elasticity is one factor in determining how to make the requisite trade-offs. As a rule there is less need to discount goods and services with low-price elasticity. This brings into sharp relief one of the perils of cheap: The more essential the good or service, and the more unique, the less elastic the price and the less likely it is to be marked down. Absolute essentials for which there are no substitutes and for which we cannot wait are almost never discounted. Transportation, health care, private education, and housing may go down in price, but unless subsidized by governments or other institutions, they are almost never cheap.

When the price of essentials goes up, the poor have no choice but to sacrifice to acquire them. In June 2008 the price of gasoline topped $4 a gallon, and average citizens of thirteen counties in Mississippi, Alabama, Kentucky, and West Virginia forked over more than 13 percent of their take-home pay for fuel. Some traded off food, health care, and housing to pay for their daily commutes, while others, no longer able to afford car payments and gas money, were forced to quit their jobs. But rising gas prices had little or no impact on the wealthy. Indeed, the wealthy feel little pain from the increased cost of essentials, for which there are few or no substitutes, while enjoying every opportunity to benefit from the low price of inessentials.

Some economists have blurred this critical distinction, even implying that the poor benefit disproportionately from discounts. Here Wal-Mart, the world's largest discount retailer, serves as a proxy for the discount category as a whole. Jason Furman, economic advisor to President Barack

Obama, once famously argued that "there is little dispute that Wal-Mart's price reductions have benefited the 120 million American workers employed outside of the retail sector. Plausible estimates of the magnitude of the benefit are enormous—a total of $263 billion in 2004, or $2,329 per household."

That is quite a bonus. Among the experts Furman cites as having done the basic work leading to this assessment is Massachusetts Institute of Technology economist Jerry Hausman, coauthor of a highly regarded study of the impact of Wal-Mart on food prices. Hausman concluded that Big Box stores made consumers "better off by the equivalent of 25 percent of food spending." For the poorest 20 percent of the population, this was estimated to be equivalent to an increase in income of 6.5 percent, a significant sum. I called Hausman to discuss this figure with him. He told me that Furman actually underestimated the Wal-Mart premium: The discounter not only offers low food prices to its own customers but forces other local supermarkets to drop their prices as well. "Even if you never shop at Wal-Mart, you are still better off with Wal-Mart nearby," he said. I asked Hausman where he buys his groceries. A city dweller, he said he lives many miles from the nearest Wal-Mart or other discount grocery and therefore shops at Whole Foods. Whole Foods is a high-priced, limited-selection supermarket, with a reputation for good service, quality, and variety, factors for which Furman said he did not control in his study. This is surprising, for without controlling for quality, how is it possible to make a meaningful comparison? How are consumers to know whether the lower price of chicken breasts at Wal-Mart signify a good deal on a superior product, or a bad deal on an inferior product? Most of the goods on Hausman's hypothetical shopping list were generic items that vary widely in variety and quality from store to store.

Discounters sell mostly what they can buy cheaply and in great bulk, so it is no wonder that the goods in Hausman's theoretical market basket—chicken breasts, ground meat, apple juice, and the like—were cheaper at Wal-Mart, which, thanks to its size, and power, can purchase these things at deep discount, and, thanks to its business model and employment policies, can sell them more cheaply than most other outlets. Generic goods like these are highly price-elastic. When the price goes up, the demand tends to go down. Discount stores keep prices on inelastic goods low, since customers quite literally can take them or leave them. If apple juice is too expensive this week, they'll switch to grape. Unique goods or goods for which there are no substitutes—such as specific brands of cereal or soft drinks—though they may be reduced in price, are far less likely to be deeply discounted unless they are "on sale," which they are equally likely to be at a traditional supermarket.

**EMEK BASKER,** an economist at the University of Missouri who focuses on the retail sector, is described by at least one analyst as the country's leading "Wal-Martologist." Basker earned her PhD from MIT and is a faithful empiricist, interested not in speculation but in verifiable facts. "The goal of my research is to shed light on recent changes in the retail sector: their causes and consequences and implications for the wider economy," she told me. "I try not to approach these questions from a particular position (pro or con) but rather focus on understanding what's going on and why." Basker's study on Wal-Mart pricing was meticulous. She gathered price data on ten specific products, including men's Dockers "no wrinkle" khakis, 11-ounce bottles of Johnson's Baby Shampoo, and cartons of Winston cigarettes, king size. The data were collected over a period of twenty-one years, from 1982 through 2002, in 165 cities across the United States. To control for seasonality she took four readings each year, one for each season. Then she checked to see how prices changed in these communities after Wal-Mart's arrival, controlling carefully for inflation and a host of other factors. Using regression analysis and other analytical tools, she concluded that Wal-Mart does indeed have low prices and tends to lower them in other nearby stores. No surprise there. Perhaps less predictable was that Wal-Mart does not lower prices on everything. Drugstore standards such as shampoo and toothpaste were cheaper than average after Wal-Mart came to town. But the vaunted "Wal-Mart effect" on cigarettes, Coke, and no-wrinkle khakis was either weak or nonexistent. When I asked Basker what might account for this, she responded that in the absence of data she could only guess, and sensibly declined to do so. But her data alone reveal a dirty little secret of bargain retailing.

A midsized Wal-Mart supercenter may offer for sale one hundred thousand different items or stock-keeping units (SKUs). The general public knows the going price of only about 1 to 2 percent of these items, generally things we buy most frequently. As we now know, discounters tend to discount most deeply frequently purchased generic items—such as generic lettuce and ground meat—rather than items we buy only occasionally. When discounters carry well-known, highly-sought-after big-ticket items, the discount is often extremely modest. For example, when Wal-Mart started stocking the Apple iPhone in the final week of 2008, it knocked only $2 off the full price. Much touted "everyday low prices" are applied selectively, often on inexpensive high-volume goods that are essentially thinly disguised loss leaders. Wal-Mart actually has higher than average prices on about one-third of the stock it carries. On those items for which prices are lower, the average savings is 37 cents, with about one-third of items carrying a savings of no more than 2 cents.

DISCOUNTERS lower the overall price of the average market basket by lowering prices on the things we buy most frequently: generic paper supplies, canned vegetables, dishwashing detergent. The small stuff matters. A 5 cent discount on a bottle of ketchup can woo customers, especially when accompanied by a 5-cent discount on related items such as hot dog buns and paper towels. So discounters position low-priced, high-volume items such as these in high-visibility areas, both to encourage consumers to buy them and to leave the impression that everything in the store is cheap. Since most of us need paper towels and many of us buy ketchup and hot dog buns, discounters do in fact save us money. But this is low-hanging fruit, loss leaders designed to lure us into stores we might otherwise avoid. Discounters generally offer less variety in any given category than do traditional stores. In one study of organic food, Wal-Mart, currently a leading seller (by volume) of organics, had by far the lowest prices, but selection was so limited that a comparison with other stores was almost impossible. The study authors concluded: "For all the hoopla, Wal-Mart is truly stocking only a very small number of organic SKUs. But they are some of the highest-volume products in the industry, so they will likely have quite an impact." While Wal-Mart was selling an enormous volume of low-priced organics, the bulk of it came in the form of one product, milk, some of which was organic in name only.

America's discount behemoths have in recent years been hailed as sentries against a frightening prospect: inflation. *Business Week* reported in 2002 that "one reason the Federal Reserve is less concerned about inflation than the European Central Bank . . . is the deflationary impact of America's more competitive retail environment." Wal-Mart, Dollar Stores, Big Lots, and the like help keep inflation in check, which seems a very good thing indeed.

Inflation is a prominent and recurring source of public anxiety the world over: In 2008 a sharp rise in the price of fuel and food led to political unrest and hardship in India, China, and elsewhere around the globe. Those of us who came of age in the 1970s, when America experienced what some economists contend was the nation's first and only experience of peacetime inflation, are all too familiar with its dangers. At the time, inflation was targeted—in the words of economist James Galbraith—as a "public evil" that "inspires public citizens to oppose it with an energy and perseverance devoted to few other tasks." In 1978 the Humphrey-Hawkins Act mandated that inflation be reduced in ten years from the then-current level of 9 percent to zero. The Federal Reserve Bank under both Paul Volcker and Alan Greenspan strove tirelessly to achieve this ambitious goal by controlling employment levels through the manipulation of interest rates. Volcker and Greenspan reasoned that too great a demand for workers would lead to an increase in wages, which both economists deemed inflationary. When the unemployment rate fell below 5.5 or 6 percent, or seemed headed in that direction, the

Fed raised interest rates to inhibit economic growth and by extension, hiring. As a result of this strategy, the unemployment rate climbed to 9.6 percent in 1983, its highest level since the Great Depression, greatly enlarging the pool of people seeking work and substantially diminishing the power of most workers to demand an increase in wages and benefits. Wages flattened, and if workers wanted to buy more, they took out a loan, often in the form of credit card debt.

Wage stagnation and growing indebtedness made discounting all the more attractive, a way to level an increasingly uneven playing field. Influential University of Chicago economist Christian Broda, a darling of the financial press here and in the United Kingdom, has argued that thanks to discounters America's astonishing income disparity was not nearly as damaging as people assumed. "The reason is simple," he wrote. "How rich you are depends on two things: how much money you have, and how much the goods you buy cost. If your income doubles but the prices of the goods you consume also doubles, you are no better off. Unfortunately, the conventional wisdom on U.S. inequality is based on official measures that look only at the first half, the income differential. National statistics ignore the fact that inflation affects people in different income groups unevenly because the rich and poor consume different baskets of goods."

Broda pointed out that between 1994 and 2005 price inflation for the richest 10 percent of American households was six percentage points higher than for the poorest 10 percent of households. The poor buy roughly twice as much of their nondurable goods in discount superstores than do the rich. The rich spend far more on durable goods and services, such as education and transportation, which are usually less subject to competition and therefore less elastic. Hence, Broda reasoned, it is the rich—not the poor—who are losing ground in the world of cheap goods. "Trade sceptics who suggest that there is no point in buying cheaper goods if you have lost your job should check America's unemployment rate," Broda concluded in July 2008. "It is about 5 percent, close to a record low."

There are several things Broda appears to misunderstand. For one, that

5 percent unemployment rate. In Broda's calculation, anyone who works is employed. This might include, say, a machinist laid off from his $40-an-hour job and currently making $220 a week at the local Quicky Mart. This is hardly helpful. According to the Bureau of Labor Statistics, fully 9.4 percent of Americans were without *sustaining* jobs in May 2008— that is, jobs that could support them and, if they had one, a family. This figure includes not only the officially unemployed (at the time 5.5 percent of the population) but also marginal and part-time workers searching for full-time work, like our hypothetical pal at Quicky Mart.

But we need not look that deeply to notice that something is amiss in Broda's assessment. By his reasoning, what we buy is necessarily what we want to buy. Do the poor shop at discount stores because they really prefer to shop at discount stores? There is no research on this question that I know of, but there are clues. Given that getting to a discount store often entails a cost in time and inconvenience, most of us shop at discount stores not because we prefer the merchandise or the ambience but because we believe it will save us money. The poor have no choice. The wealthy do have a choice, and some shop at discount stores for *some* things. What marketers call "price-sensitive affluents" regularly shop at discount stores to take advantage of the price elasticity of nondurable goods such as paper and office supplies, cleaning products, diapers, and cosmetics. But while the affluent can and do shop at discounters, the poor and working class cannot expand their incomes to accommodate the growing cost of essential goods and services. So it is hardly convincing that a low price on T-shirts, toilet paper, and lettuce truly compensates for the soaring costs of health care, education, and transportation.

The worst economic disaster in U.S. history, the Great Depression, was characterized not by inflation but by deflation, particularly income deflation. Similarly, deflation of financial assets brought many Americans to their knees in 2008. When unemployment and the risk of unemployment keeps wages low, deflation in the price of consumer goods may seem like a panacea. But this is an illusion, because cheap consumer goods do not constitute the bulk of our expenses. Just before Broda published his findings, the *New York Times* reported that medical bills alone accounted for almost one-fifth of the average family income—a whole lot of "lettuce," cheap or not, in almost anyone's book.

And health care is only one component of this disturbing trend. Harvard Law School professor Elizabeth Warren has made clear just how disturbing. Warren's biography defies Ivy League cliché. A native Oklahoman, she married at nineteen and entered Rutgers School of Law with a two-year-old toddler in tow. Not born or raised in privilege, she sees the world a bit differently than do many of her colleagues. Warren is an expert on bankruptcy and has a particular interest in the factors that inflict it on so many hardworking people. She is thrilled that women today are working and contributing to the well-being of their families, and she is frustrated that this correlates in time with so many American families falling behind. Average household income in 2003 was higher than it was in 1971 when relatively few women were working outside the home, yet household debt in 2003 was much higher. Adding to this puzzle was that in 2003 we Americans spent 32 percent less on clothes, 52 percent less on appliances, and 18 percent less on food than did our parents.

Warren took a close look at this apparent paradox and found that any savings from low-priced consumer goods was more than wiped out by the rising costs of nondurable goods and services: a 76 percent increase in mortgage payments; a 74 percent increase in health insurance costs; a 25 percent increase in tax costs; and, because it barely existed in 1971, a monumental increase in child care costs. In the 1970s, American middle-class families—with only one working parent—spent just half of their income on fixed expenses. Thirty years later, American middle-class families with two working parents spent three-quarters of their income on fixed expenses. This meant that after paying for essentials, middle-class families had a lot less money than they once did to spend on T-shirts and lettuce—certainly far less than economists like Broda imply. This is particularly true of families eking out a living laboring in the fields of cheap consumer goods, but it is also true for middle-class consumers who maintained a shaky grip on shrinking lifestyles by mortgaging their homes to the hilt and incurring record levels of credit card debt.

WHILE PRICE INFLATION is certainly not a great thing for consumers, wage deflation and unemployment are to many minds worse. For retailers, cutting jobs, salaries, and benefits is often the first step on a long, dark road to nowhere. Circuit City, the midsized electronics discounter, offers a harrowing example. In March 2007 the company announced that it was hemorrhaging money and fired without notice 3,400 experienced salesclerks with the reassuring promise that after a ten-week unpaid "cooling-off period" the employees could reapply for their old jobs at lower pay. The company had hobbled through a very, very bad period—sinking from a $140 million profit in the 2006 fiscal year to a $12 million loss in 2007. Naturally, it was hoping a slash in staff and wages would aid recovery.

Circuit City declined to share specific details of its new business plan, but to cite one example, employees working in the computer department were let go if their wage exceeded $15.50 an hour, regardless of seniority. Company executives were not affected by the layoffs and pay cuts. Nor were they affected in 2003 when 20 percent of the Circuit City workforce either lost their jobs or had their commissions cut. Meanwhile, customers stayed away in droves. Without skilled staff, what was once a full-service electronics retailer shriveled into a glorified delivery service shuffling product from factory to store to customers. The company continued to lose money, and in the final months of 2008 it filed for bankruptcy protection.

Circuit City's 2007 "wage management initiative" was reported only feebly by the press, which by then was inured to skilled workers being trampled in a stampede of cost reductions. The news then was not of falling wages but of rising consumer prices. The Consumer Price Index— a measure of the average change in prices over time of goods and services including food, clothing, shelters, fuel, transportation fares, and health care—increased 4.2 percent from May 2007 to May 2008. A closer look reveals that these increases were not evenly distributed across all product and service categories. The cost of housing was up 3.3 percent, food up

5.1 percent, and energy up an alarming 17.4 percent. But the cost of cloth-ing, which had been falling for decades, actually experienced a further decline of .6 percent. In fact, once food and energy were stripped from the equation, the Consumer Price Index increased by only 2.3 percent over that year, the largest portion of which was traced to an 8.1 percent growth in transportation costs.

Increases in the cost of food are always significant and for some people extremely painful. But to put it into perspective, the spurt in food costs in mid-2008 came on the heels of decades of sharp declines, at least relative to income. Data from the U.S. Department of Agriculture indicate that in 1929 Americans spent 20.3 percent of their disposable personal income on food at home, and an additional 3.1 percent on food away from home. In 1970 the at-home percentage had been slashed nearly in half, to 10.3 percent, while the away-from-home percentage increased only slightly, to 3.6 percent. The years that followed saw a steady decline in total food expenditures as a percentage of disposable income: In 2007, at-home food consumption had dropped to a mere 5.7 percent of income, and away-from-home had increased slightly to 4.1 percent of income. Even allowing for 2008 increases, food has for decades been a bargain in America, which is one reason that the poor have a far greater risk than the rich of becoming dangerously obese.

What we spend for food is to some degree under our control. Many of us (though certainly not all of us) who need or choose to lower our individual food costs might do so by eating out less and by reducing the amount of food we waste, which for most of us is substantial. This same sort of "trading down" also applies to most consumer goods. We can hand down T-shirts from one child to the next, buy furniture at second-hand shops, hang on to our cars for ten years rather than six, and send handmade cards or crafts instead of buying expensive gifts. These changes are not easy, but for most of us they can be made without heartbreaking disruption and hardship. This may seem a good thing, and in many senses it is. Few Americans have to concern themselves with starvation or worry about freezing to death for lack of a warm coat. But, unfortu-nately, the same cannot always be said for coping with daunting increases in the price of heating fuel, education, public transportation, rental housing and, most spectacularly, health care. For this we need income, and for millions of Americans income has not kept pace.

Thanks in part to the national insistence on low-priced consumer goods, wages and benefits have barely budged to accommodate the rising costs of most essentials. Technology-driven efficiencies have given us access to the best deals from around the world, but these deals come out of our communal paychecks. Under President George W. Bush and a compliant Republican Congress, the minimum wage was stalled at $5.15 an hour for nearly a decade. A full-time worker earning $5.15 an hour grosses $10,712 a year, well below the poverty line of $16,079 for a family of three. In 2007 the Democratic Congress raised the minimum wage to $7.25 over two years, a real victory for low-wage workers. But even this improved wage is lower in real dollars than the minimum wage of 1960. Retail workers generally make more than the minimum wage, but not enough more to allow them entry into the middle class. Nearly one-third of all working Americans living in poverty are employed in the retail sector. At this writing the average hourly wage for department store associates is $8.79, according to the U.S. Department of Labor, and the annual mean wage is $18,280—that is, except for clothing store clerks, who make less.

The minimum wage was key to President Franklin Delano Roosevelt's New Deal, a vigorous and courageous response to the horrors visited on Americans by the crash of 1929 and the Great Depression. Given soaring unemployment, and crushing homelessness, it had been clear for nearly a decade that market forces alone were unable to achieve the desired recovery and that government action was necessary, whether in the form of taxation, industrial regulation, public works, social insurance, social welfare services, or deficit spending. Roosevelt and the New Dealers built powerful protections: Social Security, unemployment insurance, welfare, housing subsidies, disability insurance, and funds for widows and orphans. Such protections gave organized labor the traction to goad big business into weaving its own safety net: health insurance, pensions, guaranteed job security, and, for some, life and disability insurance. The Fair Labor Standards Act of 1938, the final major reform of the New Deal, was hailed by Roosevelt as "the most far-reaching, far-sighted program for the benefit of workers ever adopted here or any other country."

Decades before, Henry Ford had set the bar on wages, paying his workforce (even the "sweepers") $5 a day in wages and a profit-sharing bonus—enough, he famously figured, for them to buy the Model T's his workforce assembled. We Americans revere this story as integral to the nation's legacy. (We also tend to forget that Ford engaged in some fairly repressive employment practices.) But the so-called labor aristocracy made possible by such apparent largesse and by the union movement that followed was short-lived, a veritable blip on our historical screen. Today's twenty-first-century service economy was built not on the Henry Ford manufacturing model or the union model but on the Frank W. Woolworth model. Unlike Ford, Wal-Mart and most other discounters don't manufacture products; they distribute products made by others. As Woolworth himself pronounced in 1892, cheap goods cannot be had without "cheap help." America is now awash in cheap help who distribute the cheap goods manufactured by even cheaper help working out of our sight and largely out of awareness. How lucky are we to have so many people working so hard and so cheaply to provide us with so many of life's necessities and niceties? Once again that depends on who you ask.

In April 2008 economist Emek Basker published a study entitled "Does Wal-Mart Sell Inferior Goods?" Basker meant "inferior goods" in the technical sense; that is, products and services consumers buy in times of economic stress and hardship. She found that for every 1 percent decrease in personal disposable income, Wal-Mart revenues increased by 0.5 percent. That summer, as America oozed toward recession, Wal-Mart announced a 6.1 percent rise in sales, beating Wall Street estimates. TJX, the owner of cut-rate clothing retailers T. J. Maxx and Marshall's, also enjoyed sales growth. That the corollary is obvious makes it no less troubling: Discounters profit most when Americans hit bottom. This may help explain why Wal-Mart lobbies so hard to keep unions at bay in order, it claims, to keep prices low for its customers. But it does not explain why until recent years the company lobbied against national health care reform and other protections that would benefit both its workers and its core clientele. Andrew Young, a former U.S. Congressman and U.N. ambassador turned Wal-Mart spokesman, seemed to offer an explanation: "Poverty in America," he said, "is market potential unrealized." It seems that the poor benefit the discounting industry far more than the discounting industry benefits the poor.

# CHAPTER EIGHT

# CHEAP EATS

The maxim that the "best is the cheapest" does not apply
to food.

| W. O. ATWATER, PH.D., "FOODS: NUTRITIVE VALUE AND COST"

I'm going to eat too much, but I'm never going to pay
too much.

| ADVERTISING CAMPAIGN FOR DENNY'S RESTAURANT

Potatoes have always been cheap, but they have not always been welcome. Native to the highlands of South America, they were introduced in Europe by Spanish conquistadors returning victorious from their exploits in the New World. Europeans regarded the lumpy mud-speckled objects with suspicion, and for good reason: Their flowers resembled those of deadly nightshade, and their tough, scruffy hide brought to mind skin diseases, such as leprosy and syphilis. In France, Belgium, Austria, and Germany potatoes were scorned as a pernicious, lust-inducing scourge. The Italians and British considered them a sort of punishment, food fit for pigs or prisoners, but the Irish saw things differently.

Sir Walter Raleigh brought the potato to Ireland in 1589, where it flourished. The Irish peasantry, practical by necessity, quickly embraced the staple that went from harvest to dinner plate with such aplomb and so little fuss. Wheat needed milling into flour, oats rolling or grinding, but potatoes required for palatability only a bake or a boil. Nutritious, filling, and portable, they were a near perfect food. Irish industrialists and landowners praised potatoes as "heaven-sent" food for the peasantry, cheap fuel for cheap labor. By the mid-nineteenth century 3 million Irish peasants ate almost nothing else, as many as ten or even twelve pounds a day, seasoned with buttermilk and salt, and maybe with one or two herring on the side. One historian of Ireland wrote at the time: "Cooking any food other than a potato had become a lost art. Women boiled hardly anything but potatoes."

We know the tragic corollary to this tuber fixation. In 1845 a great wind blew spores of *phytophthora infestan* from southern Europe to Ireland, where, like the potato itself, the fungus found fertile ground. Over the centuries South Americans had learned to plant potatoes in scores of genetically distinct varieties, one or more of which would surely have mounted resistance to the fungal attack. But Ireland was defenseless against this intruder, relying as it did on a single subspecies, the unfortunately named "Lumper." The Lumper, though not the best-tasting potato, grew easily on thin stony soil. It was, one might say, the cheapest of the cheap. The downside was that it rallied next to no objection to invaders. It was such easy fungal prey that it took mere days for a single infested plant to infest thousands of others, systematically curdling the nation's primary food source into a foul-smelling black slime.

The Irish potato famine is branded into historical memory as a cautionary tale of greedy landowners, helpless farmers, and bad planning. Still, it bears reminding that throughout the course of that devastating scourge the Emerald Isle was heavy with food—plenty of fish, beef, oats, and wheat. Indeed, Ireland remained a food exporter, shipping meat and grain to richer nations while a million of its own citizens starved to death and a million and a half others fled to North America. The tragedy of the great Irish famine stemmed not from a food shortage but a shortage of food deemed cheap enough to feed the poor.

Experience has taught us the recklessness of growing one crop to the exclusion of most others. We have learned the hard way that monocultures are vulnerable to whatever microbe or swarming insect comes their way. But we have not managed to shake off the presumption that for most of us food should be cheap. This is not without consequences. In September 2008 the United Nations reported that 75 million souls were added to the roll of the world's hungry, raising the total to a staggering

925 million worldwide. As it was in Ireland more than a century and a half earlier, this hunger was not traceable to an actual food shortage. The world in 2008 was richer in food than ever before; despite an uptick in population, there was more than enough to go around. But abundance was not enough. In Haiti, Burma, Ethiopia, and the Sudan people starved as the food they grew and harvested went to others. For them this was not a new story. In 1984–85 Ethiopia continued to export beans to the United Kingdom while famine killed a million of its people. Despite the continued threat of famine in 1989, Sudan sold 400,000 tons of sorghum to the European Community for animal feed. Today, despite continued food shortages, in Ethiopia much of the best land is devoted to growing coffee (which comprises more than 50 percent of that country's exports) and in Sudan to growing cotton (50 percent of exports). This is not to suggest that exports and cash crops are not vital to these economies; they are, of course. But by focusing on one or two crops and making trade a priority, these nations greatly increase their risk of food insecurity, just as Ireland did two centuries ago. It is a terrible irony that the global demand for ever cheaper food has pushed the most vulnerable—poor families in the developing world—to the brink.

ANYONE WHO HAS laid eyes on a modern factory farm knows that factory—not farm—is the operative term. Agribusiness and the technology powering it enable efficiencies beyond the dreams and reach of any ordinary farmer. Livestock genetically engineered in the lab, fattened on corn and growth hormones in confinement facilities, and pumped with antibiotics grow into spectacular specimens. Crops grown from scientifically optimized seeds and lavished with petroleum-based fertilizers and herbicides do, too. All this makes for extremely cheap food not only in the United States but in much of the world. Between 1974 and 2005 food prices on world markets fell by three-quarters, meaning that in real terms food was much cheaper in 2005 than it was a generation earlier. Technology-driven efficiencies are one reason that food prices fell so far. Another is government-supported protections and subsidies for mega-farms.

The U.S. Department of Agriculture handed out $177.6 billion in farm subsidies between 1995 and 2006, with three-quarters of the largesse concentrated in the hands of only 10 percent of the recipients. The top beneficiary was Riceland Foods of Stuttgart, Arkansas, the largest rice miller and marketer in the world. You have probably eaten Riceland rice in a cafeteria at work or school, or maybe in a restaurant. There is a good chance the "private label" rice at your local supermarket came from there, too. Riceland is responsible for one-third of the entire United States crop, and the cooperative exports rice to Europe, Saudi Arabia, Mexico, and Cuba. Still, Riceland relies on a good deal of taxpayer support. From 1995 to 2006, Riceland received an astronomical $554,343,039 in government handouts. Thanks to this, Riceland can set the bar for low price: In 2005 the world market price for rice was 20 to 34 percent less than what it cost the average U.S. farmer to grow.

Larry Matlock is a fifth-generation farmer in Kansas and president of the American Agriculture Movement, a national lobby representing the interests of small farmers. Matlock is not a fan of government subsidies, which he said "suck the lifeblood out of every family farmer in the world." While there is little evidence of actual blood-loss, most independent American family farmers gave up long ago. Some can and do compete by offering "boutique" products, such as organically grown crops and meat, or by diversifying. American and European farmers can also go into the business of value-added products such as specialty cheeses and smoked meats. But in the developing world, local producers rarely have these options. And it is in the developing world that America's penchant for cheap food has the most devastating impact.

Michael Morris is lead agricultural economist at the World Bank, currently stationed in Madagascar, a large island state where people eat rice two or three times a day, much of it imported. Morris assured me that the price of food in American supermarkets does not reflect the true cost of production of rice, wheat, corn, or the livestock that fatten on it. "The low prices are there partly because of first-world efficiencies, but mostly thanks to subsidies," he said. "And subsidies have a depressing effect on producers in developing countries. They sharply reduce incentives." That is, when developing countries are pushed to import Western-subsidized food, they are likely to lose the knack of growing their own.

Haiti, the poorest nation in the Western Hemisphere, offers a telling illustration. In 1995, Haiti reduced tariffs on rice imports from 35 to just 3 percent in response to pressure from the International Monetary Fund (IMF) and the United States. Rice imports grew by 150 percent, and Haitian rice farmers could not compete. Some tried cultivating other crops but eventually abandoned their land and moved to the city in a desperate search for work. Henri Bazin, head of the Haitian Economists Association and a former IMF employee, told one reporter, "Cheap imports and the government's failure to support peasant farmers are driving them off the land and into the cities to burgeoning slums."

Haiti once exported rice. Today, three-quarters of the rice on Haitian dinner plates comes from the United States. When farms are neglected, native farming traditions and practices are lost. This, in turn, increases local demand for imported food. Paying for those imports requires cash, and acquiring that cash usually means getting a job providing the First World with something it wants—either raw materials, such as timber, minerals, or coffee, or cheap mass-manufactured goods. Farmers leave their land to find work in mines or factories, further reducing local food production. Without land or with only marginal plots, those who cannot find jobs join the poorest of the poor. Some of them flee—often to the United States. This helps explain why U.S. immigration reached an all-time high of over 37 million in 2007.

The rap against "agribusiness" is not new. Antiglobalists protest the destruction of agrarian economies and the "de-peasantization" of the developing world. Journalists, too, tend to take this view, contending that globalization has destroyed a vibrant and vital way of life. Although well meaning, these claims are simplistic and reflect their adherents' ideology more accurately than the experience of the rural poor. The story of cheap food is far more complicated than advocates on either side make it out to be.

History has rarely been kind to peasants, for whom farming is not necessarily a source of satisfaction or, for that matter, a decent living.

Small subsistence farmers comprise 75 percent of the world's poor, and few can rely on their farms as an exclusive source of income. Even under the best of circumstances, subsistence farming is not a job for the future, because the land simply will not sustain it.

Let's say a farmer makes a decent living growing sorghum on a ten-acre plot. The farmer grows old and bequeaths his farm to his three sons. In a healthy expanding economy, two sons might leave the farm to work in another trade, while one son stays back to run the farm. But in many poor countries the economy is not growing, and all three sons must rely on that plot to make their living. The same ten acres must now support three families. When these men grow old, they bequeath the land to their sons. Eventually, and probably soon, there is no longer enough land to support the string of generations.

For the vast majority of the rural poor, farming is just one component of a highly diversified working life. The myth of the "noble peasant," though increasingly popular, is no more real today than it was in medieval times. Scratching a living out of an unforgiving earth is a dicey business for most people in the developing world and offers a lifestyle that many are eager to escape. University of London development scholar Henry Bernstein points out that the vast majority of rural farm workers make their living by finding work where they can, both on and off the farm, and had done so long before globalization brought multinational interests into play.

Still, the demands of today's global marketplace—and the influence of multinational corporations—have made it even more difficult for Third World farmers to maintain what little power they once exerted over their own lives or to plan for the future. When food prices soared in the early 2000s, few small farmers were prepared to take advantage of it. Many were just as shocked as the rest of us.

Blame for the price hike landed on a number of culprits: price spikes in the fossil fuels needed for farm machinery, transportation- and petroleum-based fertilizer; the ill-considered biofuels fad that rocketed demand for corn and soybeans and, indirectly, other grains; storms, droughts, and political unrest in Australia, Russia, and other food-exporting nations; a sustained decline in the dollar leading to a spurt in commodity speculation as a hedge; and growing prosperity in the developing world that contributed to demand for high-value foods such as meat and dairy products. Each of these played a significant role, but it would be natural to assume that the final variable—growing affluence in developing nations—would compensate for rising food prices. After all, higher prices should lift the incomes of farmers, and a wealthier citizenry should be better able to pay the bill. Unfortunately, things have not played out that way.

Once again, rice, a staple for more than half the world's population, makes a good example. Prior to the most recent "global food crises," India for nearly two decades had been a reliable exporter of rice—and often the world's largest, after Thailand. Given that impressive track record one would think India would be self-sufficient in rice and be in a strong position to keep rice prices within reasonable limits for its own people. Underlying circumstances make that outcome seem even more likely. In 2008, India produced 94 million metric tons of rice, an increase of more than 2 million metric tons over the year before and more than 20 million metric tons more than 2003's crop. As for the poor, India's government-run free rice distribution unit purchased 25 million metric tons from both domestic growers and importers, a substantial increase from the 20.6 million metric tons it bought the year previous. Making things look even better was that global rice production had reached an all-time high. Indeed, grain harvests in general were stupendous, up 5 percent from the previous year. Bluntly put: There was no shortage of rice in India and no shortage of food in the world during the "food crises" of 2008. Yet millions of Indians—as well as Africans and Asians—suddenly found themselves stranded on the edge of starvation.

What had changed was not rice but the rice trade. Historically, the Indian government had kept a firm grip on rice stores and maintained a policy of food self-sufficiency that discouraged exports. In the 1990s that policy was softened, and Indian rice was made available on the world market. Indian farmers and traders auctioned their wares to the highest bidder, with the result that rice which had once sold domestically or was stockpiled by the government was sold abroad. Over time this practice increased price instability. When world rice prices started to climb in 2006 and India started to pull back on exports in 2007 and ban them entirely in 2008, panic ensued. Those who could afford to hoarded rice, which led to scarcity, and in April 2008 prices leaped from $750 to $1,100 a ton. Suddenly, rice was unaffordable.

And, of course, it was not only rice. April of that year was an altogether terrifying month for a hungry world. The price of meat, milk, wheat, and corn skyrocketed. Most other things did, too. Yet the prices were not the highest they had ever been—far from it. Despite stratospheric increases, the price of staples was only about half of what it had been in 1973–74 and no higher than average prices throughout the 1960s. These facts were of little comfort to the hundreds of millions of poor in the developing world or to budget-strapped consumers in the West. But they were inescapable—and key. The spike in food prices in 2008 was a result, at least in part, of the unsustainably low prices that preceded them.

ON ITS FACE, cheap food is a godsend, especially for urbanites and the rural landless. But frequently this benefit is short-lived. Over the long term, overreliance on cheap food contributes to food dependency, complacency, and—when prices rise as they have in recent years—social unrest and devastation. "All things being equal, if agricultural prices were higher, incentives in the developing countries would have been greater, and there would have been more food production in the developing world," Michael Morris said.

Prior to 2001, cereal prices were on a stuttering decline for nearly a century and on a steady decline since the early 1980s. Stanford economist Peter Timmer, an expert on global agricultural markets, explained what happened when prices dropped too far. "They sent investment signals to governments, donors and research institutions, encouraging them to walk away from the agricultural sector as a crucial source of productivity growth and poverty reduction." Low prices provoked government policies directed not at increasing food production and supporting farmers, but reducing surpluses. Food was so cheap and so plentiful that there seemed little reason to store much of it or find better ways to grow or harvest it. Stockpiles dwindled as nations relied on a just-in-time approach to getting food to markets. Governments operated as though food, like T-shirts or DVD players, would always be available at a low price.

"Reduced investments in agriculture and rural infrastructure throughout the 1980s and 1990s resulted in falling productivity growth," Timmer said. "Eventually, growth in food production fell behind growth in food consumption, scarcity reemerged, and market prices spiraled higher. The world food crisis in late 2007 and early 2008 had its roots directly in this earlier neglect of agricultural investments."

Agricultural investments are not always well placed or even well meant. Titans of industrial agriculture—including U.S.-based multinationals such as Monsanto, Archer Daniels Midland, and Cargill—have long pushed for increased production through the introduction of "inputs"—designer seeds, chemical fertilizers, and herbicides—that small farmers can ill afford. Increased efficiencies achieved by these improvements brought great benefit to the world's hungry but also demanded consolidation of small farms into mega-farms, forcing marginal producers—small farmers in particular—onto smaller plots and then, when they could last no longer, off their land. "The consolidation of food production has led to economies of scale and lower production costs, which have contributed to the long-term secular decline in real food prices," Morris explained. "But consolidation has meant that when the large agribusiness interests decide to change course abruptly and, say, invest in biofuels, that can lead to severe disruptions in food markets in the short run."

The United States is the world's largest exporter of food and as such dominates world food policy. But in recent years we have become increasingly dependent on imports in a frantic effort to keep food prices low. Left to their own devices, global food markets pretty much follow the same "race to the bottom" model followed by other unfettered markets. Subsidies and economies of scale have made grain and everything it is made of—including the animals that eat it—increasingly cheap.

In hard times all but the poorest Americans tend not to cut back on food consumption but, rather, gravitate toward getting what we perceive to be "more for less." Responding to rising food prices and a sinking economy in the early months of 2009, Americans cut back on fresh fruits and vegetables but increased their consumption of fast food. The *New York Times* reported: "During a year when the stock market lost a third of its value—its worst performance since the Great Depression—shares of McDonald's gained nearly 6 percent, making the company one of only two in the Dow Jones Industrial Average whose share price rose in 2008. (The other was Wal-Mart.)" The popular Denny's Restaurant chain touted its Extreme Grand Slam Breakfast, consisting of three strips of bacon, three sausage links, two eggs, hash browns and three pancakes. The meal contains 1,270 calories and 77 grams of fat, and aside from the potatoes, every component is either grain-based or grain-fed. There are no tomatoes with those eggs or fruit salad or even orange juice. Humans are programmed to seek the greatest volume of food at the least energy expenditure, which in biological terms amounts to a "cost." So in times of economic stress, loading up on large amounts of low-cost foods makes sense. But in a world of industrial food, this seemingly simple strategy is neither simple nor, over the long term, safe.

IN NEW ENGLAND, seafood is king. People here think nothing of burning through a gallon of gas to drive to a plate of fried clams, or two gallons for a great lobster roll. We argue tirelessly over whether to add potatoes to clam chowder and whether Wellfleet oysters beat those from Damariscotta, Maine. But we tend not to bicker about shrimp, which we buy mostly in bags, frozen solid. We have every reason to assume that those bags are filled with crustaceans pulled out of the Gulf of Mexico off the coast of Texas, Louisiana, or Florida. But those of us who scan the fine print on the bag learn—perhaps to our surprise—that that is not the case. The American shrimp industry all but collapsed a decade ago under the weight of imports from Latin America and Asia. Spiting the laws of supply and demand, shrimp got cheaper as demand for it grew, the price dropping by half between 1980 and 2005 as consumption nearly tripled from 1.4 to 4.1 pounds per person per year. Today, 90 percent of shrimp in the United States is imported. Even if you live in Florida or Texas, the frozen shrimp in your shopping cart most likely came from Thailand.

Unlike potatoes, shrimp was not always cheap. Before the 1980s, few

Americans cooked with shrimp, and not many were fortunate enough to eat it in restaurants more than a few times a year. Many of us can still recall it as a delicacy, served in a martini glass with a side of cocktail sauce or folded tenderly into cream sauces. Shrimp was a treat: expensive because it was so devilishly hard to come by. Most shrimp sold in the United States was wild, caught in nets, an arduous job requiring strong backs, keen wits, deep knowledge, diesel fuel, and luck. Cultivation was possible but extremely difficult since farmed shrimp was plagued by deadly viruses.

Eventually, science caught up. Aquaculturists unlocked the secrets of shrimp cultivation, of hatching eggs and coaxing them through the post-larvae stage into childhood. They also learned to curb the spread of viruses with sophisticated filtration and purification systems. Millions of acres of coastal wetlands in Asia and Latin America were cleared to make way for man-made ponds where juvenile shrimp were fattened on nutrient slurries and antibiotics. Shrimp exports skyrocketed, and prices plummeted.

Today, shrimp is no longer a delicacy. Wal-Mart is the world's fastest-growing shrimp importer. Food services giant Sysco Corporation buys more than a billion dollars' worth of seafood a year, much of it in the form of mysterious "shrimp products" distributed to hospitals and schools. If these facts are not evidence enough of the distance shrimp has fallen in the American pantheon of luxury foods, consider this: Since 2001, Americans have eaten more shrimp by weight than canned tuna fish.

As our taste for shrimp has grown, so has the business of farming it: In the past two decades the number of shrimp farms has quintupled in coastal regions and, to a lesser extent, in inland freshwater farming areas. Virtually all the world's farmed shrimp is cultivated in the global south, where most of the world's poor live, too. Slightly less than half of that farmed shrimp is exported to the United States, the world's leading importer.

At restaurants, shrimp is a no-brainer. Easy to cook, easy to eat, it's an almost foolproof crowd pleaser. Darden Restaurants, the world's largest full-service restaurant company, is the parent company of Olive Garden, Bahama Breeze, and Red Lobster, all front-runners in the casual dining category. The most popular dishes at Bahama Breeze are fire-cracker shrimp and coconut shrimp. At Olive Garden there are grilled garlic shrimp pasta and shrimp scampi. But for dedicated shrimp lovers, Red Lobster's endless shrimp parade seems by far the best choice. At this writing the deal includes limitless Cajun, popcorn, coconut, or other shrimp specialty, served with a side of potato, rice, or broccoli; a salad or coleslaw; and Red Lobster's signature "cheddar" biscuits. The cost is $15.99. How much shrimp do diners eat at one sitting? It's hard to say, but on the unofficial Red Lobster blog, waitstaff trade "you won't believe this" stories of customers waddling in and demanding twenty orders—more than two hundred shrimp—at a sitting.

Red Lobster was once positioned—and priced—at the high end of the casual dining category, a place a young couple might go to toast a special anniversary, or a family to fete a new graduate. But in 2001 when the economy softened and customer numbers fell, the chain fought back with a line of menu selections priced under $10. That list included twenty-two items, mostly chicken, pasta, and farm-raised shrimp. Half of Red Lobster's annual $90 million in seafood sales that year was farm-grown, and 80 percent of that was shrimp. Most of that shrimp was shipped, frozen in blocks, from Thailand.

If there is a heaven for shrimp, it almost certainly looks like Thailand. The country's 2,700 miles of warm, protected coastline is an ideal habitat for both wild and domesticated species. Shrimp hatch in the ocean, drift toward land with the tides, and get tangled in roots and sediment on the shoreline, where, safe from predators, they grow into juveniles and then return to open water to further mature. Thais have farmed shrimp for centuries on a very small scale, taking advantage of the creature's natural life cycle by holding it safe in coastal ponds until harvest. Shrimp was also farmed in alternate seasons from rice in paddies, again on a relatively small scale. None of this changed the landscape or made much of a dif-ference in the quality of the shrimp. But it didn't make for high efficien-cies, either. Shrimp was still a luxury.

In the late 1970s, shrimp farmers turbocharged the age-old shrimp-farming process by adding to their ponds post-larval shrimp caught in the wild or raised in hatcheries. They supplemented natural feeds with nutrient slurries, chemicals, and antibiotics. Efficiencies skyrocketed, and the shrimp rush was on.

The World Bank, the Asian Development Bank, and other lenders poured hundreds of millions of dollars into shrimp, as did private investors. Racked with debts, the Thai government encouraged this development. By the mid-1980s farmers up and down the Thai peninsula had converted their rice paddies—and thousands of square acres of coastline—into teeming shrimp operations, veritable seafood gold mines. While traditional shrimp farms yielded less than 450 pounds per acre, the new factory-style outfits harvested as much as 89,000 pounds per acre. Production grew and then exploded—from 33,000 metric tons in 1987 to an astonishing 240,000 metric tons in 1995.

Shrimp farming was cheered by the World Bank and others as a surefire path out of poverty, and for some it was: Shrimp was substantially more profitable than rice and other crops, and not a few farmers got rich. But the party didn't last long. As corporate and government interests took tighter hold, pushing demands higher, ponds started to break down and fail. What followed was ruinous debt, environmental degradation, horrifying human rights abuses, and violence that left millions destitute. It was almost as if the shrimp itself was taking revenge for being diminished to the status of a cheap commodity.

Shrimp comes in hundreds of varieties, only a few of which can be tamed. On Thai farms, warm water types dominate—notably Pacific white shrimp, *P. vannamei*, and black tiger shrimp, *P. monodon*. White shrimp tend to be small, but tigers are the largest shrimp on record, some behemoths weighing in at just under three ounces each. To grow them, coastal or other farmland is swamped or flooded with salt water, to create a brackish pond, and surrounded by a slippery blue plastic apron to prevent frisky shrimp from escaping. (Yes, shrimp can jump.) Some inland farmers truck salt water in from the coast, while others just dump salt into freshwater ponds. Under the best conditions, these ponds are well tended, adequately monitored, and not too tightly packed. More typically, the ponds are dangerously overcrowded and indifferently managed, plagued by overfeeding, plankton blooms, and inadequate water circulation. Shrimp are carnivorous and require feed—usually fish meal—in amounts more than double their adult weight. Often, groundwater aqui-fers, domestic water supplies, and adjacent rice paddies and farm fields are contaminated with this meal and with massive volumes of waste from the shrimp itself. Waste water pumped from ponds pollutes canals, rivers, and other water sources with pesticides, antibiotics, and disinfectants. Built-up waste mixed with chemicals scraped from the bottom of the ponds is piled into ugly—and toxic—hillocks. The smell of the shrimp ponds has been likened to a hobbyist's fish tank that hasn't been cleaned in months. Beneath the smell lurks disease: As with any creatures in extremely crowded and filthy conditions, farmed shrimp are highly sus-ceptible to infection, and despite massive inputs of antibiotics, many sicken and die. As a result, roughly half of the more than million acres of shrimp farms lie abandoned. Meanwhile, the land is permanently contaminated. Paddies tainted by salt and filth are no good for growing rice or much of anything else. And on the coast the same mangrove forests that once sheltered and nourished wild shrimp have been system-atically eradicated to make way for the farmed variety.

The mangrove forest is a unique and irreplaceable tropical ecosystem and a star player in the natural history of Thailand. Stretching down roughly half of the country's coastline, the mangrove is thick with nutri-ents for fish and shellfish, and offers shelter from predators. Life in the world's coral reefs and sea grass beds—from which two-thirds of all fish are caught—rely on a critical synergy with mangroves. Creatures move back and forth among them, stirred by the winds and tides. But perhaps even more important, mangroves form a transitional buffer between land and sea, stabilizing shorelines, reducing soil erosion, and softening the assaultive impact of tidal waves. Scientists at the Mangrove Ecosystems Research Center in Vietnam have evidence that mangroves work better than concrete walls to hold back the punishing tides of tropical storms. Mangroves are perhaps best appreciated by their absence: On December 26, 2004, the great Southeast Asian tsunami pummeled the coasts of eleven nations with waves twenty feet high, killing more than a quarter of a million people and leaving millions of others homeless. The United Nations reported that clear-cutting of coastal mangrove forests for shrimp production contributed significantly to this tragic outcome.

Cheap shrimp, like all things cheap, require cheap labor. Apparently, too few Thais are willing to work cheaply enough to satisfy our demand for low-priced shrimp because the industry is served mostly by migrant workers from Burma, Cambodia, and Vietnam. The migrants, many of whom do not speak the local language and have little concept of their own rights, suffer egregious and well-documented abuses ranging from unpaid overtime to child labor, torture, and rape. Perhaps it is too big a stretch to link all this suffering and degradation to the $15.99 "all you can eat" shrimp parade at Red Lobster, or perhaps it is just a small step.

Stanford economist Peter Timmer is a measured, thoughtful scholar not given to exaggeration, but when it comes to the global markets, one thing worries him above all else. "I'm quite concerned about what the large food companies are doing to the quality and safety of our diet," he said. You need not be an economist to realize that food farmed, harvested, and processed in enormous quantities and sold at very low prices is unlikely to have been handled with great care. Lack of care can lead to sloppiness, and sloppiness to contamination, infestation, and infection. More than two hundred known diseases are transmitted by food through viruses, bacteria, parasites, toxins, metals, and prions, the protein implicated in a number of fatal neurological disorders including mad cow disease and its lethal human version, a new variant of Creutzfeldt-Jakob disease. The less we spend on food, the more likely it is that one or more of these killers will sneak into our food supply.

An estimated 76 million cases of foodborne disease occur each year in the United States, requiring 325,000 hospitalizations and resulting in 5,000 deaths. New surveillance data—and newfound links between food and disease—suggest that these are underestimates. The vast majority of food-related illness goes unreported, and the vast majority of food-related threats are likely to be as yet unknown.

Consider that until the early 1980s few thought that *Escherichia coli* posed a serious problem to human health. The bacterium is ubiquitous and in many ways essential. It resides (among other places) in the human intestine, where it suppresses the growth of harmful bacteria and plays an important role in digestion and vitamin synthesis. Its biological simplicity makes it an excellent model for genetic research, as does its harmlessness.

But that is the normal form. Mutated, E. coli can be virulent. E. coli 0157, for example, exudes a powerful toxin that turns on and attacks its host. In humans the toxin attacks the intestine, causing severe stomach cramps, high fever, and debilitating bloody diarrhea. In about 4 percent of cases the toxins enter the bloodstream, where the real damage is done. E. coli 0157 infection is linked to the most common cause of acute kidney failure in children, hemolytic uremic syndrome, and also to seizures, strokes, blindness, and brain damage.

E. coli 0157 was first isolated and characterized in 1982, and since then has been linked to what appear to be an increasing number of foodborne disease outbreaks. In 2006 more than two hundred Californians fell ill and three died after eating Dole-brand bagged baby spinach tainted with the bacterium. The bug was traced to the guts of a wild pig caught rooting around a cattle feed lot. One would think three deaths would be enough to motivate the food industry to change its ways, and perhaps in some ways it was. But the following year, in 2007, there were twenty-one beef recalls nationwide for suspected E. coli contamination, the largest number in five years. The amount of beef recalled—33.4 million pounds—set a new record. A year later, in July 2008, the dangerous strain appeared in hamburger meat packaged and distributed by Nebraska Beef Ltd., purveyor not only to Kroger Supermarkets., but, more surprisingly, to Whole Foods Market, a paragon of the natural foods movement. For reasons no one has fully explained, Whole Foods continued to sell the meat briefly even after the FDA recall. That September the strain appeared in lettuce distributed by Aunt Mid's Produce in Detroit.

Factory farming is efficient, but it is also showing signs of wear. Confined in what might be best compared to a filth-choked slum and stressed beyond reason, livestock are bait for every conceivable pathogen. We can attack them with antibiotics and other drugs, but the microbes are relentless and exact their toll. In 2000 the U.S. Department of Agriculture tracked disease on 895 hog farms, comparing farms with fewer than two thousand animals with those that had more than ten thousand. No one expected the larger farms to be healthier for the animals. Still, it was sobering to learn that when compared with smaller farms, the mega-producers had three times the incidence of mycoplasma pneumonia, six times the cases of swine influenza, and twenty-nine times the cases of a new flu strain. That young pigs tend to die under these circumstances is part of the calculus, mere collateral damage. The survivors live just long enough to stumble over the finish line—and onto our dinner plates.

Livestock doomed to this short, brutish existence exact revenge in subtle but potent ways not only through their flesh, but also through their waste. Traditional farmers fertilize their corn and alfalfa fields with manure from livestock in a closed loop system that benefits both plants and animals. But factory meat growers—the ones with hundreds of thousands of animals crammed into huge concrete-floored barns—produce far too much waste to be contained within this system.

It is quicker—and therefore cheaper—to fatten cattle on grain than on grass. Grain feeding greatly increases the capacity for E. coli and other microbes to survive in the colon of cattle, where it multiples and gets passed into manure. E. coli can survive up to ninety days in manure, making cattle feedlots fertile breeding grounds for infection. As many as one hundred thousand steers at a time fatten on a single lot, pouring out huge volumes of waste. Two feedlots outside Greeley, Colorado, together produce more excrement than the cities of Atlanta, Boston, Denver, and St. Louis combined. Trucking the stuff off is impractical. One alternative popular among big companies is to spray liquefied manure into the air and let it fall where it may, coating trees and anything else that happens to be in its path. Another is pumping the mess into lagoons. Both methods have distinct disadvantages.

Lagoons can leak during heavy rainstorms, contaminating wells, rivers, groundwater, and irrigation water. The lagoons also give off fumes of ammonia and hydrogen sulfide, a cause of respiratory and neurological disorders. Manure lagoons also concentrate cadmium, copper, zinc, and other heavy metals that can leach into the soil and eventually get sucked back into crops—and into us. And there is the smell to consider. Smithfield Foods, the largest and most profitable pork processer in the world (and among the largest beef and poultry producers), puts out 6 billion pounds of packaged pork a year. A visitor encountering one of the company's manure lagoons described it this way: "I've probably smelled stronger odors in my life, but nothing so insidiously and instantaneously nauseating. It takes my mind a second or two to get through the odor's first coat. The smell at its core has a frightening, uniquely enriched putridity, both deep-sweet and high-sour. I back away from it and walk back to the car but I remain sick—it's a shivery, retchy kind of nausea—for a good five minutes. That's apparently characteristic of industrial pig shit: It keeps making you sick for a good while after you've stopped smelling it."

In July 2007, China blocked imports of U.S. factory-grown pork on the grounds of contamination. It is unclear whether these charges were valid or simply payback for U.S. rejection of Chinese processed foods. The United States had reason to be worried about Chinese products. That September, 180 Chinese food factories were shut down after inspectors found industrial chemicals being used in food processing. The closures were part of a nationwide crackdown that also exposed the use of formaldehyde, illegal dyes, and industrial chemicals in the processing of candy, pickles, crackers, and seafood. "These are not isolated cases," Han Yi, a director at the General Administration of Quality Supervision, told a reporter. "Han's admission was significant," the report continued, "because the administration has said in the past that safety violations were the work of a few rogue operators, a claim which is likely part of a strategy to protect China's billions of dollars of food exports."

U.S. imports of Chinese agricultural and seafood products have quadrupled in the past decade. From July 2006 to June 2007, the Food and Drug Administration [FDA] rejected 1,901 Chinese shipments: dried apples preserved with a cancer-causing chemical, frozen catfish treated with banned antibiotics, prunes tinted with chemical dyes unsafe for human consumption, mushrooms laced with illegal pesticides, scallops and sardines coated with putrefying bacteria, and the ever popular farm-grown shrimp, this time preserved with nitrofurans, a class of antibiotic that has been linked to cancer. But it wouldn't be fair to imply that the Chinese have cornered the market on tainted food. During the same period, the FDA rejected almost as many shipments from India (1,787) and Mexico (1,560).

AMERICANS claim to put safety first, and one would assume that applies doubly in the case of food. But safety is not free, and we are not always willing to pick up the tab. The United States Department of Agriculture (USDA), which is responsible for inspecting meat and poultry, inspects only 16 percent of all imports. The FDA, responsible for fruits, vegetables, and most other foods, inspects less than 1 percent of imports, down from 8 percent in 1992. Given this record it takes no leap of imagination to conclude that most tainted imports manage to elude inspection and find their way onto American menus. Blaming exporters for this problem is to shirk our own responsibility. Were we to demand fresher, safer food and be willing to absorb the cost of producing it, tainted imports would be a shrinking rather than a growing threat. The Chinese understand this. Speaking in 2007, Chinese officials begged U.S. importers to communicate standards "more clearly" and "look beyond their emphasis on low prices."

As journalist Paul Roberts wrote in *The End of Food,* "Until late in the twentieth century, the modern food system was celebrated as a monument to humanity's greatest triumph. We were producing more food— more grain, more meat, more fruits and vegetables—than ever before, more cheaply than ever before, and with a degree of variety, safety, quality and convenience that preceding generations would have found bewildering." As prices declined, the sanctity of cheap food was rarely questioned until, over the last couple of decades, it became so cheap as to be both dangerous and irresistible.

At the close of the last century *overweight* overtook *malnutrition* as a health hazard in the developed world. Concern over the growing obesity pandemic incited a reconsideration of the falling price, with some going so far as to suggest that cheap food was an evil unto itself. Author Michael Pollan and the slow food movement encouraged eaters to "pay more for less and better" food. Still, when food prices began trending skyward, few thought it cause for celebration or, for that matter, contemplation. The U.S. numbers were frightening: The price of food eaten at home jumped 4.2 percent in 2007, and food eaten away from home—at restaurants, cafeterias, and the like—rose 3.6 percent. Complicating matters was that staples such as milk and eggs were the hardest hit. Milk went up 20 percent, eggs more than 29 percent. Projected food prices for 2008 were even higher. Voices were raised, and threats were made: How can we feed ourselves at these prices? The outcry tended to muffle the reality—that we Americans still spend just over 6 percent of our *disposable* income on food, about half of what the Japanese and French spend and a quarter of what the Chinese spend. Russians, Indians, and Indonesians spend much more. Still, we worry. We worry that there must be a catch, that we aren't getting the deals we deserve. And our food system struggles to comply. The motto "value for money," means not "the same for less" but "more for less." The fully loaded foot-long sandwiches at Subway cost a dollar less than they did the year before. McDonald's offered two Egg McMuffins for three-fourths of the price. The idea that Americans might actually curb their appetites was unthinkable.

Psychologist Adam Drewnowski, director of the Nutritional Sciences Program at the University of Washington School of Public and Community Health, knows why. Americans, he said, respond almost viscerally to the concept of food "value." Price, Drewnowski said, *drives* taste, because left to their own devices, Americans tend to choose what is cheap and therefore develop a taste for cheap foods. Cheap food also delivers the "bang for the buck" we have been conditioned to expect.

"Laboratory scientists aren't able to handle this concept. For them, talking about the price of food is taboo—but it's extremely important," he said. "Americans can eat pizza at about a thousand calories a dollar, or Oreo cookies at about 1,200 calories a dollar. M&Ms at about 3,000 calories per dollar are a huge bargain. Spinach is about 30 calories a dollar, not a bargain. And don't even think about lettuce or cucumbers or tomatoes or, heaven forbid, strawberries. By comparison, these foods are a rip-off!"

Given that chow for humans is not yet synthesized by scientists in laboratories, even our cheapest food must be grown, harvested, and processed. In the United States, cheap translates into anything benefiting from agricultural subsidies, meaning grain and the farm animals that eat it. Cheap food is meant to make us happier and healthier, and years ago when food costs ate up half our income, this was undoubtedly true. But the past couple of decades have brought us to a turning point at which cheap food seems to diminish rather than enhance our health and—one might reasonably argue—our happiness. We know that mountains of processed grain and grain-fed livestock—the stuff of Subway subs and Egg McMuffins—is not terribly good for us. Still, that knowledge doesn't stop us from seeking and consuming "great deals." Meanwhile, scientists writing in the *New England Journal of Medicine* linked cheap food to a startling prediction: that the next generation of Americans will be the first in human history to die younger than their parents.

One might reasonably argue that it is not price but taste that shapes food preferences. But that argument begs the question. Taste preferences develop over time through exposure, and most of us have had scant opportunity to taste food in its natural state. Those fortunate enough to sample naturally grown pork know that it shares little in common with its factory-created cousin. Naturally grown pork is succulent, firm, sweet, and savory; it is meat one can imagine coming from a pig that once roamed freely, if not in a field of daisies, then at least in a field. Factory pigs are bred to be lean, so lean that producers sometimes inject their flesh with saline marinades to make it palatable. Stressful lives tend to make factory-grown pork acidic, bleaching it pale and breaking the tissue down to something flaccid, watery, and limp. The pork industry calls this meat "pale soft exudative," or PSE. In advertising lingo it is called the "other white meat." By any name it is the cheap unbranded stuff found in most supermarket meat coolers. It is what most of us have come to think of as pork.

Likewise, anyone who has eaten ocean or freshwater shrimp caught wild knows that it shares little in common with its factory-farmed stepcousins. Wild-caught shrimp has a firm texture and a bracing, briny taste brought on by clean living. There is no whiff of antibiotic or pesticide residue, and no trail of human misery behind it. Shrimp bred in crowded, polluted ponds is slippery, even slimy, with a flat muddy taste that tells us all we need to know about its past. Still, it is what most of us have come to think of as shrimp.

Toward the end of 2008 the world spun into a deep recession from which it seemed it would take years to escape. Wages and benefits were sinking, and job security a happy memory. A focus on deregulation and unfettered free markets had made unions and their protections almost a thing of the past, particularly in the private sector. Global markets, in which goods were produced far away from the eyes and sensibilities of those who purchased them, made it difficult or even impossible to enforce environmental precautions, worker protections, or health and safety regulations. Few of us knew where our food was being grown and processed. But this ignorance was not so much a matter of not knowing where to look as of our simply averting our eyes.

Farming is and always has been a difficult business fraught with hazard. Droughts, storms, bugs, and bad luck have plagued farmers for 10 million years. Even generations ago, few American farmers could survive just by working the land. Farmers then and now subsidized their farm earnings with side jobs in town. The difference is that years ago those side jobs were in packing plants or factories with good wages and benefits, while today they tend to be low-paying service jobs, bagging groceries or stocking the shelves of discount stores. Farmers can no more shore up their farms with these uncertain low-paying jobs than city dwellers can sustain their families with them. Farmers need and deserve our support. But the vast bulk of federal agricultural subsidies and taxpayer dollars go not to small fruit, vegetable, and dairy farmers who desperately need the help but to a relative handful of giant agribusiness operators pumping out vast quantities of grain, meat, and milk.

There are more than 6 billion people on this planet and billions more to come, thanks in part to a food system built on twentieth-century technology. Without chemical fertilizers and herbicides, advanced irrigation systems, and modern animal husbandry, the world would be a far hungrier place. We need large farms to grow and process the enormous quantities of grain necessary to feed the world's exploding population. And like it or not, the world is not going to lose its taste for meat. But it is time to acknowledge that food grown on the factory model is costly—directly in the form of inputs, and indirectly in long-term erosion of our health, environment, and humanity. We need to be more honest about these costs and bear them bravely, rather than externalize them and pass them down to our children or impose them on the poor here or overseas. And we need to build a system in which small farm producers can survive and thrive.

Given the opportunity, many of us would buy naturally grown pork and wild-caught shrimp. We would likely prefer their taste, and we would certainly prefer their life story. But as Drenowski makes clear, not all of us have had the opportunity. Julie Guthman, a food scholar at the University of California, Santa Cruz, said a narrow focus by some advocates on local and organic food tends to underrate both history and most people's needs. "Everyone has a right to quality food, but we must address the inequalities that make some reluctant—and others unable—to pay more," she said. "There are historic reasons why some people don't seek out better food, and we won't get anywhere by ignoring them."

Guthman pointed to what she called our bifurcated system in which most people get their food at Wal-Mart or low-price-driven supermarkets, and a small and committed elite grow their own food, graze at farmers' markets, or patronize high-end specialty grocery chains.

"Some people believe that they are morally in the right to shop at Wal-Mart, that they are saving money, being prudent, making sure that their family gets enough," she said. "Others say they are morally right for buying organic or local. But the question to ask is this: How can it possibly be cheaper to buy garlic from China rather than local garlic from California? What are the economic structures that have made that happen? Issues of land use, labor, subsidies—all this needs to be addressed. We have to get beyond the food to what's behind it."

The recent spurt in food prices is a wake-up call. The phenomenal successes of the Green Revolution made us believe that technology would solve all the world's food problems, but as it turned out, it was only part of the solution. Given higher grain prices, we may want to consider how it is that producers manage to keep pork and beef prices relatively low, and profits relatively high. That is, really think about the compromises they are making, the corners they are cutting. Price is important—critical—but so are many other factors. Regulation, research, and long-term investment are key. We need to make sure that people can afford the basics beyond grain and grain-fed animal products. To that end we should reconsider reinstating the historical system of price supports by which farmers were guaranteed a certain price for their wares. Price supports encouraged farmers to diversify, potentially lowering the price of fruits and vegetables, and making imports less attractive. And by reducing subsidies on grain, we could afford to subsidize consumers more generously with vouchers or food stamps—giving everyone more control over what they eat and feed their families.

International trade in food is critical. Life would be far less lovely for Americans without imported coffee and bananas, and many other nations need what we have to offer. But it makes no sense to dump large amounts of cheap grain on grain-exporting nations or to dump cheap Thai shrimp on Florida. The global food distribution system needs reigning in. Rather than flooding markets in developing countries with cheap food, thereby weakening incentives to grow and process food locally, aid should be given directly to the poor to help them purchase food at fair prices, be it local or imported. And local governments and world development organizations need to help farmers capitalize on high prices when they can, by investing in sustainable growth of local agriculture.

Change, when it comes, will begin with consumers. Take Guthman's garlic example. Since the 1990s, California farmers have complained vociferously about the flooding of American markets with cheap Chinese garlic. Environmentalists, too, have warned that the transportation-related pollution from importing Chinese garlic amounts to thirty-nine times more particulate matter and six times the global warming impact of transporting the California variety. Still, Chinese garlic is cheaper, and for that reason American markets stock as much of it as—and home cooks buy more of it than—the homegrown variety. But scientists recently confirmed what serious cooks knew all along: Chinese garlic lacks the intensity of American garlic, therefore requiring that we use more of it. Meanwhile, the unpredictability of fuel costs have made exporting Chinese garlic to California (and, for that matter, exporting California garlic to Europe) increasingly less prudent. Whether Americans will reconsider their penchant for cheap garlic is hard to say, but the reasons to do so are mounting.

Food reflects our values, traditions, and beliefs. Nothing is more personal or more intimate. Americans like to think that we put our money where our mouth is, but recently our mouths haven't had all that much to say about it. Money has driven the argument. We eat what is put before us, what we know, and what we can afford. But here is something to consider: Has price become a bully? Recently, I was at a restaurant celebrating a birthday with friends. I studied the menu and considered a shrimp dish, flavored with chorizo, a Spanish sausage. I love spicy food, and the waitress assured us that this was the house "signature dish." I hesitated, in some ways not wanting to know. It sounded great, after all. But of course I had to ask: Where did the shrimp come from? The waitress looked puzzled and then amused. If I was expecting gulf shrimp, she said, I was out of touch with reality. "No one gets those anymore. We get our shrimp frozen from Asia just like everyone else." I thanked her and ordered the chicken. My friends ordered the frozen Asian shrimp, and polishing it off, they swore it was the best they had ever tasted . . . for the price.

# CHAPTER NINE

# THE DOUBLE–HEADED DRAGON

Look, I know that Americans have a hard time accepting
that sweatshops can help people.

| NICHOLAS KRISTOF, "WHERE SWEATSHOPS ARE A DREAM"

A cheap price is a shortcut to being cheated.

| ANCIENT CHINESE PROVERB

China was not always factory to the world. Until the middle of the last century the laborious process of moving large shipments from Asia was so costly as to be prohibitive. Loose cargo was baled or bundled and piled high on the backs of longshoremen to be loaded and unloaded from truck, barge, train, or ship, a slow process plagued by inefficiencies and corruption. Pilferage was so common that shipping items of value—watches, whiskey, radios, gold—was avoided. Perishables—like shrimp—spoiled. Breakage was also a factor, as was the insurance to cover it. Wages were rock-bottom low in East Asia, South America, and India even then, but for most Americans the exorbitant cost of shipping—10 to 25 percent of the total cost—put most imported goods out of reach. Back then, buying local was not a virtue, it was a necessity.

Shipping containers changed all that. The rectangular steel and aluminum boxes enabled a seamless flow of goods from truck to train to ship and back again. They reduced theft, spoilage, delays, and over 90 percent of the cost. Unloaded by crane from boat to truck to train to barge, no backs were wrenched, no whiskey or watch or gold gone missing. Today, a skeleton crew of a dozen hands can navigate a vessel freighted with up to six thousand containers, each the size and shape of a railroad car. Containers made shipping fast and predictable, enabling the just-in-time delivery system that retailers have come to depend on. In the estimations of some economists, containers made the transport of goods so cheap as to be essentially free. They certainly help make many things from China unbelievably cheap. Big Boxes, Category Killers, Bargain Basements, and Dollar Stores all owe their existence to fast boats from China and the containers they carry.

The Port of Los Angeles is the busiest container port in the United States, a veritable Ellis Island for stuff. Every year the equivalent of 8.3 million twenty-foot-long containers arrive here, the vast bulk of them from China. Some of these get loaded onto trucks and then on trains headed straight across the country. For others the journey is much shorter. I followed one truckload just half a dozen miles or so to Concord Enterprises in Vernon, California.

With fewer than one hundred residents, Vernon is the smallest incorporated city in southern California, only 5.2 square miles. This "industrial Mayberry" is a blur of furniture assembly shops, car part distributors, meatpacking plants, and taco stands. Concord Enterprises, one of the largest import/export dollar store distribution centers in the country, seems right at home here. Concord supplies dollar stores from Alaska to Panama with pallets of cosmetics, razors, toothbrushes, underwear, panty hose, turkey basters, soybased fruit drinks, and an impressive assortment of bongs thinly disguised as vases. The prices of these and the roughly nine thousand other items on display bring new meaning to the word "affordable." A pair of boys' kung fu shoes—black with a red lining—cost 41 cents. A package of twenty-four disposable razors was selling for 65 cents; a trio of toothbrushes—one each in purple, blue, and green—for 18 cents. David, a dapper man in his mid-fifties, had, when we met, worked at Concord for six years. Before that he owned a textile factory in Iran. "My wife would never have dreamed of shopping at a dollar store there," he said, declining to give his last name. "But now she does. Eventually, we all go to the dollar store."

Without China there would be no dollar store: Those 41-cent kung fu shoes, the 6-cent toothbrushes, and more than 70 percent of the rest of Concord's merchandise come straight out of the box from China. The story of China's explosive growth and the cheap labor that powers it is, of course, a familiar one. Still, how human-made objects can travel all that distance and be sold for next to nothing seems a wonder worth exploring.

China may be the factory to the world, but it is not the world's largest manufacturer. It makes only one-twentieth of the world's manufactured goods. Nor is China the only low-wage or even the lowest-wage country. A number of Latin American nations come close, and the labor in Bangladesh, India, Cambodia, and Vietnam is cheaper. Labor in many African nations is cheaper still. But no other low-wage country can match China's efficiency and reach. Germany, the world's largest exporter, is known for its quality. China makes many beautiful, sturdy, and useful things, but it is not the quality of its goods that drives business to its door. The strength of the booming Chinese export markets rests on the "China price," made possible by the country's determination to manufacture and sell shoes and toothbrushes and almost everything else at a price no developed nation can touch.

The China price has come to mean the lowest price imaginable, minus a bit. Beyond that, the China price has transformed the way we think about *things*. In *A Year Without "Made in China,"* author Sara Bongiorni chronicles her family's experience of surviving just one year without purchasing Chinese-made goods. The author's struggle to find affordable sneakers, small appliances, sunglasses, and mouse traps offers apt illustration of the power of low price to direct our behavior and thinking. Thanks to the China price we have come to expect once weighty and consequential purchases—blenders, DVD players, microwave ovens, photo albums, linens, and even shoes—to be hardly more than an impulse buy. Not even a book contract could cure Bongiorni's addiction to cheap stuff: Before the year was out, she was coercing friends and family members to "gift" her household with Chinese imports.

Despite spectacular economic growth, China is not yet a prosperous country. Yes, wealth has soared there in the past couple of decades, but the wealth is not evenly shared. In what I've seen strolling the back streets of Shanghai and Beijing and their outskirts, the poverty is palpable. In the countryside, where incomes are about a third of what they are in the city, matters are even worse. Officially, 42.3 million people live in poverty, but that figure underestimates the problem. In China the official poverty line is drawn at $156 a year, just over a third of the World Bank poverty limit of $456 a year. China's centralized government holds less sway than it might in outlying regions where corruption is a way of life. But the government's focus is not on social justice and equity for its citizens but on political stability, and to achieve that it must keep its business humming and its booming population occupied.

At a seminar I attended in Shanghai, a government official warned a roomful of foreign businessmen that the country was not interested in purchasing the latest labor-saving devices, even machines that would reduce occupational risks. There were, he said, too many hands to keep busy to allow machines to take their place. No matter the official policies about modernization and worker safety, those 1.3 billion pairs of hands could not be allowed to grow idle. China regards economic progress as the solution to most of its ills and is therefore committed to economic growth at all costs. This focus has led to incredible advance, but also to blind spots and to a policy of public defensiveness that encourages the papering over of inequities and injustice. Hu Jindou, a professor of economics at Beijing University of Technology, put it bluntly in an interview with the *International Herald Tribune*: "In order to achieve modernization, people will go to any ends to earn money, to advance their interests, leaving behind morality, humanity and even a little bit of compassion, let alone the law or regulations, which are poorly implemented. Everything is about the economy now, just like everything was about politics in the Mao era, and forced labor or child labor is far from an isolated phenomenon. It is rooted deeply in today's reality, a combination of capitalism, socialism, feudalism and slavery."

DONGGUAN, a boomtown in China's industrial Pearl River Delta region, boasts steel and glass high-rises, staggering traffic jams, and the world's biggest shopping mall. Dongguan lies a few hours' drive north of Hong Kong in Guangdong, China's most populated province and also its richest, thanks to the labor of roughly 30 million workers. Most of these are migrants, peasants from the neighboring provinces of Guangxi, Hainan, Fujian, Hunan, Sichuan, Guizhou, Yunnan, and Jiangxi. A Hainanese or Hunanese farmer stumbling off the overnight train into Guangdong is an alien in a foreign land or at least feels like one. Certainly, he or she is treated like one. Under China's restrictive Household Registration Law, it is extremely difficult for migrants to obtain official city residency or the associated privileges and protections. Among many sad discrepancies is that while 95 percent of official resident children attend school, only 50 percent of migrant children do. Migrants are likely to be illiterate, unschooled in politics, and clueless in matters of labor law. Migrant workers who are aware of their legal rights have little leverage to demand their enforcement, and those who try are regularly turned away by government labor inspectors and police. Complicating matters is the widespread perception that migrant workers are low-class and unworthy, a belief that not a few migrants believe themselves. My translator in Shanghai, a college-educated sophisticate, told me she could spot a migrant instantly: "They are badly dressed, and their faces look stupid."

As a consequence of their low status and lack of leverage, migrants are more likely to accept low-paid dangerous jobs. So Deng, a migrant to Guangdong from a mountainous region of central China, told a *Washington Post* reporter in January 2009 how he had stood knee deep in vats of hot toxic dye, seven days a week, twelve hours a day, at his job in the Overseas Fur Factory for a salary of $15 a month. Deng said many workers lost their footing or passed out in the fumes, but that did not deter him from persuading his seventeen-year-old son to sign on. In 2005, China reported 717,938 workplace accidents and 127,089 deaths, and since then the reports list more than 100,000 occupational deaths each year. But these are official government numbers; the actual numbers are thought to be much higher.

A diaspora of migrant workers who are funneled into China's industrialized south make almost everything that is cheap in America: toys, clothes, bedding, stationery, sports equipment, electronics, lunch boxes, dashboard bubbleheads, fuzzy dice, hair elastics, Christmas ornaments, pencils, pens, and so on. Essentially, these migrants are America's indentured servants. Uprooted from their home villages, scraping together the fare to travel by train or bus hundreds or even thousands of miles and sometimes standing the whole route, migrants arrive in China's great cities dazed, broke, and ready to take whatever jobs they can find under any conditions. Bosses assign them to dormitories and deduct room and board from their wages. Work contracts are sporadic and unpredictable. In news reports these workers are as cavalier about the dangers of their workplace as they are about the quality of the products they make. "In China no one worries about things lasting a long time," my translator said. "Labor is so cheap that if something falls apart, we just make another one."

LIKE MANY American companies, RC2 Corporation, based in Oak Brook, Illinois, has a motto: "Compelling, passionate parenting for all ages." On its Web site the company boasts building "consumer loyalty by fulfilling passions of targeted consumers with branded toys, collectibles, hobby or infant products that encourage repeat purchases and are fun to own and use." Selling toys to encourage the buying of more toys is an ingenious strategy, though most parents would probably prefer it not be targeted to them specifically. Safe to say this message was meant not for parents, however, but for RC2 shareholders, apparently with little worry that the two categories would overlap.

The toys made for RC2 in Dongguan—Thomas the Train sets aimed at children ages three to five—were finished with a liberal spraying of lead paint. Lead is a neuron-toxin known to lower the intelligence quotient of children who ingest it. Adults who inhale lead dust can suffer brain damage, kidney failure, memory loss, and miscarriage. This leads to the puzzling question of why an American company would purchase lead-painted toys from any factory, let alone one where underage workers without face masks spend their days spraying lead paint on children's toys.

RC2 had a history of difficulties with its Chinese suppliers. It had recalled other products, like the Shake 'n Jingle Keys and John Deere Real Keys, baby toys with a tendency to break into a choking hazard. The company was also forced to recall the Learning Lamaze Activity Toy, due to its contamination with *pseudomonas aeruginosa* and *pseudomonas putida* bacteria. Considering this bleak record, it is sobering to consider that 80 percent of all the toys in the world today—most of them marketed by American and multinational companies—are made by migrant workers in Chinese factories.

Substandard and fake goods are so common in China that the Chinese have an expression, heixin (pronounced *hey-sin*), to describe those who make, sell, or profit from them. Heixin roughly translates as "black heart." The Chinese, though perhaps not comfortable coexisting with these black hearts, appear to be resigned to them. The problem is not confined to exports but to the things Chinese use themselves, including food. Writing in *The New Yorker* magazine, Chinese food expert Fuchsia Dunlop quotes restaurateur Dai Jianjun: "You just can't trust the ingredients you buy in the markets. Vegetables laced with chemicals. Fake birds' nests held together by glue." For his own elegant restaurant Jianjun assures safety by sending assistants out to the countryside to buy food directly from farmers or even to forage for it themselves in the wild.

The Chinese government has taken steps to deal with the problem of tainted goods, most dramatically with the very public 2007 execution of Zhen Xiaoyu, the director of the China Food and Drug Administration who was convicted of taking bribes from drug companies. (His corrupt practices were linked to forty deaths in Panama from cough syrup that contained diethylene glycol in place of glycerin.) But efforts to improve conditions for the Chinese people themselves, particularly Chinese workers, have been slow in coming. America's demand for cheap encourages and enables this complacency.

AMERICAN COMPANIES claim to source from responsible factories with health and safety protections, and fair wages and working hours. But in China graft is rampant, and transparency is not. After a decade of monitoring Chinese factories, most outsiders have no idea what goes on once the inspectors go home—and some prefer not to know. Often, dummy or model factories serve as the public face for other illegal factories operating completely off the books. *New York Times* correspondent David Barboza covered the Chinese factory beat for several years. "Everything is linked," he told me. "Factories that observe the rules outsource to factories that observe only some or none of the rules. But, anyway, enforcement of rules is not a priority."

Americans don't like tainted dog food or exploding tires or other dangers traced to Chinese manufacturers. We prefer our milk straight, not laced with melamine to artificially boost its protein content. We do not approve of spraying children's toys with lead paint. Still, increasingly, we are not willing to look too deeply at the causes or real solutions of these problems. Responding to the lead paint incident, *New York Times* business columnist David Leonhardt wrote, "This isn't really about replacing toy trains. It is about the realities of offshoring, and it doesn't yet have a tidy, Thomas-style ending. What happens in Chinese factories determines how good—how reliable and how safe—many products are. So there is no way for executives to distance themselves from China without also distancing themselves from their own product."

Sellers of consumer goods of all kinds typically obscure the pedigrees of their products, making it difficult for consumers to know just what it is we are getting. Tracing the lead-painted Thomas the Train caboose to the Ohio-based RC2 Corporation, one would assume it was made in the American Midwest, not the Pearl River Delta. The same might be said for many other toy manufacturers. How are we consumers to know where our purchases come from when even Mattel's iconic American Girl Doll is made in China?

And the pricier the purchase, the more difficult it is to trace—be it to China, Vietnam, India, or Latin America. Executives at high-end shirt maker Tommy Bahama may not want customers to know that its $100 Tortola Trance shirts are made by Oxford Industries, the same parent company that makes $12.99 Mercerized Simple Luxury Polos for Dockers. Nancy Cleeland won a Pulitzer Prize for her reporting on the working conditions in factories where companies like Oxford do their manufacturing. Her focus was on Latin America, which, being closer than China to the United States, is where many manufacturers of fashion goods once preferred to locate—at least until price pressures sent them elsewhere. "I went to San Pedro Sula, Honduras, and saw big sewing factories there," she said. "There was a huge flow of women coming in from the countryside—always women, because they are supposed to be better workers than men." At the Oxford Cosmos clothing factory Cleeland spoke with Isabel Reyes. Reyes was an eleven-year veteran of the factory. She sewed sleeves on shirts at a rate of twelve hundred a day for a wage of $35 a week. Her arms were too sore to keep working or even to pick up her daughter without daily doses of pain medication. She was exhausted from overwork and sleep deprivation. But the kicker Cleeland told me was this: Reyes lost her job. Apparently $35 a week was too high to accommodate Oxford's low-price demands. The company had assigned a manager, Chuck Wilburn, to scout out a new location. Wilburn was very unhappy about having to lay off thirteen hundred workers in San Pedro Sula. Years before, he was equally unhappy about laying off even more workers in North Carolina where Oxford closed all forty-four of its factories.

Richard Locke, professor of Entrepreneurship and Political Science at the Sloan School of Management at the Massachusetts Institute of Technology, is an expert on economic development, comparative labor relations, and political economy. To his mind, he said, there is worldwide only one force powerful enough to enforce workers' rights and protection: guilt. And there is only one institution capable of evoking that force: the Vatican. So far the Vatican has not gotten into the factory inspection business, but no other entity on earth, Locke said, can prevent global industry from exploiting and abusing global labor. "There is no enforced international law on the books that limits and sets hours, child labor, or anything else," he said. "The laws are not enforced because there is no global governing institution. In this vacuum there are many private codes of conduct by individual companies, but there is neither the will nor the capacity to monitor, to see whether companies are living up to these codes."

Locke explained that even when an overseas factory is audited, the information does not often lead to change. "If you look at audit scores of factories, they go in and out of compliance all the time," he said. The offending factory is given time to improve and often does on the factor for which it is cited. The problem is that in the next inspection, new and different violations pop up to take their place. "Bad audits," Locke said, "have no consequences."

A handful of multinationals badly burned by embarrassing publicity have created what they claim is a vigorous system of auditing their suppliers. Locke oversaw a famous case study of one of these companies, Nike, and to his surprise found that the longer a foreign supplier was associated with this "enlightened" company, the worse it treated its workers. Nike invested $11 million in audits and other measures over two years, yet according to Locke's findings, conditions in their suppliers' factories improved only marginally. This disappointing performance, Locke said, is typical across industries and across the developing world.

In 2006 the Fair Labor Association released a study based on unannounced audits of eighty-eight factories in eighteen countries and found an average of eighteen violations in each—of excessive hours, underpayment of wages, health and safety violations, and worker harassment. The association cautioned that this number was probably far too low as "factory personnel have become sophisticated in concealing noncompliance related to wages. They often hide original documents and show monitors falsified books."

Auditing is important, but it is not enough. "What's critical," Locke said, "is rule of law." There is a clear correlation between the purchasing power of a nation's citizens and the power of the rule of law in that country. Countries with better incomes are more lawful, and countries with lower incomes are less so. "All studies show that when rule of law strengthens, working conditions improve," Locke said. "So the United States might be wise to work with [low wage] nations to improve their rule of law," and working conditions, presumably, will follow.

But logic does not link rule of law with low price. Indeed, the preferred option for many multinationals is to relocate to countries where there is little or no rule of law, where workers have little or no leverage. Some argue this trend may look bad to Western eyes, but that it has greatly benefited workers in China, India, Vietnam, and other low-wage countries. Ira Kalish is director of Global Economics and Consumer Business for Deloitte Research. "A lot of people criticize the labor standards in places like China as unacceptable," he told me. "But they have to compare these to the lives migrant workers led before they came to the factories. The point is they are moving one rung up the ladder."

Certainly there is truth to this argument. Life in rural China is extremely difficult and the flight from the countryside remarkable: In 1978 only 18 percent of Chinese were urban dwellers; by 2008 that figure had leaped to 40 percent. China's rural population suffers from shortages in health care, schools, and opportunity. Chinese farmers on average are poorer than city dwellers, at least in cash. Most Chinese leave their farms not because anyone forces them to but in pursuit of a better life in the city or to earn money to send back home to sustain relatives in their native village. Influential New York columnist and old Asia hand Nicholas Kristof put it bluntly: "Anyone who cares about fighting poverty should campaign in favor of sweatshops." In January 2009, Kristof wrote that Cambodia has "pursued an interesting experiment by working with factories to establish decent labor standards and wages. It's a worthwhile idea, but one result of paying above maker wages is that those in charge of hiring often demand bribes—sometimes a month's salary—in exchange for a job. In addition, these standards add to production costs, so some factories have closed because of the global economic crises and the difficulty of competing internationally." Kristof reminds us that just a century ago the United States suffered similar growing pains on its march toward industrialization and prosperity.

Such arguments, while compelling, tend to oversimplify historic events. Workers' rights in this country were forged in a crucible that was highly visible to consumers. The Triangle Shirtwaist fire of 1911, the worst workplace disaster in the history of New York City for ninety years, ignited the American labor movement for the very reason that the victims of this tragedy were within sight of other Americans, most of them workers themselves. It is this identification that led to the strikes, riots, and union efforts that forced reform. But the thousands of similar tragedies killing and injuring workers in Cambodia, China, and other low-wage countries happen out of sight—and out of mind—of the American and European consumers who purchase the fruits of their labor. All we see is the price, and few of us stop to think about how it got to be so low.

Robert Pollin, a professor of labor economics at the University of Massachusetts at Amherst, does not agree with Kristof and other observers that sweatshops are a necessary stage in the growth of developing economies. Sweatshops, he said, are thuggery and a form of theft. "It's a complete failure of imagination to say that the choice is between sweatshops and starvation," he told me. "Are we saying that a country is better off with no labor standards, no rights? The cost of wages matter; the cost of labor matters." Yes, better treatment of workers does lead to increased production costs, as Kristof states, but this should not deter us from insisting on improvements. Pollin has done the math and calculated that increasing the wages of, for example, apparel workers in Mexico by 25 or even 30 percent would raise the price of a shirt in the United States by 1.2 percent. That is, a 30 percent increase in wages for the workers results in a leap in price of a $20 shirt to $20.24. Surveys indicate that most American consumers are willing to accept this additional cost without fuss, especially if they understand the reasons for it. So far, several small producers have taken up the challenge, but few multinationals have been willing to put it to the test.

University of Michigan political scientist Mary Gallagher told me that in China laws are increasingly more attentive to critical social problems but that they are likely to fail at the implementation and enforcement stages. The reason, she said, is foreign demand for low price. "The American manufacturers, like Nike and Reebok, do not own their factories," she said. "They use Chinese suppliers and try to get them to comply with labor and environmental standards. But they also insist on very low prices, so the profit margins are very thin. This makes it nearly impossible to raise wages or benefits or improve working conditions, and the workers get really squeezed."

Like IKEA, which claims to demand legally harvested wood but won't pay a premium for it, American companies claim to demand social responsibility of their suppliers but aren't willing to pay the price to make it happen. Basic economic principle dictates that when workers refuse to work at a given wage, the wage should go higher. But this principle does not hold true in a global economy. In China when workers make too many demands, factories can simply move inland, sometimes building new factories on farmland confiscated for the purpose by the Communist Party. Political economist Jeff Riedinger, dean of International Studies and Programs at Michigan State University and a specialist in Asian agriculture, has studied the migration of farm workers to the city. When we spoke he said that in China land grabs are common, and their impact can reach far beyond the individual farmers involved.

"What happens is that local governments collude with outside investors in order to build a housing subdivision or a factory and essentially steal the land," he said. This is supposed to happen only for "public purposes," but this rule is not enforced. In the best cases, the farmer is reimbursed for his land, and the village is better off. In the worst cases the farmer gets nothing or his land is "redistributed," giving the farmer a bit of everyone else's land so that he can start anew. Unfortunately, this reduces the land holdings of all farmers, sometimes making every farm in the village nonsustainable. Land grabs make poor farmers feel even more insecure, and even less likely to make long-term investments in their farm. When farmers see their plots shrink, they have little choice but to send their children to work in factories—at any wage. This vicious cycle has poor farmers pouring into cities to make 41-cent shoes for Concord Enterprises, while the price of food in China rises due in part to the decline in farming.

Internationalism—the spread of economic exchange across geographic boundaries—is as old as human history. It exploded when seventeenth century colonial empires sailed the globe in search of raw materials and new markets. Colonies provided resources and sometimes human capital in the form of slaves. Today's globalization is a variation of this inexorable trend, abetted by far more efficient communication and transportation systems. But contrary to the writings of Tom Friedman and others, the world's playing field is not always flattened by this effort. Quite the contrary, in at least one sense it has become lumpier: More than 80 percent of the people in the world live in nations with growing income disparity. Urbanization made possible by world trade is no panacea: Slum growth is outpacing urban growth by a wide margin.

In 2001, China became the newest member of the World Trade Organization (WTO), signaling its full acceptance into the global economy. WTO rules require *unconditional* Most Favored Nation status (MFN) be granted to all its members. The U.S. endorsement of China's entry into the WTO meant that Congress would no longer conduct an annual review of China's status as a trading partner. Officially, then, the United States and other WTO members have endorsed China's labor practices, upon which foreign corporations continue to build their own practices. Roughly two-thirds of the increase in Chinese exports over the past dozen years can be traced to non-Chinese-owned global corporations and their joint ventures—with Wal-Mart being the largest.

THE AMERICAN CHAMBER of Commerce in Shanghai (AmCham) and the U.S.–China Business Council, while publicly supporting China's reforms, have quietly lobbied fiercely against them. Just a month after serious reforms were proposed in March 2006, AmCham sent a forty-two-page document to the Chinese government on behalf of its 1,300 members—among them Microsoft, Wal-Mart, Dell, Google, UPS, Nike, AT&T, Ford, and Intel—demanding a list of revisions and reversals of what it termed "rigid" regulations. Among other things, AmCham objected to rules making it more difficult to fire workers or to hire so-called temporary workers on multiple-year contracts. They objected also to guarantees that permanent workers have some sort of binding agreement of employment that ensures timely payment at a minimum rate. This final reform is particularly critical in China where labor law is predicated on written labor contracts signed either individually or collectively. In theory all workers in China are required to have contracts, but in reality untold millions of workers—in particular migrants—do not, leaving them completely vulnerable to exploitation and abuse. Without a written contract, Chinese laborers have no evidence that they are employed, and employers can simply deny their existence.

Laced throughout AmCham's objections were thinly veiled threats to curtail investment and hire fewer workers in China if the new law was implemented. The strategy worked. According to a lawyer who represented American business interests: "Comments from the business community appear to have an impact. Whereas the March 2006 draft offered a substantial increase in the protection for employees and a greater role for union than existing law, [the new draft] scaled back protections for employees and sharply curtailed the role of unions." Outraged global human rights organizations shamed some players—notably Nike and the European Union Chamber of Commerce—into reversing their stands. But AmCham held firm, and its tireless efforts weakened key provisions, sharply scaling back protections for employees and limiting the role of unions—this despite AmCham's boast of "universal principles" that "American business plays an important role as a catalyst for positive social change by promoting human welfare and guaranteeing to uphold the dignity of the worker and set positive examples for their remuneration, treatment, health and safety." Siva Yam, president of the U.S.–China Chamber of Commerce, summed matters up with some reluctance "As long as consumers are looking for the lowest possible costs," he said, "[regulations are] not going to have a long-term impact."


ROUGHLY 25 PERCENT of the global workforce is now Chinese. Given such enormous firepower, China inevitably sets the norm for wages and working standards in the global supply chain. American corporate interests have chipped away at those standards and wages in order to maximize profits and influence, and to serve their shareholders. The chronic disregard for workers' rights in China's foreign-invested private sector threatens wages and working conditions around the globe, including the hard-won gains of American workers.

Labor scholar Robert Bruno, a political economist at the University of Illinois, has observed that most Americans tend not to think of themselves as "workers." This demands some level of cognitive dissonance because most of us do work for a living. But in a society where salesclerks in discount stores are called "associates" and garbage collectors "sanitary engineers," the term "worker" has lost meaning. Bruno is certain that this is no accident, and explained why in one of several conversations we had over many months.

"The Labor Department classifies 45 percent of Americans as 'working class,' but Americans all consider themselves part of the middle class. It's hard in America to be working class. There has been such a concerted effort to 'disappear' that concept, to bury the very idea of the working class. If you compare our culture now with the 1930's and 1940's, there's been an 'erasure' of the working class. Labor issues just aren't talked about, not by most people. Take the newspaper. There's a business section but very little about labor issues. There used to be a good number of labor reporters, but now I think there are about two. And kids don't read about the labor movement in high school textbooks. And how many ministers preach sermons about the sanctity of labor on Labor Day Sunday? I can tell you: not many. We identify as consumers, as citizens, as members of a religious group or ethnic denomination. We get worked up about cultural issues—not work issues. We don't identify around class, and that leads many of us to lobby against our own best interests.

"Corporate giants have become our heroes," he continued. "We are so focused on the dream of wealth that we identify with billionaires, with whom we have nothing in common. Where fifty years ago we had labor identity that pit workers against management, today we have a system that pits worker against worker. And that includes workers in the United States against workers in the developing world."

Mark Barenberg, a professor of law at Columbia University and a renowned expert on international labor law, authored a trade petition on labor rights in China for United States representatives Benjamin L. Cardin and Christopher H. Smith in conjunction with the AFL-CIO in 2006. In it he argued that Chinese labor practices enable the exploitation not only of the Chinese but of workers throughout the developing world.

Barenberg told me that the "very success of China makes it all the more difficult for smaller, poorer countries" to get or sustain a grip on manufacturing opportunities. China lures manufacturers with an undervalued currency and serious tax incentives, but the low labor costs—about one-quarter the cost of Mexican workers—is the real draw. Americans feared that the passage of NAFTA in 1994 would suck American manufacturing jobs southward, and to some extent it did. But since that time Mexico has lost hundreds of thousands of jobs to China. U.S. Department of Commerce data reveal that from 2002 to 2003 Mexico lost market share in thirteen of its top twenty export industries, nearly always to China. With fewer jobs at home, Mexicans are finding it all the more compelling to cross the border into the United States in search of work. No fence is high enough to bar workers desperate to feed their families.

Labor arbitrage, the contracting out of work to the lowest bidder, has lowered prices, and it has also made workers—including American workers—increasingly vulnerable. China has a reported 780 million peasants (some argue that figure is unreliably low), and as many as a third of these people are what economists call "excessive," that is, living in dire poverty. People this poor are primed for any sort of employment, regardless of the circumstances or working conditions. For decades to come, 10 million to 20 million of these very poor Chinese will enter the nonagricultural workforce every year. Put another way, every year China will add more workers to its payrolls than the total manufacturing workforce of the United States. Economic theory dictates that in free labor markets workers earn their marginal productivity—that is, they earn what their output is worth. "But the assumptions underlying this simple theory," Barenberg wrote, "crumble against the hard realities of China's political economy. China's inflation-adjusted wages for the majority of factory workers have fallen or remained flat in the last fifteen years . . . while labor productivity has rapidly increased from year to year—creating an enormous 'wedge' between wage and productivity growth that flatly contradicts naïve economic theory."

Some would quibble with this analysis, pointing out that millions of Chinese have worked their way out of poverty in recent years. Yet, while the nation as a whole has grown wealthier, China's poor have grown poorer. World Bank economists reported in 2006 that the real income of the poorest 10 percent of China's 1.3 billion people had fallen by 2.4 percent between 2001 and 2003, to less than $83 per year. And this was during a period when the economy grew by 10 percent and the income of the country's richest grew by more than 16 percent. China today has greater income inequality than does the United States or, incredibly, Russia. The rich are decidedly richer, and the poor unimaginably poor.

The shotgun wedding of capitalism and Communism has not resulted in the best of times for scores of millions of Chinese laborers. As Shanghai journalist Wang Chang Chu told me, "We do not yet have the luxury to concern ourselves too much with things like human rights." But this begs the question of whether the West should continue to regard the working conditions of China's workforce as "collateral damage," a situation to be ignored, tolerated, or—in some regrettable cases—even encouraged for the sake of low price.

Workers in China and the United States have more in common than many Americans would like to admit. In both countries real wages for manufacturing workers have stagnated and job security has weakened in the past decade, even when productivity soared. In 2004, the AFL-CIO filed a petition showing how denying workers' rights in China had severe negative repercussions for workers in the United States. The petition demanded that President Bush impose restrictions on Chinese-manufactured goods as long as China failed to comply with internationally recognized workers' rights. President Bush denied the petition, and the Department of Labor signed letters of understanding with the Chinese government promising "cooperation" in occupational safety and in wages and hours regulation, in which the United States pledged to "fully respect the national laws and legal provisions" of China. Rather than demanding that the Chinese improve their labor practices, the United States agreed to "fully respect" the Chinese status quo. Two years later, in February 2006, a report from China's own Work Safety Administration conceded that aggregate unpaid wages had risen to record levels, setting off thousands of demonstrations, labor shortages, and increased child labor as adults refused to accept the growing injustices. Meanwhile, the vast majority of foreign-invested and domestically owned enterprises have no health or safety controls at all.

The world may not be flat, but it is integrated and interdependent. With mega-retailers demanding ever lower prices of their vendors, manufacturers have no choice but to move their operations to where they can find cheaper and more compliant workers. Holding the line is not an option, particularly when some of the largest chains have begun contracting directly with foreign factories. Best Buy, Home Depot, and Lowe's all have sourcing offices in China. Wal-Mart has its global procurement headquarters in Shenzhen.

All this might be happening out of sight and earshot of most Americans, but it is not without serious consequence to us. Global corporations squeezing labor in China and other developing countries are today brandishing the threat of low-wage competition to roll back decades of hard-won gains in wages, benefits, and dignified treatment for workers in the United States. As Americans lose traction in an increasingly uncertain economy, Mark Barenberg's parting words take on a special resonance. "The severe exploitation of China's factory workers and the contraction of the American middle class," he told me, "are two sides of the same coin." Those 41-cent pairs of shoes, "free with rebate" computer printers, and two-for-the-price-of-one pen-and-pencil sets are costing us a lot more than we know.

## CHAPTER TEN

# THE PERFECT PRICE

The frugal man has the advantage over the man of pleasure
in facilities for self-improvement, for doing his duty to his
country, and for securing general happiness.

| PLATO, SOCRATIC DISCOURSES

If you hang around economists long enough, you hear a good deal about
their intellectual heroes: John Stuart Mill, Adam Smith, John Maynard
Keynes. Among the more controversial of these heroes is Joseph A.
Schumpeter, the Harvard economist who in 1943 published the iconic
*Capitalism, Socialism, and Democracy*. The seventh chapter of that work,
entitled "The Process of Creative Destruction," is for many academics a
sacred text. "The process of creative destruction," Schumpeter writes, "is
the essential fact about capitalism. It is what capitalism consists in and
what every capitalist concern has got to live in." Creative destruction is
an elegantly simple idea describing the industrial mutation of old structures into new ones. The department store evolves from and "creatively
destructs" the country store; the auto industry evolves from and replaces
the horse and buggy business, automation makes many factory and farm
jobs obsolete but creates new jobs in information technology, engineering,
healthcare, and biotech.

Creative destruction is a critical and necessary driver of progress. In
the stampede toward ever greater efficiencies we have come to expect
that institutions will get torn down, factories closed, stores shuttered,
workers made redundant, and lives detoured. And that is as it should
be: Nostalgia aside, we know deep down that the good old days were

not always so good. Few of us would want our own children operating a dangerous machine in a hot, dirty factory or spending blistering summers under the sun behind a plow. But in the Age of Cheap we have lost our balance: Creative destruction is as destructive as ever. It's the creative part that is in doubt.

"One of the great insights of twentieth-century economics is that you need excessive profits to create innovation," Harvard trade economist Robert Lawrence told me. "When prices are kept too low, innovation is nearly impossible." Underlying this is what economists call "perfect competition," a state characterized by a multitude of buyers and sellers, many products that are essentially interchangeable, and few if any barriers to entry in a given market. Under this condition, prices are determined by supply and demand, which sounds like a good thing. But when price is the only distinguishing characteristic among products, competition does not necessarily lead to the innovation of better products or to stronger, more highly evolved industries. Often it leads where we wish it would not go: to a price war that discourages the very creativity, entrepreneurship, and invention that we revere.

Low price was made possible by massive innovation in distribution and information exchange, computer-driven supply chain wizardry, and streamlined transportation systems. These new efficiencies brought many things within reach of consumers around the world and powered titanic progress. But in today's global market, producers have far less leverage than they once did to bargain: If a company increases its selling price, consumers can turn to the nearest competitor for a better deal. Hair-trigger price sensitivity shrinks profit margins, and when margins get too thin, producers don't have the means or the will to be creative.

University of California historian Nelson Lichtenstein said that in the last decade, discount retailing had replaced General Motors as the "template industry of our era." Given the difficulties faced by GM, this may sound like a good thing, but looking closer, the challenges become clear. Thanks to their enormous power, discounters have set de facto wage and benefit standards, subordinating the manufacturing sector. Discounters have generated, Lichtenstein said, the "most profound transformation in the spatial and demographic landscape since the emergence of suburbia in the immediate post–World War II years." In this new environment, many manufacturers are essentially penalized for innovation.

Innovation is by definition risky, and it is made all the more so when stockholders overlook the long view and demand a jump in profits every quarter. When competition is mostly about price, innovation too often takes a backseat to cost cutting. Laying off workers and hiring cheaper ones is one sure way to enhance the bottom line. Another is to scour the world for low-wage workers, especially those in countries with lackluster enforcement of environmental and workers' rights regulations. Neither of these tactics is innovative, and neither in the long run contributes to growth. And both contribute to an erosion of income that leads to debt and a decrease in spending.

Technology-powered globalization is often touted as a boon for business and citizens alike. There is no question that this has been true for the consumer side of us, the bargain-hunting side. Without steady access to the fruits of low-cost labor from abroad, Wal-Mart, dollar stores, and other discounters couldn't exist. Globalism has served our consumer side well, but for the citizen side of us—and the worker side—globalism has been a decidedly mixed bag. Lawrence Summers, one of President Obama's top economic advisors and a vocal booster of free trade, acknowledges that globalism has a troubling aspect. "As the great corporate engines of efficiency succeed by using cutting-edge technology with low-cost labour, ordinary, middle-class workers and their employers— whether they live in the American midwest, the Ruhr valley, Latin America or eastern Europe—are left out. This is the essential reason why median family incomes lag far behind productivity growth in the U.S."

Summers and most economists agree that on the most basic level, trade should make everyone richer by enabling us to buy goods at the best possible price. Bolstering this claim is the principle of competitive advantage, first proposed in 1817 by influential British political economist David Ricardo, in his landmark *Principles of Political Economy and Taxation*. By Ricardo's calculations, individual nations in a global economy are most efficient—and most prosperous—when they both produce and trade. To illustrate the point, Ricardo outlined a hypothetical case. Suppose in Portugal it takes fifty workers to make a certain value of cloth and twenty-five workers to make an equivalent value of wine. Suppose that in England it takes fifty workers to make a similar value of cloth and one hundred to make the wine. From this it would seem that Portugal, with its competitive advantage in both arenas, should export both cloth and wine, while England should import both. But in a brilliant stroke, Ricardo showed why it would be better for Portugal to make only wine and England only cloth, and for the two countries to trade their wine and cloth.

Ricardo's argument went roughly like this: If Portugal transferred twenty-five workers out of the cloth business and put them to work making wine, it would produce one more unit of wine and one-half unit less of cloth, for a total one-half unit increase in overall productivity. If England took one hundred workers out of the wine industry and put them to work making cloth, it would have one unit less of wine and two additional units of cloth, for a total of one unit improvement in productivity. By focusing on what each does best, the two nations in aggregate produce more of both wine and cloth, thereby improving efficiencies and lowering costs. Ricardo concluded that Portugal is far better off trading wine for cloth, and England cloth for wine, than continuing to produce both on their own—showing how trade between nations can increase efficiencies even when one country has a natural advantage over the other.

The law of competitive advantage applies not only to trade but to everyday life. Consider a small law practice comprised of one lawyer and one secretary. Let's say filing papers each day takes the lawyer one hour and the secretary two hours. Now let's say the lawyer makes $200 an hour and the secretary $25 an hour. Clearly, the business is better off having the lawyer stick to legal work and the secretary to filing even though the lawyer is more efficient at both tasks.

Applying this reasoning to the twenty-first century, free trade evangelicals have argued that it is more efficient for America to outsource many functions to low-wage countries such as India and China. Harvard economist Gregory Mankiw, chairman of the White House Council of Economic Advisors in the Bush administration, could not have been more clear on this point. "When a good or service is produced more cheaply abroad, it makes more sense to import it than to make or provide it domestically. This can be difficult for workers who are displaced and need to find jobs in new growing industries. But the economy overall benefits." Mankiw's comments echoed those made by former Federal Reserve Chairman Alan Greenspan, by which he reassured workers hurt by outsourcing by saying they "can be confident that new jobs will displace old ones as they always have."

This brand of "creative destruction," Mankiw, Greenspan, and others have argued, will allow Americans to focus on what we do best: invention and entrepreneurship. On the surface this seems to make sense. The United States is an innovative powerhouse, a place where ideas are born, raised, and coaxed into profitable ventures. Indian and Chinese workers indeed do good work, and they do it cheaply. But what held true for the trade of wine and cloth in the eighteenth century does not necessarily hold true in the post-Internet age.

The assumption that America is the land of endless innovation begs a critical question: Can the majority of us be—or do we want to be—constantly creative and inventive? Even if this unlikely prospect were the case, Americans hold no monopoly on entrepreneurial zeal, creativity, or intellectual firepower. Jared Bernstein, the chief economic advisor for Vice President Joseph Biden, is an expert on international labor markets. "It's pure hubris to say that we have the market cornered on talent and brains," he told me. Hubris is probably understating it. India, China, and other low-wage economies are ramping up scientific and engineering research with a vengeance. They are also educating their workforces. It is estimated that only 15 percent of the world's PhD's in 2010 will be conferred on Americans, down from 50 percent in 1975. Nearly one-third of those in graduate programs in science and engineering in the United States are foreign students, many of whom return to their home countries, set up businesses, and surpass their American rivals. Other foreign-born graduates stay here, competing for jobs. This, in turn, has made science and engineering less attractive to American students.

*New York Times* columnist Thomas L. Friedman wrote in his best-selling *The World Is Flat*, "The Indians and Chinese are not racing us to the bottom. They are racing us to the top—and that is a good thing." Well, yes and no. It is a very good thing that globalization has to some degree

redistributed the spoils of innovation and that India and China are supporting educational and technological advance and building human capital. It is a very good thing that millions of people in the developing
world are being lifted out of poverty, some into positions of responsibility and influence. But it is not such a good thing that skilled jobs and
opportunities are being commodified with little thought and almost no
regard for the consequences. For despite the hopeful projections of global-
ists, the demand for even the most skilled workers is not endless, and
the idea that more and more Americans can reinvent themselves into ever
more challenging work is a pipe dream. Harvard trade economist Richard
Freeman made this case persuasively in a speech delivered to the Boston
Federal Reserve conference in 2006: "By giving firms a new supply of
low-wage labor, the doubling of the global workforce has weakened the
bargaining position of workers in the advanced countries and in many
developing countries as well. Firms threaten to move facilities to
lower-wage settings or to import products made by low-wage workers if
their current workforce does not accept lower wages or working conditions, to which there is no strong labor response."

While Freeman does not believe that U.S. wages will be ratcheted
down to the China price anytime soon, he points out that how workers
fare in China and India and other rapidly developing countries will determine to a great degree the wages and working conditions for the rest
of us. Technological advance, combined with the threat of outsourcing
and downsizing, has neutered unions and given employers unbeatable
leverage in almost every job sector. Caterpillar, the quintessentially American maker of tractors and earthmoving equipment, offers a stark illustration. Based in Peoria, Illinois, the company once set a gold standard for
wages and benefits. Its machines helped build the Hoover Dam and
topple the Berlin Wall. In 1982, Caterpillar was featured among the "excellent" companies, in business guru Tom Peters's best-selling *In Search of
Excellence*. But after losing more than $1 billion thanks to competition from
Japan in the 1980s, the company decided to change course. First it farmed
out work to nonunion shops. Then it adopted a "southern strategy,"
moving some of its manufacturing to "right-to-work states" where labor

laws provide fewer protections for workers to organize. Finally, it strong-armed the remaining unionized workers into a two-tier agreement that slashed in half wages and benefits for all new hires. Before the changes, the typical compensation package for unionized Caterpillar factory workers was $40 an hour including benefits. Today a worker in the same job is getting $13 to $18 an hour plus $9 in benefits. To put it bluntly, Caterpillar's young employees labor under a contract their fathers would have laughed at.

"Caterpillar is a powerful symbol," University of California, Berkeley, labor economist Harley Shaiken told the *New York Times.* "It dominates its field. It is one of America's largest exporters, and it is very profitable. If there ever was a company that could bring back the social contract of the mid-twentieth century, it is Caterpillar. But it chooses not to."

Caterpillar CEO James W. Owens insisted that choice had nothing to do with the changes. The new wage structure was essential to the company's survival in the United States, he said, a way to ensure that the factories stayed in Illinois rather than being forced overseas. It is hard to know whether this is a fair assessment or a thinly veiled threat. What is certain is that company profits soared under the new low-wage scheme, to $3.5 billion in 2006, up 74 percent from two years earlier. This windfall worked out to roughly $37,000 per employee, but the employees did not get a raise. Caterpillar executives did: Owens received $14.8 million in 2007 compensation, a jump of 17 percent from the previous year. Caterpillar sales declined that year, and by November 2008, Owens was fretting publicly over the company's future. By then the world was less inclined than it once was to buy earthmoving equipment, the sort of machines that, among other things, dig foundations for new homes. As one factory worker said at the time, "I don't understand how you're supposed to be able to buy a house and live the American dream when you work for one of the biggest companies in the United States and it's paying you just twelve dollars an hour." It was as if Owens and his shareholders had been too caught up in their own dreams to notice that most Americans were being rudely awakened from theirs.

"Because of the low-cost imperative, you have a vicious cycle,

Robert Bruno, labor scholar, p. 203

squeezing workers up and down the value chain," Robert Bruno said. "This impoverishes them and makes it impossible for them to achieve social mobility. What's happening is that we are creating low-income workers who become low-wage consumers who seek low-priced goods. Stores are built strategically to cater to these low-wage earners, filled with products that are there for the single reason that they are affordable. This is a diabolical strategy, an evil strategy. What it comes down to is one group of workers eating another while the big boys in corporate sit back and watch the carnage. This thing could take us down."

HENRY FORD is lionized for connecting the dots between worker prosperity and profitability. He understood that when workers are paid enough to purchase the fruits of their labor, companies thrive and communities prosper. When workers no longer have the means to buy what they make—or, for that matter, what other decently treated workers make—companies fail and economies crumble. In a sense that is what happened to Caterpillar and to many other companies in the economic downturn of late 2008. Consumer confidence faltered as unemployment peaked, housing prices fell, and credit became scarce. Consumer spending accounts for 70 percent of the nation's gross domestic product, so when Americans stopped spending, the economy came to a crashing halt.

Anticipation of President Obama's jubilant inauguration did little to ease pessimism as commodity prices tanked and energy consumption withered. Fear gripped the world's markets, credit tightened to a stranglehold, unemployment crept higher, and consumer confidence was at an all-time low. As the United States fell into its worst economic downturn in generations, then-Wal-Mart CEO H. Lee Scott Jr. couldn't help but gloat. "In my mind there is no doubt that this is Wal-Mart time," he said. "This is the kind of environment that Sam Walton built this company for." Dollar stores, too, were booming. There is no question that when the country is in pain, the discounters gain. Discounters do not have to innovate to gain profit share; they simply squeeze their employees and suppliers a bit harder, and lower prices.

The year before, Wal-Mart had announced a new scheduling system that created unconventional shifts for its 1.3 million employees. Under the new plan, minimum wage workers were expected to be on call several days a week and would be sent home—without pay—during a lull. Schedules would change from day to day or even hour by hour, meaning that employees would have difficulty arranging babysitters for their children and predicting what their income would be from month to month. The following year a number of other retailers followed Wal-Mart's lead and installed similar systems. In September 2008 the *Wall Street Journal* reported: "The systems stand to have a broad impact on the work lives of Americans. Some 15 million people work in the U.S. retail industry, making it the nation's third largest private-sector employer. The work isn't especially lucrative. Many jobs are part-time, the pay is low, and most sales jobs aren't unionized." Still Wall Street lauded the new system's unquestionable efficiency. "Retailers as a whole are embracing this technology," Rick Rubin, an analyst at Mercantile Bankshares Corp., told the *Los Angeles Times*. "It's probably the right decision from a customer service standpoint." But he added, "It may not make employees all that happy."

As the United States plunged deeper and deeper into recession, cut-throat price competition became the norm. Still, the crises got Americans thinking about what had gotten us into the mess. *New York Times* readers flooded the Internet with commentary in response to a *New York Times* opinion piece entitled "Obama's Biggest Challenge." Wrote a typical responder: "the reliance upon low-cost and poor quality imports from abroad has actually been counterproductive for the consumer. . . . I would be happy to pay a little extra for an article that lasts longer and is not tainted with health hazards." There were other signs as well that public awareness was on the upswing, signs that the creepy upstairs/downstairs synergy between discount retailers and high-end purveyors was starting to fall apart.

As 2008 sputtered to a close, the *New York Times* reported that the demand for organic food after growing by double digits for years was on the decline. As an example it cited Whole Foods Market, the world's largest retailer of natural and organic foods. At the time, Whole Foods was struggling to stay afloat through the toughest stretch in its twenty-eight-year history. The company stock was in free fall, down by more than 70 percent in ten months, and analysts were not optimistic that matters would improve soon. The *Times* interpreted this as a public retreat from quality, writing: "It turns out that when times are tough, consumers may be less interested in what type of feed a cow ate before it got chopped up for dinner, or whether carrots were grown without chemical fertilizers . . . "

Well, maybe. Or maybe the deepening recession had jolted the public to its senses, and led us to question whether the Whole Foods premium was worth paying. For years, customers had complained that the chain was paying less attention to quality than to public relations. Looking closely, there seemed to be some truth to this: The Whole Foods nearest my home sells very little locally grown produce or meat and, though situated in New England, surprisingly little local seafood. It does sell shrimp farmed in Thailand and lamb from New Zealand, while most of the produce is trucked in from huge California farms. The company's much vaunted quality standards were called into question by the revelation that in 2008 it sold beef tainted with dangerous bacteria. But the public's real beef with the chain some call "Whole Paycheck" is its inattention to value.

**WHOLE FOODS** is the largest nonunion supermarket chain after Wal-Mart and exerts profound demands on its suppliers to cut costs. Yet until sales started to slip, the company largely declined to pass those savings on to consumers. At Whole Foods, a loaf of Heart Gluten-Free bread costs $7.50, and the salad bar $7.99 a pound for (among other things) lettuce, carrots, coleslaw, deep-fried tofu cubes, and hard-boiled eggs. That's eight bucks a pound for shredded lettuce and eggs! "They charge a premium, and people are willing to pay it," Mike Griswold, research director at AMR Research, told the *Los Angeles Times*. "They've conditioned the market to believe that if you want high-quality natural foods, you have to pay more for it." No surprise, then, that when the economy tanked, Whole Foods lost credibility and market share. What some mistook for a retreat from quality might be more accurately described as a return to common sense.

Cheap is a two-sided coin. Tails is Whole Foods and other chains promoting the oxymoronic ideal of affordable luxury. Heads is Wal-Mart, Target, outlet malls, dollar stores, and other low-price brokers. These supposedly opposing entities actually bolster each other, creating the false impression that quality and everything that goes with it must by definition be expensive. This, of course, rationalizes both business models: If we want quality, we go one way; if we want value, we go the other. What is missing here is what we used to take for granted—what my mother called "the happy medium."

This is true not only of groceries but of every retail sector from electronics to clothing to children's toys to sporting goods. On one side are the quaint boutiques and high-end chains offering service, quality, and (one hopes) social responsibility up and down the supply chain. On the other side are the discounters, Big Box stores, and category killers that devalue service, skimp on quality, and treat their workforce like a disposable commodity. Consumers are left to choose between discount retailers whose practices they find questionable and high-end stores whose prices they cannot afford. Given that these same consumers are laboring in a low-price/low-wage economy, their choice is not really a free one. "Voting with your feet" doesn't apply when your values are so completely out of line with your budget.

It has been well over two hundred years since Adam Smith, the father of modern economic theory, coined the term "enlightened self-interest." A professor of moral philosophy, Smith was a deist who believed that world events are guided by a benevolent system of natural laws. He reasoned that the common good was best served not by government regulation but by individuals making economic decisions that served their own interests. Given this, he said that good would be done as if by an "invisible hand." In his words:

> Every individual intends only his own security; and by directing that industry
> in such a manner as its produce may be of the greatest value, he intends only

*his own gain, and he is in this, as in many other cases, led by an invisible hand to promote an end which was no part of his intention. Nor is it always the worse for the society that it was not part of it. By pursuing his own interest he frequently promotes that of the society more effectually than when he really intends to promote it. I have never known much good done by those who affected to trade for the public good. It is an affectation, indeed, not very common among merchants, and very few words need be employed in dissuading them from it.*

Smith's work is frequently evoked by free-market evangelists promoting deregulation, but their arguments seem to ignore the obvious: that Smith's world was quite different from ours. In the late 1700s, most money-making operations were small family-run businesses where labor, capital, and management all gathered under the same roof—or at least in the same village. Most people lived and worked on farms too small to have much of an influence on the marketplace as a whole. Generally, market transactions involved a direct interchange between buyer and seller, and as a consequence, personal reputation was key to success. You can only cheat your neighbor once. A dishonest merchant was unlikely to remain in business for long, and acts of unfettered greed were kept in check by strong cultural and moral standards enforced by laws so draconian that even debtors were jailed. Smith railed vehemently against monopolies by which merchants might conspire to cheat the public, and he had no tolerance for a society in which the welfare of the poor would be ignored by men of means. As he wrote, "No society can surely be flourishing and happy, on which the far greater part of the members are poor and miserable. It is but equity besides, that they who food, clothe, and lodge the whole body of people should have such a share of the produce of their own labour as to be themselves tolerably well fed, clothed and lodged."

Smith would not have thought kindly of the low-wage economy. Like Henry Ford, he advocated a system by which the worker earned a sufficient wage to purchase a decent life. Smith did not—could not—foresee a world in which multinational corporations dominate every sector of local and global economies, and where the basic units of labor, capital, and management are distanced not only philosophically but literally by thousands of miles. Nor could he have predicted a marketplace where producers and merchants do not know their customers—in fact, do not see them—and where consumers know so little about the things they buy. The great irony is this: In Smith's time, most adults could not read, let alone use technology to access information. Yet consumers then generally knew more about what they purchased than do consumers in the Internet age where information is both ubiquitous and free.

Smith's hero was the prudent man who behaved virtuously even when it was in his material interest to do otherwise. A prudent man, a practitioner of "frugality, and even some degree of parsimony" would likely not squander $7.99 a pound at the Whole Foods salad bar. But that doesn't mean he has no interest in where his food is grown or in his community, or is out of reach of the "invisible hand." Rather, a prudent man is likely to shop where his interests are best served. In Boston, for example, he might be at the Haymarket, a raucous open-air market favored by foodies on a budget. Every Friday afternoon and Saturday morning fifty or so vendors vie for business by hawking fruit, vegetables, and fish from ramshackle stalls. The place is packed with regulars, many of them newcomers to the United States who would no more patronize Whole Foods than they would a Rolls-Royce dealership.

The Haymarket has its own logic and its own rules. When tomatoes cost 50 cents a pound, you don't argue, and those foolish enough to squeeze that tomato or test its weight are lucky to avoid getting cursed while the offending object is wrenched from their hand and dumped back onto the pile. There are rotten tomatoes at the Haymarket but also excellent tomatoes, and the prudent man knows where to find them. Generally, this means seeking vendors who charge a reasonable price— maybe 65 cents rather 50 cents a pound. And that is precisely what the prudent man does: He uses his knowledge and instincts to ferret out value for himself and, by extension, for society.

Like the Haymarket vendors, discounters prefer that customers do not poke too hard at their merchandise. But unlike the Haymarket, discounters don't employ a two-tier system whereby knowledge and prudence pay off. Discounters shroud their offerings, selling virtually identical products as different brands, and B-grade versions of national brands. Or, like IKEA, they hide shoddy construction—and questionable practices— with clever image making and design. The cheaper the goods, it seems, the harder retailers work to keep us from knowing about them. And the more narrowly we focus on price, the easier we are to fool.

Sixteenth-century British merchant Thomas Gresham had some thoughts on this. You may recall Sir Thomas, the friend of Queen Elizabeth who devised the theory to explain how bad money drives out good. The example he used was watered milk. If customers know the milk is watered, there is no problem; they pay less for it and get precisely what they bargained for. Customers who prefer their milk without water can choose to pay a higher price. No one is cheated, no one is fooled. But when dishonest brokers add water to the milk and sell it for less without telling customers they've watered it, the unwitting public believes it is getting a great deal. If enough dishonest merchants water their milk, more and more customers will forget what normal milk tastes like and buy only the cheaper—watered down—variety. Eventually, honest brokers are forced to water their milk, too, or get pushed out of business. Whole milk becomes no longer available, and eventually the price of watered milk goes up. Good money and good milk are driven out.

After years of experiencing little else, American consumers grew accustomed to watery milk, developing if not exactly a taste for it, then at least a tolerance. Shoddy clothes, unreliable electronics, wobbly furniture, and questionable food have become the norm. We pay less for these products than we would for their quality counterparts, but not so much less that we are getting a really good deal. As good stuff drives out bad, the market for quality goods shrinks, making the good stuff all the more costly.

"CHEAP MERCHANDISE," President William McKinley said over a century ago, "means cheap men." Cheap undermines us, gives us less control over our lives, and weakens our resolve. It cloaks concerns of ethics, sustainability, and social responsibility in a shroud of unaffordability. Yes, we'd prefer to enforce environmental protections and human rights; yes we'd prefer to eat wholesome food and purchase well-crafted, long-lasting goods. But aren't these luxuries for the few? In times like these, how can we afford to put our money where our hearts are?

This argument begs Smith's point, that the prudent man is a thrifty fellow who follows his head and his heart on a path toward prosperity. But the prudent man had protections. In his day social norms determined what was acceptable and what was not. The choices were clear. Today, societal norms are much less compelling, and we rely far more heavily on the blunt instrument of law to determine right from wrong. Stretching morality to the breaking point, businesses rationalize their behavior by insisting they are "within the law." What was impossible in Smith's day is, in the Age of Cheap, a matter of course.

As I said in this book's introduction, in the Age of Cheap, we are all tourists. The ever escalating demand for lower prices puts us under extraordinary pressure to be ruthlessly competitive and engage in endless self-deception to feel okay about it. But that era is passing. We know from painful experience that a cheap world—with cheap food, cheap fuel, cheap credit, and cheap men and women—is not sustainable. With even China shuttering its factories and laying off millions of its workers, we have no choice but to find an alternative route to progress.

Regulation is vital, of course, but it does not set a simple path. We cannot overnight undo the wrongs of decades of steady deregulation. Tariffs to keep out foreign-made goods may offer a short-term fix, but over the long term the United States would be poorer and weaker were we to snub international markets. Unions offer workers protections, set minimum wages and benefits, and enforce job security. But what worked for the manufacturing economy has not found wide favor in the information age: Fewer than 8 percent of private sector jobs are unionized. Despite recent gains in some sectors and surveys that show public support for organized labor, it is unlikely that unions will retrench to their glory days anytime soon, if ever. Given these realities we must set a new course for the twenty-first century.

The genie of globalism has escaped the bottle, and it will never squeeze back in. Trade is and must be free. But globalism means more than the system of mutual exploitation it has become. Preying on the developing world's vulnerabilities to feed our penchant for Cheap is neither defensible nor sustainable. As Ricardo so elegantly revealed, nations thrive in a symbiotic—not parasitic—relationship. International environmental and human rights protections should be enforced and over the long term must be enforced, but doing so will require the mustering of public will around the world and an enormous infusion of funds unlikely to be available in the short term. For now we must begin at home.

A first step is to revisit Adam Smith's concept of enlightened self-interest, the idea that fulfillment of individual wants in the aggregate can serve society's needs. Smith lived in a smaller world that had more sharply defined boundaries. He could not have anticipated the relentless pursuit of low-cost labor around the globe or a disposable economy. Still, his idea is flexible enough and universal enough to expand to fit our time. There are many examples of enlightened individuals and organizations working toward this goal, but for brevity's sake I will focus on just one to offer evidence of both Smith's enduring good sense and what the end of the Age of Cheap might look like for all of us.

ON A DREARY Sunday morning in November, Wegmans Food Markets was preparing to celebrate the grand opening of its newest store in the small city of Manassas, Virginia. The opening was not really grand. No bands played, no ribbons were cut, and rumors of a free breakfast were quickly laid to rest. Still, as the morning mist gave way to a tentative sun a steady procession of pickup trucks, sedans, and minivans, headlights blazing, pulled into the parking lot and disgorged a rumpled sleep-deprived cargo. Piling out were college-aged kids in hooded sweatshirts, young families with baby carriages, and middle-aged couples in baggy jeans—husbands in baseball caps beside wives hugging windbreakers close against the chill. Some were from far away, and others were from the neighborhood. Most stood in a silent daze, shuffling their feet, drinking coffee from paper cups, checking their watch or cell phone. A few gathered in clusters to chat. After a while, a trio of women stepped forward in response to the essential question: Why rise hours before dawn to queue up outside a supermarket? "We're small-town folk," one said, smiling. "This is an event for us." Manassas is only 25 miles west of Washington, D.C., a commuter town. Things were plenty eventful—for one, Barack Obama was scheduled to be in Manassas the following night, presiding over his final campaign rally. Come clean. What was their real reason for coming? Looking a tad flustered, even embarrassed, one hurriedly confessed: "Okay, I guess it's just that we love Wegmans." The white-bearded guy standing behind her let go with a hearty "Damn straight."

At 6:45 the line snaked around the building as a phalanx of police officers in knee-high leather boots kept watch from a safe distance. At 7:00 a sharp roar rose from inside the store. Those near enough to the entrance squinted through the glass to catch a glimpse of Wegmans' employees with name tags and aprons waving their arms in what looked like a parody of a Village People routine: "Give me a W!" "W!" "Give me an E." "E!" "What does that spell?" "Wegmans!" Bells pealed (it was Sunday morning, after all), the automatic doors slid open, and the cheering throng pushed forward into a carnival. Shopping carts nearly collided at the brass and marble patisserie, where a brick oven filled the air with smells of cinnamon and caramel. At what might pass for a Parisian fromagerie, a distinguished-looking "associate" in a black beret offered advice and samples of brie-slathered apple bread. In the seafood department another associate opined on the art of grilling tilapia, while in the eight-thousand-square-foot wine shop, customers toasted one another with complimentary mimosas. Beaming company reps in suits shook hands and slapped backs.

Wegmans is not a new company; far from it. Founder Jack Wegman got his start in 1916, peddling fruits and vegetables from a pushcart, while his brother, Walter, hawked groceries out of the front room of the family home. The Rochester Fruit and Vegetable Company grew into a full-scale grocery operation, and in 1930 the brothers opened a twenty-thousand-square-foot self-service showplace, complete with refrigerated food display windows, a water vapor spray for produce, and a three-hundred-seat cafeteria. Walter died in 1936, and his son, Robert, a Marine

Corps veteran, built the business into a regional empire. He is credited with, among many other things, being one of the first to introduce optical scanners and bar coding to the supermarket sector in 1974. A tireless innovator, he assiduously avoided competing on price. In a 1967 speech he said,

> I am a merchant, and I have therefore my own philosophy about merchandizing. That is, to do something that no one else is doing and to be able to offer the customer a choice she doesn't have at the moment. This is the only reason for being in business. . . . I think that uniqueness gives one an opportunity to profit. If you are doing the same thing that everyone else is doing, your opportunity for a substantial profit is materially reduced because of the price ceiling your competition will impose. Thus, good merchandizing resolves itself into rendering a service in such a way as to be difficult for your competitors to emulate.

Wegmans was phenomenally successful. In 1994 a supermarket industry analyst told the *Wall Street Journal:* "We consider them the best chain in the country, maybe the world." This sounds extravagant, but it is hard to argue. Entering a Wegmans market is not unlike strolling into the vaunted Harrods Food Halls in the posh Knightsbridge neighborhood of London. Like Harrods, Wegmans is a tourist attraction. I know this because my mother, a resident of upstate New York, took out-of-town visitors on tours of the store near her home. But unlike Harrods, Wegmans is no luxury emporium. Writer S. S. Fair once compared the chain to Whole Foods by writing in the *New York Times* that it was a "corporate behemoth branding itself as a phenomenon: the largest chain of natural food stores in the world. The other [Wegmans] consists of regional supermarkets that quietly satisfy persnickety tastes with mellow prices. Both hawk designer apples and pluperfect oranges, and both excel at leading us into temptation, where so many of us have permanent lockers. [But] one stinks of Zen, the other doesn't."

The Wegmans mystique is that it has no mystique at all. Loyalists are of the salt-of-the-earth variety, the sort inclined to throw tailgate parties in the store parking lot wearing "Wegmaniac" T-shirts. The chain gets thousands of mash notes each year from smitten customers pleading for a store to be built closer to their homes. In Internet chat rooms Wegmans gets almost nothing but accolades. A typical entry in the We Love Wegmans blog begins: "Is it possible to be obsessed with a grocery store? If you live in the Northeast, you know it is. People who move away miss it: friends and family who come to visit want to see it. We are four friends who love Wegmans, and this blog is where we write about all the things we love most at the store we can't live without."

Robert Wegman died in 2006, thirty years after his son Danny had taken the reins. Like his dad, Danny got his start in the meat department. Also like his dad, he is borderline obsessed. Every year between Thanksgiving and New Year's he makes a pilgrimage, dropping in on every one of his seventy-two stores, most of them in the suburbs of New York, Pennsylvania, New Jersey, Virginia, and Maryland. Each store is distinctive, with a mural along the back wall representative of the region. In Manassas it is the Shenandoah Mountains, cherry blossoms, and the Battle of Manassas, known to some as the Battle of Bull Run. George Lawrie, a principal analyst for Forrester Research, explained that Wegmans, in sharp contrast to discounters, builds an individual persona for each of its stores. "Rather than fill all the stores with the same cheap stuff, they build a portfolio of products that's intriguing for the customer," he said.

Danny says that's true, but it's not the whole story. Each Wegmans store is individual, he says, because the people are what make it. "We build the stage," he said. "Our people (employees) perform on those stages. They bring in the products that the customers want—our job is to give them the freedom and opportunity to know what the customer wants."

Danny majored in economics at Harvard, where he once wrote a paper on the economics of a large store. Like IKEA, he builds very big stores—80,000 to 130,000 square feet—but unlike IKEA, not all of them have the same floor plan or the same game plan. As an example, Danny points to his outpost in Ithaca, New York. Ithaca is a college town, home to both Cornell University and Ithaca College, and perhaps as a consequence has more than its share of vegetarians. Wegmans hired cookbook author Julie Jordan, a pioneer in the American vegetarian movement, to create a huge array of exotic and everyday vegan and vegetarian selections and a Wings of Life salad bar. Also apt for a college town, the store carries something like six hundred different varieties of beer.

"Coming from western and central New York, high prices are not something our customers can afford," he told me. In 2002 the chain switched from the "high/low" pricing model common to most grocery stores, in which products are priced high until put on sale, to what Danny calls "consistent low prices." Rather than offering the lowest possible price on selected items at selected times, Wegmans negotiates with suppliers to offer consistent prices across its inventory, accepting that it will sometimes be undersold. Wegmans pursued this policy partially in response to a threat from Wal-Mart, but company spokesperson Jo Natale claimed the company adopted it for reasons Wal-Mart might have difficulty understanding. "Some of our own employees were finding prices on some items too high," she said. "This was not acceptable to us." Still, it took nearly nine months for Wegmans' customers to adjust to the change. Sales dropped by roughly 4 percent, and the company lost between $30 million and $50 million, which took time to recoup. "If this were a public company, I would have been fired for making that change," Danny said. "But since we don't have to worry about stockholders, we can concentrate on what we care about, which is our people."

In 2005, Wegmans snagged the number-one spot on *Fortune* magazine's "100 Best Places to Work," and it has remained fairly close to the top ever since. The company spends $4,000 per employee on training—about twice what other retailers spend—and offers a panoply of benefits that includes health insurance (even for part-timers), a generous retirement plan, and tuition remission and a college scholarship program. For this it is rewarded with an attrition rate of roughly 6 percent, compared with an industry-wide employee turnover of more than 30 percent. (Wal-Mart is a bit coy on this point, but industry experts put Wal-Mart employee attrition at between 50 and 70 percent.) Souha Ezzedeen, a business professor at York University in Toronto who specializes in human resource issues, said that Wegmans' track record with employees is extraordinary. "Supermarkets are generally ruthless, not a great place to work," she said. "Wal-Mart symbolizes that, with poor wages and low benefits. Wegmans takes the opposite approach, putting its employees first and its customers second, knowing that if you take care of your employees, your employees will take care of the customers."

Wegmans runs cooking classes, nutrition seminars, and wine tastings at its stores, on the theory that broadening customer palates will grow demand. Education is an integral part of the company mission. Employees are empowered to figure out what customers want and need, and to provide them with what Danny calls "telepathic service." But Wegmans' outreach goes beyond its own stores into the community. When Robert Wegman learned that entry-level employees in Syracuse and Rochester were quitting within a year, he found that the quitters were mostly high school kids from the inner city. "The only models of success these kids had were pimps, prostitutes, and drug dealers," Danny said. "We knew we had to do something." Wegmans launched a "work scholarship connection" program through which high schoolers who earn decent grades are awarded scholarships. Wegmans hired some of these kids to work in his stores, hired a full-time advocate to supervise their progress, and paired them up with adult employee mentors. Roughly 80 percent of participating students graduate from high school, compared to less than 50 percent for students not participating. "We got the kids to stay in school and, in some cases, stay working for Wegmans," Danny said. "Many of them have careers with us now. Instead of paying thousands of dollars to train new people, we spend money on the people we have, with what we think are pretty good results."

Knowing full well that its customers can't afford to be wide-eyed idealists, Wegmans nonetheless identifies with the local food movement. For more than two decades the store has quietly sourced as much local produce as possible, buying from eight hundred small farmers throughout the northeast. Danny Wegman, who grew up on a farm in Greece, New York, said he would prefer to source all his food locally, not because it is politically correct but because it is so simple. "These guys have the most sophisticated ordering systems. No paper is exchanged at all except for a check," he said. "I wish my other suppliers—Proctor and Gamble, Coca Cola—had such a clean and simple system."

The right-leaning Cato Institute once characterized Wegmans as a "Living Poem to Capitalism." This was before Danny banned the sale of tobacco in his stores, but, still, the Cato scholars were onto something. A true follower of Adam Smith, Danny does nothing he believes won't result in a payoff. "Profit is critical," he said. "It's essential for everything we want to do, everything we can do. But for us it is a measure, not a goal. If we don't make a profit, we feel we've done something wrong for our employees and, therefore, for our customers. We prefer to focus on our employees and let profit take care of itself."

IN 1986 stock speculator Ivan Boesky declared, "I think greed is healthy. You can be greedy and still feel good about yourself," and his audience at the University of California Berkeley School of Business Administration cheered. Money is what makes the world go around, they say, and at the time the world was spinning wildly. But a year later, when Boesky's comment was echoed in the infamous "Greed . . . is good" line uttered by Michael Douglas in the movie *Wall Street,* the audience booed. By then the market had crashed. Boesky was on his way to prison for insider trading. Yes, greed motivates us to push the limits, take risks, and aim high. But greed is also a distraction. In business as in sports, focus is everything. Wegmans succeeds because it remains keenly fixed on its mission—a mission that starts with treating even pimply, gum-snapping sixteen-year-old grocery store clerks as valued colleagues and potential customers.

Wegman argues that his philosophy—and his business model—is eminently scalable, and there is evidence that he is right. Costco Wholesale Corporation of Issaquah, Washington, now the fifth largest retailer in America, pays employees an average wage of nearly $18.15 an hour, 68 percent more than its main competitor, Wal-Mart. It covers 88 percent of employee health care costs and has a generous dental health plan and an optical plan that pays for eyeglasses. Costco works on anemic profit margins (1.75 percent versus Wal-Mart's 3.34 percent), and makes most of its money on membership fees. But it also keeps costs down the old-fashioned way by retaining its employees and by keeping executive compensation in check.

Neither of these institutions is perfect. Wegmans has come under criticism from some suppliers who decry what they describe as unreasonable demands, and its practice of building fewer but larger stores means customers must drive more gas-burning miles to reach them. Costco offers a far smaller assortment than traditional retailers, sells some brand-name items at inflated prices under its own model numbers, and forces consumers to buy many things—even fresh produce—in bulk, thereby contributing to waste. Yet the success of both companies gives evidence of the power of enlightened self-interest to bolster the bottom line.

In November 2008, two days after Wal-Mart CEO Lee Jones announced his retirement, New York Times language columnist William Safire announced his "hot" word of the year: frugalista. Frugalista is defined by the New Oxford American Dictionary as "a person who lives a frugal lifestyle but stays fashionable and healthy swapping clothes, buying secondhand, growing own produce, etc." Safire traced the term back to 2005, but had he searched a bit more, he would have found that it is not a new word at all but a form of the very old "frugalist." More than a hundred years ago, economist Simon Nelson Patten, chair of the Wharton School of Business at the University of Pennsylvania, made lavish use of the term. Patten is best known for predicting the national shift in emphasis from production to consumption, contending that as the American economy advanced from scarcity to abundance, workers freed from degrading factory work would enjoy both more leisure and more opportunity to consume. This, he argued, would not only enhance our quality of life but encourage the growth of a more cohesive, less class-bound society. Patten assumed in his optimistic prediction that business interests would eventually be reined-in to serve the worker as well as the consumer and that unbridled capitalism would be outdated by a pragmatic "frugalism." In 1899 he compared the two worldviews:

*The typical capitalists are lovers of power rather than sensual indulgence, but they have the same tendency to crush and to take tribute that the cruder types of sensualism possess. The discipline of the capitalist is the same as that of the frugalist. He differs from the latter in that he has no regard for the objects through which productive power is acquired. He does not hesitate to exploit natural resources, lands, dumb animals and even his fellowman. Capital to such a man is an abstract fund, made up of perishable elements which are constantly replaced. . . . The frugalist . . . stands in marked contrast to the attitude of the capitalist. The frugalist takes a vital interest in his tools, in his land, and in the goods he produces. He has a definite attachment to each. He dislikes to see an old coat wear out, an old wagon break down, or an old horse go lame. He always thinks of concrete things, wants them and nothing else. He desires not land, but a given farm; not horses or cattle and machines, but particular breeds and implements; not shelter, but a home. . . . He rejects as unworthy what is below standard and despises as luxurious what is above or outside of it. Dominated by activities, he thinks of capital as a means to a particular end.*

Patten's prescient analysis is even more apt today than it was when he first published it over a hundred years ago. Capitalism has indeed become an abstraction in which financial "instruments" are cleverly crafted to serve the interests of the few while exploiting the weaknesses of the many. No matter where we stand economically a decade or five decades from now, we will not forget the meltdown of the current decade or how we got here. Our fixation on all things cheap led us astray. We have blundered before and risen chastened but stronger. From this latest fiasco we have learned the hard lesson that we cannot grow a country and a future on a steady diet of "great deals."

Americans love a bargain, and that is not about to change. But sometimes what looks like a bargain is really just a bad loan. The latest economic meltdown gave evidence that a globally integrated world economy is not secure when built on a shaky foundation of "more and more for less and less." Cheap "no money down" mortgages with low introductory interest rates seemed like a good way for more people to get into the housing market, until the "teaser" rates gave way to higher rates, loan holders defaulted, and thousands of homes went on the block. Buy-now-pay-later schemes sound great until the bill comes due, larded with exorbitant retroactive interest. Cheap flights are enticing, but delays and cancelations cost us plenty, as do the noxious fumes pluming through the crowded sky. "Too cheap to fix" electronics seem less attractive when their life span only briefly exceeds that of their warranty and their broken innards leak heavy metal into our landfills.

"Everyday low prices" are built on everyday crumby lifestyles, not only for Mexican cloth cutters and Thai shrimp farmers and Chinese toy makers but for all of us. There is nothing innovative about building business plans on the backs of an insecure, low-wage workforce, about depleting resources and polluting environments to cut costs, about squeezing producers until they fail or quit or cheat. Shuttling the American middle class out of town on a rail of low prices is not the path to prosperity or growth.

Globalism is our reality and our future, and it brings with it a sober responsibility. Free markets are important—essential—but they are only free if we make them so. We are consumers, certainly, but also citizens of the world whose needs and wants are linked to—and dependent on—the needs and wants of others. Our practice of scouring the world for cheap resources and cheap labor is not sustainable. It is a great relief to know that in a true global village we can love a bargain without compromising our standards or values.

The next consumer revolution will be bloodless, requiring neither bullets nor even bullhorns. We have the power to enact change and to chart a pragmatic course. That power resides not only in the voting booth but in our wallets. Bargain hunting is a national pastime and a pleasure that I, for one, will not relinquish. But knowing that our purchases have consequences, we can begin to enact change. We can set our own standard for quality and stick to it. We can demand to know the true costs of what we buy, and refuse to allow them to be externalized. We can enforce sustainability, minimize disposability, and insist on transparency. We can rekindle our acquaintance with craftsmanship. We can choose to buy or not, choose to bargain or not, and choose to follow our hearts or not, unencumbered by the anxiety that someone somewhere is getting a "better deal." No longer slaves to the low-price imperative, we are free to make our own choices. As individuals and as a nation we can turn our attention to what matters, secure in the knowledge that what matters has never been and will never be cheap.

# ACKNOWLEDGMENTS

This book began as a conversation with my editor, Eamon Dolan, a man with the intellect of an Oxbridge don, the manners of an aristocrat, the VO2 max of a Sherpa, and the work ethic of Bill Gates. Eamon pushed me to expand my thinking beyond what I thought were its natural limits, tightening my focus and forcing me to carefully consider—and reconsider—every assumption. Eamon is the sort of editor all authors dream of but few are lucky enough to know in their waking life.

Among the hundreds of experts and colleagues who helped shape my thinking on this project, a few stand out as being particularly influential. I am deeply grateful for the great generosity of Daniel Ariely, James B. Duke Professor of Behavioral Economics at Duke University; Mark Barenberg, professor of law at Columbia University; Jared Bernstein, chief economic advisor to Vice President Joseph Biden; Robert Bruno, associate professor of labor and industrial relations at the University of Illinois Urbana-Champaign; Peter Cappelli, George W. Taylor Professor of Management at the Wharton School, University of Pennsylvania; Lizabeth Cohen, Howard Mumford Jones Professor of American Studies at Harvard University; Robert Lawrence, Albert L. Williams Professor of International Trade and Investment at Harvard's Kennedy School; Nelson Lichtenstein, professor of history and director of the Center for the Study of Work, Labor and Democracy at the University of California, Santa Barbara; Robert Pollin, professor of economics and founding co-director of the Political Economy Research Institute at the University of Massachusetts, Amherst; and Peter Timmer, visiting professor in the Program of Food Security and the Environment at Stanford's Woods Institute for the Environment. Others who were kind enough to share their thoughts and insights at some length include Martin Neil Bailey, former Senior Fellow, Institute for International Economics; Emek Basker, assistant professor, Department of Economics, University of Missouri; W. Sushi Chandra, assistant professor of marketing, Boston University; Sucharita Chandran, assistant professor, Boston University School of Management; Altha Cravey, associate professor of geography, University of North Carolina; Erica Dawson, assistant professor of organizational behavior, Yale School of Management; Pamela Gordon, CEO, and Charlie Bernhardt, analyst, at Technology Forecasters; Lisa Bolton, assistant professor of marketing at the Wharton School, University of Pennsylvania; Dan Clawson, professor of sociology, University of Massachusetts, Amherst; Nancy Cleeland of the Economic Policy Institute; Sean Cooney, associate professor of law, The University of Melbourne; Matthew Crawford, fellow at the Institute for Advanced Studies in Culture at the University of Virginia; Peter Doeringer, professor of economics, Boston University; Peter Fader, professor of marketing, Wharton School, University of Pennsylvania; Kathryn Fitzgerald of FKF Applied Research; Ellen Frank, senior economic analyst for the Poverty Institute at Rhode Island College; Mary Gallagher, associate professor of political science at the University of Michigan; Julie Guthman, associate professor of sociology, University of California, Santa Cruz; Jacob Hacker, professor of political science and Resident Fellow of the Institution for Social and Policy Studies, Yale University; Gregory Hess, vice president for academic affairs and dean of the faculty, Robert Day School of Economics and Finance, Claremont McKennan College; Ron Hira, assistant professor of public policy, Rochester Institute of Technology; Steven Hoch, Patty and Jay H. Baker Professor, professor of marketing, Wharton School, University of Pennsylvania; Ira Kalish, director of consumer business, Deloitte Research; Brian Knutson, associate professor of psychology and neuroscience, Stanford University; David Laibson, Robert I. Goldman Professor of Economics, Harvard University; Donald Lichtenstein, professor at Leeds School of Business, University of Colorado, Boulder; Richard Locke, Alvin J. Siteman (1948) Professor of Enterpreneurship, professor of political science,

Sloan School of Management, Massachusetts Institute of Technology; Sarah Maxwell, associate professor of marketing, Fordham University; Kent Monroe, professor emeritus of business administration at the University of Illinois, Urbana-Champaign; Read Montague, professor of neuroscience, Baylor College of Medicine; Bethany Moreton, assistant professor of history, University of Georgia; Michael Morris, agricultural economist at the World Bank; David Neumark, professor of economics, University of California, Irvine; David Parkes, Gordon McKay Professor of Computer Science, Harvard University; Misha Perovic, assistant professor of sociology, National University of Singapore; Souha Ezzedeer, Assistant Professor of Business, York University; Rama Ramakrishnan, former chief analytics officer and vice president of product development, analytic products, Oracle Retail; Robert Reich, professor of public policy, University of California, Berkeley; Jeff Riedinger, dean, International Studies and Programs, Michigan State University; Pietra Rivoli, professor of finance and international business, McDonough School of Business, Georgetown University; Alan Sanfrey, assistant professor of psychology, University of Arizona; Robert Schindler, professor of marketing, Rutgers School of Business; George Laurie, principle analyst, Forrester Research; Tim Silk, assistant professor of marketing, Sauder School of Business, University of British Columbia; Merritt Roe Smith, Leverett and William Cutten Professor of the History of Technology at the Massachusetts Institute of Technology; Gail Tom, professor of marketing, Sacramento State; Daniel Viederman, executive director, Verite; Joel Waldfogel, chair of business and policy, Wharton School, University of Pennsylvania; Barton Weitz, executive director, David F. Miller Retailing Education and Research Center, University of Florida.

Master craftsmen Brent Hull of Brent Hull Architectural Design in Fort Worth, Texas; Peter Korn, executive director of the Center for Furniture Craftsmanship in Rockport, Maine; and Neil Kaufman, director of the National Center for Craftsmanship in Fort Collins, Colorado, helped set me straight on what it takes to build objects of lasting value, as did Richard Sennett, professor of sociology at both New York University and the London School of Economics, and author of the marvelous book *The Craftsman*. Robert Kanigel, professor of science writing at the Massachusetts

Institute of Technology, informed my thinking on the history of technology, as did cultural historian Roz Williams, Robert M. Metcalfe Professor of Writing in the department of Science, Technology and Society at MIT, president of the Society for the History of Technology, and a dear friend whose insights, support, and soulful cooking have sustained me for over two decades.

At Wegmans I am grateful to Jo Natale for making things happen and to Danny Wegman for taking time out of his insane schedule to speak with me at length. I would also like to thank Brien Williams, oral historian and videographer, for rising before dawn on a chilly Sunday morning to tape the "grand opening" of a supermarket, as well as Carol Ruppel for accompanying him and asking the hard questions.

In China I would like to thank the dozens of workers, scientists, and public health professionals kind enough to speak with me off the record, in particular Y.Y. in Taizhou, who asked that his name be forgotten but whose courage I will never forget. As well I would like to thank Dr. Yuan Dong, chief of the unit of Environmental Health, the Shanghai Municipal Center for Disease Control and Prevention; and Wang Chang Chu, assistant editor of *China Business News*. David Barboza, China correspondent for the *New York Times*, was most generous with his thoughts on business as usual in China, which significantly informed my own. I hope someday to repay the generous hospitality of Gail and Colin Lawrence in Shanghai. Thanks to Jamie Shreeve and *National Geographic* magazine for subsidizing the trip to China and to the editors at *Audubon* magazine for their support as well.

In Sweden I owe a serious debt to IKEA spokeswoman Charlotte Lindgren, who served tirelessly as guide, companion, and cultural interpreter, and whose kind offer to join her for a traditional Swedish midwinter sea sauna and ocean dip I never quite declined but now do. In Sedona I want to thank my friends at the Journalism and Women Seminars (JAWS), vortex skeptics and shoppers extraordinaire. In Las Vegas I am grateful to Gillian Naylor, associate professor of marketing at the University of Nevada, Las Vegas, for convincing me that discount outlet stores are a gamble not worth taking and that comparison shopping for higher education is no gamble at all.

At Boston University my deep thanks go to dear friends Susan Blau, Caryl Rivers, and to my old pal and partner in so many things Doug Starr. They also go to my research assistants Rachel Blumenthal, Joe Caputo, Arsineh Aghazani, and the scores of hardworking graduate students who make teaching such a challenge—and a pleasure.

Thanks to the Brain Trust: June Kinoshita, Karen Wright, and Nicole Reindorf, whose faultless and fearless appraisal of all things literary helped keep me on my toes, and to Robin Marantz Henig, Andrew Lawler, and Charles Mann, extraordinary writers, colleagues, and friends who see through it all—but gently. Thanks to my brother Richard, a scholar and athlete whose good sense I will never take for granted, and to my brother David, whose strength stands as a model for us all.

To my agent, Todd Shuster, who dons a velvet glove to play hardball, and whose confidence in my work exceeds my own.

Bill Whitworth, my old editor at *The Atlantic Monthly*, helped sharpen my prose and my thinking, as did my editors there—Corby Kummer, Amy Meeker, Barbara Wallraff, and Toby Lester.

This book owes everything to the patience, support, and wise counsel of my little family. Joanna, my material girl, kept my fashion sense as sensible as anyone could (given the obvious constraints) and kept me laughing. Alison, budding cognitive scientist, dared me to look deeper and to take nothing on its face. Marty, challenging as he is loving, is always there for me every step—and misstep—of the way. Thanks so much, guys.

# NOTES

While I relied chiefly on firsthand reporting and research for this book, I also benefited greatly from the hard work and expertise of others. In the body of the book I credited everyone I quoted directly and mentioned many from whose work or thoughts I gleaned insights. Notable among these was Lizabeth Cohen, whose *A Consumers' Republic* offers a fine overview and historical analysis of the politics of postwar mass consumption. For China, in addition to my own reporting in Shanghai, I relied on the work of several China hands, among them *China Inc.* by Ted C. Fishman and the fascinating *Oracle Bones* by Peter Hessler. For thoughts on the state of the American worker I was enlightened by *The Big Squeeze* by Steven Greenhouse, *The Disposable American* by Louis Uchitelle, *Behind the Label* by Edna Bonacich and Richard P. Appelbaum, and *The Great Risk Shift* by Jacob S. Hacker. Robert Reich's *Supercapitalism* was of particular help on the perils of growing income disparity and what he calls "turbo-charged" global capitalism. Robert Pollin's incisive *Contours of Descent* offered careful documentation and analysis of the decline of the middle class and the real wage in the face of growing productivity under neoliberal restructuring. On all things Wal-Mart there is probably no better guide than Charles Fishman's *The Wal-Mart Effect*, and no more thorough analysis than that offered by the many authors of *Wal-Mart: The Face of Twenty-First-Century Capitalism* edited by Nelson Lichtenstein. Jason Zweig's *Your Money and Your Brain* is a nice lay introduction to neuro-economics, and Daniel Levitin's *This Is Your Brain on Music* is an excellent reference on the physiology of perception. Of course there were scores more books—and hundreds of other thinkers—whose influences this book reflects. I hope that I have managed to credit all of them in the notes that follow.

## NOTE TO READERS

xiv *with cheap stuff we may have forgotten we own:* According to the Self-Storage Association, a Virginia-based trade group with more than six thousand members, one in ten United States households rented self-storage units in 2007, up from one in seventeen in 1995. Nearly sixty thousand storage facilities in the U.S. satisfy that demand, annually generating $20.1 billion in revenue.

xiv *key economists have endorsed this view:* Paul Volcker, chairman of the Federal Reserve under Presidents Jimmy Carter and Ronald Reagan and chief economic advisor to President Barack Obama's political campaign, worked tirelessly to keep prices in check, as did his successor, Alan Greenspan.

## INTRODUCTION: GRESHAM'S LAW

1 *attractively packaged but inferior in content:* Alan W. Watts, *The Book: On the Taboo Against Knowing Who You Are* (New York: Collier Books, 1996), 75.

2 *family spending on basic expenses grew $4,655:* See, for example, Harvard Law Professor Elizabeth Warren's testimony before the U.S. Congress Joint Economic Committee, "How Much More Can American Families Be Squeezed by Stagnant Wages, Skyrocketing Household Costs, and Falling Home Prices?" July 23, 2008.

2 *corporate profits doubled:* See, for example: "American Corporate Profits: A Turn for the Worse," *The Economist,* September 11, 2008.

3 *the world has been turned on its head:* quoted in Chris Farrell, *Deflation: What Happens When Prices Fall* (New York: Harper Collins, 2004), 18.

3 *have been trending downward for decades:* Food prices increased sharply in 2007 and 2008, but, adjusting for inflation, remained below 1984 levels. Fuel prices spiked radically, but, adjusted for inflation, were not much higher than they were at the previous peak, in 1981. Of course, by the end of 2008, the price of oil had dropped substantially, and food was not far behind. By way of historical perspective, it is interesting to consider 1918 when the nominal price of gas at the pump was 25 cents, equivalent to $3.52 today, a real price that according to economists was not exceeded until the spring of 2008. At the same time, increased fuel economy actually lowered the average cost of driving a car between 1972 and 2008, although some Americans continued to choose low-mileage vehicles. For specifics on this it is helpful to have a look at Inflation.data.com (http://www.inflationdata.com/inflation/images/charts/Oil/Gasoline__inflation __chart.htm.

3 *24 percent less on owning and maintaining a car:* Elizabeth Warren, "The New Economics of the Middle Class: Why Making Ends Meet Has Gotten Harder." Testimony before the Senate Finance Committee, May 10, 2007.

3 *tarnish the reputation of their own brands:* Anne D'Innocenzio, "Retailers Slash Prices, but At What Cost?" Associated Press, September 2, 2008.

4 *the central experience of life in the bazaar:* Clifford Geertz, "The Bazaar Economy, Information Search in Peasant Marketing," *Supplement to the American Economic Review,* May 1978: 28–32. Geertz, an anthropologist, spent decades observing bazaar life in Morocco and Indonesia.

4 *sell for more than thirteen times their production price:* See Dana Thomas, *Deluxe: How Luxury Lost Its Luster* (New York: Penguin, 2008) This delicious exposé of the

real cost and decline of luxury reveals—among many, many other things, that the average markup of a handbag is ten to twelve times its production cost. A Vuitton bag, however, is marked up as much as thirteen times.

5 *in the same terms as he to them:* Clifford Geertz, "Bazaar Economy."

6 *illustrates the problem with a thought experiment:* George A. Akerlof, "The Market for 'Lemons': Quality Uncertainty and the Market Mechanism," *Quarterly Journal of Economics* 84, no. 3 (1970): 488–500.

## CHAPTER ONE: DISCOUNT NATION

7 *or generate even as much power as a horse:* Robert Kanigel, *The One Best Way: Frederick Winslow Taylor and the Enigma of Efficiency* (New York: Viking, 1997), 95–96. Kanigel shared his thoughts on the importance of mass manufacture on price over a drink at the annual meeting of the American Association for the Advancement of Science in Boston.

8 *for firepower in the latter half of the eighteenth century:* Merritt Roe Smith, "Eli Whitney and the American System of Manufacturing," in Carroll W. Pursell (ed.), *Technology in America: A History of Individuals and Idea.* (Cambridge, Mass.: The MIT Press, 1990.) Professor Smith, historian of technology at the Massachusetts Institute of Technology, is arguably the world's expert on the colonial munitions trade. He was kind enough to discuss the history of mass manufacturing with me at length.

8 *peace of mind if not survival:* See, for example, George C. Neuman, "Hunting Guns in Colonial America," *American Rifleman,* http://www.nrapublications.org/TAR/Colonial.asp. Neuman explains that hunting in England in the 1700s was legally restricted to the gentry. Land was scarce and valuable in England, and only landowners were allowed to own guns to prevent commoners from poaching. In the North American colonies, by contrast, land was readily available to all and Neuman wrote that the possession of guns was "universal as hunting with a firearm was a primary means of survival." Interestingly, this class distinction remains today. In the United Kingdom, hunting is a sport of the elite, while in the United States, hunting is often more strongly associated with the middle and working classes.

8 *often with the help of an apprentice:* Readers with an interest in witnessing this process might view the excellent documentary *The Gunsmith of Williamsburg, The Story of a Master Craftsman,* produced by the Colonial Williamsburg Foundation (1969). It is truly remarkable to watch master gunsmith Wallace Gusler fashion a gorgeous flintlock rifle out of iron and brass with what appears to be little more than a hammer, files, and the heat of a forge.

8 *what the average person of the time made in a month:* Interview with historian Merit Roe Smith.

8 *"both arms and ammunition are much wanted"*: Neil York, "Clandestine Aid and the American Revolutionary War Effort: A Re-Examination," *Military Affairs* 43, no. 1 (February, 1979): 26–30.

8 *imported from France were of high quality*: Ibid., p. 29. York writes that France, hoping to benefit from Colonial turmoil, joined with Spain to supply the American army with 21,000 muskets and 100,000 pounds of crucially needed gunpowder in March 1777.

8 *arms industry felt pressed to do better*: Joel Mokyr, *The Lever of Riches: Technological Creativity and Economic Progress* (New York: Oxford University Press, 1992).

8 *yet another war with England*: The Jay Treaty of 1794 negotiated by Chief Justice John Jay averted war between the United States and Great Britain by settling several previously unresolved issues from the American Revolution.

9 *"his title as father of mass production"*: See Edwin A. Battison, "Eli Whitney and the Milling Machine," in Eugene S. Ferguson, ed., *Bibliography of the History of Technology* (Cambridge, Mass.: Society for the History of Technology and MIT Press, 1968), 299.

9 *and its corollary, mass production*: David Hounshell, *From the American System to Mass Production, 1800–1932* (Baltimore, Md.: The Johns Hopkins University Press, 1985), 28.

9 *"much better as it is quicker made"*: Ibid., 28.

9 *"any other pistol of the twenty thousand"*: From Houshell (op cit) as quoted in S.N.D. North and Ralph H. North, *Simeon North, First Official Pistol Maker of the United States: A Memoir* (Concord, N.H., 1913), 81.

10 *led to an emphatic boost to the slave trade*: The Eli Whitney legend has come under scrutiny over the past few years, and there is some dispute over the role of his gin in the transformation of the history of the South. Notably, historian Angela Lakwete, author of *Inventing the Cotton Gin: Machine and Myth in Antebellum America* (Baltimore, Md.: The Johns Hopkins University Press, 2003), argues persuasively that the "invention" of the cotton gin was a complex process involving many players that began hundreds of years earlier in India and China, and that they were used in the South prior to Whitney's invention." That said, it is widely agreed that the automation of the cotton production process significantly boosted the demand for cheap labor and rejuvenated the waning slave trade.

10 *and other "dry goods" was well under way*: David Brion Davis, *In Human Bondage: The Rise and Fall of Slavery in the New World* (New York: Oxford University Press, 2006), 184–86.

11 *"quality range for which it was originally designed"*: Edgar Augustus Jerome Johnson et al., *The Journal of Economic History* (Baltimore, Md.: Economic History Association at Johns Hopkins University, 1954), 367. In this compilation an essay

by John Sawyer, "The Social Basis of the American Manufacturing System," credits this quote to the trade publication *Management Accounting*.

12 *its first grand department store:* See, for example: Harry E. Resseguie, "Alexander Turney Stewart and the Development of the Department Store, 1823–1876," *The Business History Review* 39, no. 3 (Autumn 1965): 301–22; and LeRoy Ashby, *With Amusement for All* (Lexington: University Press of Kentucky, 2006), 118.

12 *"by the improved condition of persons employed":* John Wanamaker, "The Evolution of Mercantile Business, Corporations and Public Welfare." Addresses at the Fourth Annual Meeting of the American Academy of Political and Social Science, April 19–20, 1900. *Supplement to the Annals of the American Academy of Political and Social Science* (May 1900), 123–34.

12 *the working and middle classes feel rich:* William R. Leach, "Transformations in a Culture of Consumption: Women and Department Stores, 1890–1925." *The Journal of American History* 71, no. 2, (September 1984).

12 *when the* Titanic *sank:* "Radio" by David Sarnoff as told to Mary Margaret McBride, *The Saturday Evening Post*, August 7, 1926, 141–42.

12 *putting smaller merchants out of business:* As described by Malcolm P. McNair in his essay "John Wanamaker, On the Department Store, 1900," in Daniel J. Boorstin ed., *An American Primer* (Chicago: The University of Chicago Press, 1966), 637.

14 *those out of favor paid more:* A. T. Stewart, proprietor of a huge dry goods store in New York City, is thought to have instituted one of the first fixed price policies in 1846. Stewart was far more explicit than Wanamaker in his association of fixed prices and cheap labor. Of his salesclerks he once said, "Not one of them has his discretion. They are simply machines working in a system that determines their actions." Stewart was quoted by Harry E. Resseguie in his article cited above: "Alexander Turney Stewart and the Development of the Department Store, 1823–1876."

14 *lowest possible prices to attract customers:* See Malcolm McNair's essay on Wanamaker in Daniel Boorstin's *An American Primer*. Also, for an exhaustive account of Wanamaker's life and career, see Herbert Erskowitz, *John Wanamaker, Philadelphia Merchant* (Cambridge, Mass.: Da Capo Press, 1998).

15 *became the cornerstone of his business:* See Karen-Plunkett Powell, *Remembering Woolworth's: A Nostalgic History of the World's First Five and Dime* (New York: St. Martin's, Griffin, 2001), 28–43.

15 *goods had to be continually added:* T. F. Bradshaw, "Superior Methods Created the Early Chain Store," *Bulletin of the Business Historical Society:* 17, no. 2 (April 1943): 35–43.

15 *across the Atlantic to his American stores:* See this and other fascinating facts about Woolworth and the history of his stores at the Woolworths Virtual Museum, http://museum.woolworths.co.uk/1919s-ww1impact.htm.

15 *but make a bigger show:* Quoted in T. F. Bradshaw, "Superior Methods," 41.

16  *Hailed as the "Napoleon of Commerce"*: Alan R. Raucher, "Dime Store Chains: The Making of Organization Men, 1880–1940," *Business History Review* 65 (Spring 1991): 130–63.

16  *king of American mass production*: See "A Short Biography of Frank W. Woolworth" in the Woolworths Virtual Museum.

16  *our clerks ought to know it*: John K. Winkler, *Five and Ten*, 110.

16  *as much as $50,000 annually*: Alan R. Raucher, "Dime Store Chains," 145.

17  *were constantly forced to grapple*: Ibid., 138.

17  *as well as in their personal lives*: Fred B. Barton, "The Company Point of View," *Chain Store Age* 5 (December 1929): 36–38 ff.

17  *Woolworth demanded marble*: Robert A. Jones, "Mr. Woolworth's Tower: The Skyscraper as Popular Icon," *The Journal of Popular Culture* 7, (1973) no. 2: 408–24.

17  *money on everything you buy from us*: See John E. Jeuck, "Richard Warren Sears Cheapest Supply House on Earth" in Daniel J. Boorstin, ed., *An American Primer*, 552.

17  *agricultural implements, plumbing equipment, and cameras*: Susan Strasser, "Woolworth to Wal-Mart: Mass Merchandising and the Changing Culture of Consumption," in Nelson Lichtenstein, ed., *Wal-Mart: The Face of Twenty-first Century Capitalism* (New York, The New Press, 2006), 41.

18  *hold the attention of the customers it brings into the store*: Anonymous, "Extending Sale of Cheap Goods," *New York Times*, February 22, 1915.

18  *onetime luxuries, such as clocks*: Merritt Roe Smith told me about a monograph he had read of a British visitor traveling around Illinois and Missouri in 1834, expressing surprise that every dirt floor cabin he entered had an "eight-day brass clock" on its mantel. Clocks, handmade by the thousands in large workshops, were status symbols at the time. Smith said they sold for about $1.50 apiece and were considered a luxury.

18  *criminal tendency to cheap goods*: David Monod, *Store Wars: Shopkeepers and the Culture of Mass Marketing 1890–1939* (Toronto: University of Toronto Press, 1996), 235. Here Monod is quoting from an article in *Canadian Grocer*, 1904.

18  *"vile, awful sweatshop"* . . . *"plenty of the bargains"*: Ibid., 292.

18  *integral to its concept of community*: Paul Ingram and Hayagreeva Rao, "Store Wars: The Enactment and Repeal of Anti-Chain-Store Legislation in America," *American Journal of Sociology* 110, no. 2 (September 2004): 446–87.

19  *"would-be dictators"*: National Association of Retail Druggists Journal, April 2, 1936, 397, as cited in Paul Ingram and Hayagreeva Rao, "Store Wars."

19  *"chain-store system fosters must be eradicated"*: Carl G. Ryant, "The South and the Movement Against Chain Stores," *The Journal of Southern History* 39 (1973): 208.

19 *than the operators of chain stores*: Robert Spector, *Category Killers: The Retail Revolution and Its Impact on Consumer Culture* (Boston: Harvard Business School Press, 2005), 17.

19 *"first step in the development of totalitarianism"*: Jonathan J. Bean, *Beyond the Broker State: Federal Policies Toward Small Business, 1936–1961* (Chapel Hill: University of North Carolina Press, 1996), 5.

19 *heavy graduated taxes on the chains*: In the Pacific Northwest, activist Montaville Flowers attacked the chains in a series of thirty-six half-hour radio broadcasts, and Portland, Oregon, became the first community in the country to pass a municipal antichain store law.

20 *Sears shipped merchandise shrouded in plain brown wrappers*: Leon A. Harris, *Merchant Princes: An Intimate History of Jewish Families Who Built Great Department Stores* (New York: Harper & Row, 1979) 319.

20 *"very cheaply and roughly made"*: Robert Kanigel, *The One Best Way*, 496.

20 *marvel at this criticism*: Although Ford is credited with putting mass production into high gear in his car assembly facilities, he did not personally popularize the term. That distinction belongs to Ford Motor Company spokesman William J. Cameron, who ghost-wrote an article on the subject under Ford's name that appeared in the *Encylopaedia Britannica* in 1925.

20 *to keep his overstressed workforce happy*: Steven Babson, *Working Detroit: The Making of a Union Town* (Detroit, Mich.: Wayne State University Press, 1986), 29–31.

20 *of its workforce every month*: See John R. Lee, "The So-Called Profit Sharing System in the Ford Plant," *Annals of the American Academy of Political and Social Science*, 65, Personnel and Employment Problems in Industrial Management, (May 1916): 297–310. This astonishing document, prepared by a Ford manager, outlines a remarkable social engineering scheme created by Ford to maintain control over his employees. Lee describes the eligibility criteria for the Ford profit sharing plan. Workers were disqualified if it was determined that the lavish sum of $5 a day would "make of them a menace to society" and "no man was to receive the money who could not use it advisedly."

21 *automakers were forced to follow suit*: See, for example, Stephen Meyer III, *The Five-Dollar Day: Labor Management and Social Control in the Ford Motor Company, 1908–1921* (Albany: State University of New York Press, 1981). For an excellent online synopsis of this period in Ford history, see "The Assembly Line and the Five Dollar Day" at http://www.michigan.gov/hal/0,1607,7-160-17451_18670_18793-53441—,00.html.

21 *five-dollar day; and low prices*: Ibid., 263.

21 *to $290 in the early 1920s*: Steven Babson, *Working Detroit*, 30.

21 *that placed goods and spending at the center of social life*: Charles McGovern, *Sold American: Consumption and Citizenship, 1890–1945* (Chapel Hill: .The University of North Carolina Press, Chapel Hill, 2006).

22 *"promise of greater freedom, democracy and quality"*: Lizabeth Cohen, *A Consumers' Republic* (New York: Knopf, 2003). I am also obliged to Dr. Cohen, professor of sociology at Harvard University, for speaking to me at length on the rise of the American consumer movement.

22 *but with the more forward-looking "Low prices"*: Don Humphrey, "Price Reduction as a Stimulus to Sales of Durable Consumer Goods," *Journal of the American Statistical Association*, 34, no. 206 (June 1939): 252–60.

22 *corporate greed-heads from pushing them even higher*: See, for example, Cohen, 21–23. Cohen writes: "By the end of the depression decade, invoking 'the consumer' would become an acceptable way of promoting the public good, of defending the economic rights and needs of ordinary citizens."

22 *every American believed that he or she had a claim to ownership*: Ibid., 22.

22 *"America's opportunity to serve progress"*: "Who Serves Progress Serves America," General Motors advertising campaign published in the *Saturday Evening Post*, October 28, 1936, 48–49.

22 *"geography, religion, or politics, but by spending"*: Charles McGovern, *Sold American*, p. 5.

22 *at the very same low price*: In 1904, Sears Roebuck distributed one million catalogs. By 1927, that number grew to 23 million copies—while the U.S. population hovered at just over 19 million.

23 *and downward spiraling prices*: "Resale Price Maintenance: The Miller-Tydings Enabling Act," *Harvard Law Review* 51, no. 2 (December 1937): 336–45.

24 *paid fair prices for high-quality goods*: Thanks to YouTube and other online video providers, clips of this film can be seen gratis from any computer with Internet access.

24 *first in the nation in private home ownership*: Harold Meyerson, "In Wal-Mart's America," *Washington Post*, August 27, 2003, A25.

24 *and even used cars*: Lizabeth Cohen, *A Consumers' Republic*, 64.

25 *surroundings with new goods and services*: Christopher Lasch, *The Culture of Narcissism: American Life in an Age of Diminishing Expectations* (New York: W.W. Norton, 1979), 138.

26 *"both may lead to a totalitarian state"*: Malcolm P. McNair, "Marketing Functions and Costs and the Robinson-Patman Act," *Law and Contemporary Problems* (Durham, N.C.: Duke University School of Law, June 1937).

26 *had exploded reaching 25 million homes*: For a comprehensive timeline of television in the United States see "Television History, the First 75 Years" online at http://www.tvhistory.tv/index.html.

26 *spurred record levels of consumption*: research indicates that media foster commercial attitudes and motivate consumption. See, for example, Heejo Keum et al., "The Citizen-Consumer: Media Effects at the Intersection of Consumer and Civic Culture," *Political Communication* 21, no 3, (July–September 2004): 369–91.

26  *"wants that previously did not exist"*: John Kenneth Galbraith, *The Affluent Society*. (Boston: Houghton Mifflin, 1958), 60.

26  *"the Sears, Roebuck catalogue"*: Ibid.

27  *"sizeable chunk of our business"*: Carl Riser reporting in "The Short Order Economy," *Fortune*, August 1962. The quote comes from General Foods marketing executive Herbert M. Cleaves.

27  *region to carry a particular brand*: Stephanie Strom, "Department Stores' Fate; Bankruptcies Like Macy's Overshadowing Strong Consumer Loyalty, Experts Assert," *New York Times*, February 3, 1992.

28  *legal barriers to price-cutting were gone*: In fact, in 1961 four officials of the General Motors Corporation and several General Motors agencies were indicted of conspiring to prevent sales of cars through discount stores.

28  *were the most impatient and impulsive shoppers*: Charles E. Silberman, "The Revolutionists of Retailing," *Fortune* (April 1962): 260. Silberman points out that discount stores in particular were catering to a new wave of male shoppers by opening auto supply, sporting goods, and hardware departments. He writes: "Today men naturally become interested in shopping, for consumption has become too important to be left exclusively to women."

29  *frugal America to a nation in debt*: See, for example, Lizabeth Cohen, *A Consumers' Republic*, 124. The author points to a 1959 Department of Labor study, "How American Buying Habits Change," confirming that ordinary workers who once strove to save now regarded debt as the norm. By 1957 two-thirds of American families carried some kind of debt, and about half of all families owed money for installment plan purchases.

29  *an astonishing $5 billion*: D. B. Deloach, "Marketing Through Discount Stores," *Journal of Farm Economics*, 44, no. 1 (February, 1962): 169–77.

29  *women's clothing, shoes, furniture, and jewelry*: Robert Spector, *Category Killers: The Retail Revolution and Its Impact on Consumer Culture* (Cambridge, Mass.: Harvard Business School Press, 2005), 22.

## CHAPTER TWO: THE FOUNDING FATHERS

30  *stockholder of E. J. Korvette*: Charles Silberman, "Revolutionists of Retailing," 99.

30  *which means "sell" in Yiddish*: Peter Y. Meddling, *Coping with Life and Death: Jewish Families in the Twentieth Century* (New York: Oxford University Press, 2000), 56.

31  *tips no higher than 10 percent*: Sam Walton's personal habits are detailed in numerous profiles and books, but on this and many other things related to Wal-Mart, one particularly reliable source is Charles Fishman, *The Wal-Mart Effect* (New York: Penguin Books, 2006).

31 *"the most unorthodox tycoon in the land"*: Murray Gart, "Everybody Loves a Bargain," *Time*, July 6, 1962.

31 *second-story loft on East 46th Street*: Robert Spector, *Category Killers*, 18.

32 *"eight Jewish Korean War veterans"*: This myth has been debunked repeatedly, but perhaps the most authoritative source is Paul Dickson and Joseph C. Goulden, *There are Alligators in Our Sewers and Other American Credos* (New York: Delacorte, 1984).

32 *to avoid legal hassles with the navy*: Gart, "Everybody Loves a Bargain."

32 *the dreary into the fabulous*: An advertisement for Ballantine Ale appearing in *Life* magazine (February 1, 1943, 70) portrays a middle-aged man in suit, tie, and fedora covering his wife's eyes with one hand and with the other brandishing a brand-new electric mixer—clearly a surprise for her. The ad copy reads: "And how American to want something better—in kitchen equipment or airplanes or threshing machines or what have you. Why, we're even fighting a war over the promise of a better tomorrow."

32 *"forget that kitchen drudgery forever"*: N. W. Ayer Collection, Series 3, Box 245, Drawer 303, Folder 1943–47, Archives Center, National Museum of American History, Smithsonian Institution, Washington, D.C., as cited in Charles McGovern, *Sold American*.

32 *shop for more low-price goods*: Gail Collins, *America's Women: 400 Years of Dolls, Drudges, Helpmates and Heroines* (New York: HarperCollins, 2004), 403.

33 *"secure the utmost for their money"*: Advertisement in *Ladies' Home Journal* 37 (March 3, 1920), 57.

33 *A freezer sold for close to $400*: See, for example, this history of appliances: http://www.thepeoplehistory.com/50selectrical.html.

33 *median annual income for a family*: U.S. Census Historical Income Tables, Table F-7: All Races by median and mean income, 1947 to 2005, at census.gov/hhes/www/income/histinc/f07ar.html.

33 *department stores such as Macy's and Gimbels*: Brian Trumbore, "Discount Retailers," StocksandNew.com, 2001.

33 *a million-dollar profit selling a million refrigerators*: David Halberstam, *The Fifties* (New York: Villard Books, 1993), 151.

33 *"parasite and a bootlegger" and, most degrading of all, a "discounter"*: Robert Spector, "Category Killers," 18.

33 *An almost pathologically honorable man*: In his book, *More Than They Bargained For: The Rise and Fall of Korvettes* (New York: Lebhar-Friedman Books, 1981), *New York Times* business reporter Isadore Barmash portrays Ferkauf as compulsively competitive, volatile, and loyal. Apparently he denied only one childhood buddy a job—a man who as a kid had violated the honor code of their neigh-

borhood softball team by substituting his own name for Ferkauf's on a chalk-board of players.

34 *a supermarket, and a toy store*: unsigned editorial introduction, "Everybody Loves a Bargain," *Time* magazine, March 10, 1961.

35 *mass manufacture with mass distribution*: Marketing consultant Frank Meissner speaking to reporter Murray Gart in the *Time* magazine cover story, July 6, ' 1962.

35 *was worth $50 million*: Silberman, "Revolutionists of Retailing," 99.

35 *"self-selection and checkout counters"*: Godfrey Lebhar, *Chain Stores in America, 1859–1962* (New York, Chain Store Publishing Corp., 1963).

36 *"everything directed at you and no one else"*: Letitia Baldrige, "I Shopped Them All," *New York Times*, Op-ed, March 8, 2005.

38 *"I've pushed my last baby buggy"*: Curt Wohleber, "The Shopping Cart: The Invention That Made Giant Economy Size Possible," *American Heritage* 20, no. 1 (Summer 2004).

39 *shopping cart to put it in*: Britt Beemer, chairman of the market research firm America's Research Group, Inc., as quoted in Joseph B. Cahill, "Hot Wheels, The Secret Weapon of Big Discounters: Lowly Shopping Cart," *Wall Street Journal* (November 24, 1999), A1.

39 *dominated the general merchandise sector*: For this, and for many other insights on the history of discounting, I am grateful to Misha Petrovic, assistant professor of sociology at the National University of Singapore. Dr. Petrovic was kind enough not only to speak with me at length on the history and politics of discount stores in the United States, but also to share an as-yet-unpublished monograph on the subject that was extremely helpful.

39 *brand or provenance of these items*: This advertisement is available as a charmingly nostalgic tribute to discount stores of the 1960s developed by David P. Johnson at www.wtv-zone.com/dpjohnson/6osdiscounstores/pag3.html.

39 *"rather than upon planned assortments"*: William R. Davidson and Alton F. Doody, "The Future of Discounting," *Journal of Marketing*, 27, no. 1 (January 1963): 36–39.

40 *'Thick on the best, to hell with the rest'*: Sol Canton, president of Interstate Department Stores quoted in *Time* magazine, February 2, 1962.

42 *choked off the money flow*: Adam Gopnik, "Under One Roof: The Death and Life of the New York Department Store," *The New Yorker*, September 22, 2003.

42 *bottom tier of the American steel market*: Japanese steel makers managed to scare away most of the American competition in this sector and then pursued American manufacturers into the higher tiers of the steel market. Today, Japan makes some of the highest quality steel available.

42 *manufacturing sophistication and business savvy*: See, for example, Clayton Chris-
tensen, Thomas Craig, and Stuart Hart, "The Great Disruption," *Foreign Affairs,*
March/April 2001, 80.

43 *one-third of their workforce overseas*: For a penetrating and thought-provoking analysis of early union support of imports and the Buy American campaign see
Dana Frank, *Buy American: The Untold Story of Economic Nationalism* (Boston: Beacon Press, 1996).

43 *more than a third of all department store sales*: In Misha Petrovic's monograph, drawn
from a citation from *DSN Retailing*, 2002.

44 *routed to a truck for delivery to the designated store*: Frederick H. Abernathy, John
Dunlop, Janice H. Hammond, and David Weil, *A Stitch in Time: Lean Retailing
and the Transformation of Manufacturing-Lessons from the Apparel and Textile Industries*
(New York: Oxford University Press, 1999), 57.

45 *"the right to grasp for ourselves some advantage over others"*: President Jimmy Carter,
televised speech, July 15, 1979.

46 *only 29 percent of sales*: Walter Salmon, "Organizational Barriers to Department
Store Success," Harvard Business School Case 9-581-027 (Boston: Harvard Business School, 1980).

46 *only twenty survived that decade*: Abernathy et al., (op cit) 49.

47 *double pack of Wrigley's chewing gum in 1974*: Stephen Brown, *Revolution at the Checkout
Counter: The Explosion of the Bar Code* (Cambridge: Harvard University Press, 1997).

47 *react instantly to price fluctuations in their markets*: See, for example, Charles Fishman
(op cit).

49 *average employee earned in a lifetime*: My thinking on this benefited by a telephone
conversation with Robert B. Reich, professor of public policy at the Goldman
School of Public Policy at the University of California, Berkeley. Reich's book,
*Supercapitalism: The Transformation of Business, Democracy, and Everyday Life* (New
York: Knopf, 2007) was also extremely helpful. See also Larry M. Bartels, "In-
equalities," *New York Times Magazine*, April 27, 2008.

49 *by the news media and touted by the company*: See "The Price Impact of Wal-Mart
Through 2006, an Update," *Global Insight*, September 2007. At this writing the
report was available on the web at http://www.livebetterindex.com/2007Glob
Report.pdf.

49 *was built on faulty statistics and self-interested analysis*: See for example Jared Bernstein
and L. Josh Bivens, "The Wal-Mart Debate: A False Choice Between Prices
and Wages," *Economic Policy Institute*, EPI Issue Brief #223, June 15, 2006.

49 *"Save money. Live better"*: This influence was evident by the large number of
editorials and opinion pieces built around the counterintuitive notion that
Wal-Mart had improved wages as well as lowered prices, thereby improving
the lives of untold millions of Americans.

51 *"best company to work for"*: See "Fortune Annual Ranking of America's Largest Corporations," *CNNMoney.com*, http://cgi.money.cnn.com/tools/fortune/custom _ranking_2008.jsp.

51 *8 percent of the private-sector labor force*: Tamara Draut, "Economic State of Young America," *Demos*, Spring 2008.

52 *"Celebrity Style for $8.98"*: Eric Wilson, "Is this the World's Cheapest Dress: How Steve & Barry's became a $1 billion Company Selling Celebrity Style for $8.98," *New York Times*, May 1, 2008, E1.

53 *"a virtue I could never acquire in myself"*: Walter Isaacson, *Benjamin Franklin: An American Life* (New York: Simon and Schuster, 2003), 78.

54 *"maze of urban streets and city blocks"*: William L. Nunn, "Revolution in the Idea of Thrift," *Annals of the American Academy of Political and Social Science* 196, Consumer Credit, March 1938, 52–56.

## CHAPTER THREE: WINNER TAKE NOTHING

56 *but not all of them are golden*: E. M. (Mick) Kolassa, PhD, chairman and managing partner of Medical Marketing Economics and an expert on pricing in the pharmecutical industry, told me that while it's impossible to know precisely how much is spent on pricing globally, the drug industry spends hundreds of millions each year and is only one industry among hundreds of industries that do pricing research. Hence, the extrapolation to billions seems more than justified.

57 *"was the price for which it could be sold"*: Diana Wood, *Medieval Economic Thought* (New York: Cambridge University Press, 2002), 135.

57 *"yet is not required by strict justice"*: Ibid., 136.

57 *Americans are intimidated by numbers*: See, for example, John Allen Paulos, *Innumeracy: Mathematical Illiteracy and Its Consequences* (New York: Hill & Wang, 2001) and Joel Best, *Damned Lies and Statistics: Untangling Numbers from the Media, Politicians, and Activists* (Berkeley: University of California Press, 2001).

58 *all other numerals have a precise meaning*: Stanislas Debaene, *The Number Sense: How the Mind Creates Mathematics* (New York: Oxford University Press, 1997), 108.

58 *"only small, round numbers"*: Ibid., 77.

60 *"condensation occurs as a matter of course"*: Anna Freud, *The Ego and Mechanisms of Defense: The Writings of Anna Freud* (Madison, Conn.: International Universities Press, 1967), reprint edition.

60 *can be evoked by even minor distractions*: Baba Shiv and Alexander Fedorikhin, "Spontaneous Versus Controlled Influences of Stimulus-Based Affect on Choice Behavior," *Organizational Behavior and Human Decision Processes* 87, no. 2 (March 2002): 342–70. In this well-known experiment, researchers asked subjects to memorize either a short or a long list of numbers and then presented them

with a choice of chocolate cake or fruit. Those who were asked to memorize a long list were much more likely to choose chocolate cake, which the authors theorize indicates that their higher order brain is swamped in thought, allowing their lower order, more impulsive brain to assert itself.

60 "*response to block the cognitive assessment*": Jodie Ferguson, "Beliefs of Fair Price Setting Rules: Pervasiveness in the Marketplace and Effects on Perceptions of Price Fairness," dissertation delivered in abstract form at Fordham Pricing Conference, September 28, 2007, Fordham University, New York.

61 "*the laws of society, is not altogether without it*": Adam Smith, *The Theory of Moral Sentiments* (1790, 6th edition), Part 1, Sec. 1, Ch 1:9.

62 "*An Analysis of Decision Under Risk*": Daniel Kahneman and Amos Tversky, "Prospect Theory: An Analysis of Decision Under Risk," *Econometrica* 47, no. 2 (1979): 363–91.

63 *are projected far into the future*: See, for example, D. Soman et al., "The Psychology of Intertemporal Discounting: Why Are Distant Events Valued Differently from Proximal Ones?" *Marketing Letters* 16, nos. 3/4 (2005): 347–60.

63 *the distance estimated by the students*: Plenary lecture at the annual meeting of the American Association for the Advancement of Science, February 15, 2008, in Boston.

64 "*for a new field of research*": As announced in the press release from the Royal Swedish Academy of Science, October 9, 2002, available at http://nobelprize. org/nobel__prizes/economics/laureates/2002/press.html.

65 *when making financial transactions*: Thaler compressed and compiled many of these cases into a book. See Richard Thaler, *The Winner's Cure: Paradoxes and Anomalies of Economic Life* (New York: The Free Press, 1992). My description of the Ultimatum Game was informed by Thaler's chapter on the subject (pp. 21–36) and also by conversations with Dr. Patrick Kaufman, chairman of marketing at Boston University School of Management.

66 *Emotion, Reason, and the Human Brain*: Antonio R. Damasio, *Descartes' Error: Emotion, Reason, and the Human Brain* (New York: Harper Perennial, 1995).

66 *true not only for humans*: There is a rich scientific literature giving evidence that humans are biologically programmed or "hardwired" to be fair and to demand fairness in others. See, for example, E. Fehr and B. Rockenbach, "Detrimental Effects of Sanctions on Human Altruism," *Nature* (March 13, 2003): 137–40.

66 *but for other primates*: Megan van Wolkenten, Sarah F. Brosnan, and Frans B. de Waal: "Inequity Responses of Monkeys Modified by Effort," Proceedings of the National Academy of Sciences 104, no. 47 (November 20, 2007): 18854–95. See also Sarah F. Brosnan and Frans B. M. de Waal, "Monkeys Reject Unequal Pay," *Nature* 425 (2003): 297–99.

**68** *"don't talk to each other much"*: Splendid unpublished profile of Daniel Ariely by journalist Andrea Baird.

**69** *"correlation did not exist"*: Ibid.

**70** *lead us to fits of impulsiveness*: This insight came thanks to a discussion with Alan G. Sanfrey, professor of psychology at the University of Arizona.

**73** *not their execution*: Emily Singer, "The Real Pain of Dread," *Technology Review* (May 18, 2006), available online at http://www.technologyreview.com/Biotech/16887/page1.

**73** *nucleus accumbens went quiet*: In addition to my interviews with Dr. Knutson, I referred to Brian Knutson et al., "Distributed Neural Representation of Expected Value," *Journal of Neuroscience* 25, no. 19 (May 11, 2005): 4086–12.

**74** *in exchange for getting it over quickly*: Gregory S. Berns et al., "Neurobiological Substrates of Dread," *Science* 312 (5775) (May 5, 2006): 754–58.

**74** *called by Antonio Damasio*: Antonio R. Damasio, *Descartes' Error*, 173–174.

**76** *"illusion of objectivity"*: See, for example, Emily Pronin, Thomas Gilovich, and Less Ross, "Objectivity in the Eye of the Beholder: Divergent Perceptions of Bias in Self Versus Others," *Psychological Review* 111, no. 3: 781–99.

**77** *that behavior after it occurs*: George Lowenstein, "The Creative Destruction of Decision Research," *Journal of Consumer Research* 28, no. 3 (December 2001).

**79** *concluded in their assessment*: On Amir and Erica Dawson, "Motivating Discounts: Price-Motivated Reasoning," June 2007. At this writing, this was a work in progress, available at http://ssrn.com/abstract=997474.

**80** *almost impossible to predict*: A. Tversky and D. Kahneman, "Judgment Under Uncertainty: Heuristics and Biases," *Science* 185: 1124–31.

**80** *customers will consider fair*: Gretchen B. Chapman and Eric J. Johnson, "Incorporating the Irrelevant: Anchors in Judgments of Belief and Value," in T. Gilovich, D. W. Griffin, and D. Kahneman (eds.), *The Psychology of Intuitive Judgment: Heuristics and Biases* (New York: Cambridge University Press, 2002).

**80** *those external clues might be*: Kristina Shampanier, Nina Mazar, Dan Ariely, "Zero as a Special Price: The True Value of Free Products," *Marketing Science* 26, no. 6 (December 2007): 742–57.

**81** *factors such as rabid discounting*: Thanks to Harvard computer scientist David Parkes, an expert on the mathematics of auctions, for speaking with me on this issue.

**81** *bidder's heat or auction fever*: Young Han Lee and Ulrike Malmendier, "The Bidder's Curse," NBER Working Paper No. W13699, December 2007. Available at SSRN: http://ssrn.com/abstract=1080202.

**82** *had their money returned*: Christopher Shea, "eBay-nomics: Modern Economists Have Assumed That People in Auctions Behave Rationally. Then Came eBay," *Boston Globe*, June 10, 2007.

**82** *"profit-leaking paradox"*: Rafi Mohammed, *The Art of Pricing* (New York: Crown, 2005), 24.

**82** *"opposition to one of their various judgments"*: Janet Landman, *Regret: The Persistence of the Possible* (New York: Oxford University Press, 1993), 116.

**85** *the response was a resounding no*: Daniel Kahneman, Jack L. Knetsch, and Richard H. Thaler, "Fairness as a Constraint on Profit Seeking: Entitlements in the Market," *American Economic Review* 76 (September 1986): 728–41.

**85** *got pretty much the same response*: Raymond Gorman and James B. Kehr, "Fairness as a Constraint on Profit Seeking: Comment," *American Economic Review* 82, no. 1 (1992): 355–58.

**85** *"biggest mistake was getting caught"*: David Wessel, "How Technology Tailors Price Tags," *Wall Street Journal*, June 21, 2001.

**86** *early birds deserved to pay more*: On the *Wired* magazine blog network, one gleeful "late adapter" wrote: "The early iPhone buyers paid a premium precisely to be among the first and the 'coolest.' Now the price has dropped, tough cookies." Writing on the same blog, an early adapter took a different view: "LAME!!! All I can say to you Steve is you've lost one of your most enthusiastic early adopters. I'll never buy another Apple product until it's been out at least 90 days. That way I won't get screwed out of money and have to deal with a buggy product at the same time. Hopefully Apple will keep churning out great products, but I, for one, won't get burned again. Fool me once, shame on you; fool me twice, shame on me!" See http://blog.wired.com/business/2007/09/steve- jobs-to-a.html.

### CHAPTER FOUR: THE OUTLET GAMBIT

**90** *Europe, Japan, and Hong Kong*: James Fallon, "First European Designer Mall in England Is a Hit," *Daily News Record*, June, 1995; Jacy Meyer, "A New Showcase for Brand Names," *The Prague Post*, October 18, 2006.

**90** *Turkey, Dubai, and South Africa*: For basic statistics on outlet malls, I used *Value Retail News* at http://www.valueretailnews.com.

**90** *growing segments of the* travel *industry*: Edwin McDowell, "America's Hot Tourist Spot: the Outlet Mall," *New York Times*, May 26, 1996.

**90** *worth of outlet visits each year*: Outlet Malls, *Consumer Reports* 63, no. 8 (August 1998): 20.

**91** *what appears to be wild abandon*: Margaret Crawford, "The World in a Shopping Mall," in Malcolm Miles and Tim Hall, eds. with Iain Borden, *The City Cultures Reader*, second ed. (New York: Routledge, 2004), 127.

**91** *real estate is cheap and the tax incentives sweet*: See, for example, Thomas W. Hanchett, "U.S. Tax Policy and the Shopping Center Boom of the 1950s and 1960s," *American Historical Review* (October 1996): 1082–1110. Hanchchett traces the explosion in shopping malls to a loophole in the tax code that allowed for "accelerated depreciation," which transformed real estate development into a lucrative tax shelter for developers.

**91** *avoid angering full-price retailers:* Parke Chapman, "Bargain Hunters Keep Outlet Malls Humming," *National Retail Estate Investor* 45, no. 4 (2003): 15.

**92** *"sky and landscape seemed to dance":* Zola modeled his fictional store after Le Bon Marche in Paris. Opened in 1852, it is widely referred to as the first modern department store.

**92** *"phobia of entering a store":* M. Jeffrey Hardwick, *Mall Maker: Victor Gruen, Architect of an American Dream* (Philadelphia: University of Pennsylvania Press, 2004), 32.

**93** *with brightly colored birds:* Biographical information on Victor Gruen was obtained in *"Victor Gruen: A Register of His Papers* in the Library of Congress," prepared by Harry G. Heiss, 1995. Available at http://lcweb2.loc.gov/service/mss/eadxmlmss/ eadpdfmss/2001/ms001017.pdf; Malcolm Gladwell, "The Terrazzo Jungle," *The New Yorker*, March 15, 2004. Gladwell cites M. Jeffrey Hartwick's biography of Gruen, *Mall Maker*, as an important source for his piece.

**93** *malls would be modeled and are still:* Margaret Growford, "Suburban Life and Public Space," in David J. Smiley, ed., *Redressing the Mall* (New York: Princeton Architectual Press, 2002), 24–25, available on the Web as part of the series Sprawl and Public Space at http://www.arts.gov/pub/Design/SprawlPubSpace. pdf.

**94** *"for suburbia's community life":* Lizabeth Cohen, "From Town Center to Shopping Center: The Reconfiguration of the Community Marketplaces in Postwar America," *American Historical Review* (October 1996): 1050–81. See also Victer Gruen, "Introverted Architecture," *Progressive Architecture* 38, no. 5 (1957): 204–208.

**94** *it was the driving force:* An interesting essay on Gruen from a socialist perspective can be found in Anette Baldauf, "Shopping Town USA: Victor Gruen, the Cold War, and the Shopping Mall," *Documenta Magazine*'s online journal, August 2007, at http://magazines.documenta.de/frontend/article.php?IdLanguage =5&NrArticle=1736.

**94** *"the longer people will stay":* Mary Ann Galante, "Mixing Marts and Theme Parks," *Los Angeles Times*, June 14, 1989, quoting mall developer Bill Dawson.

**94** *in 1960 to nearly three hours in 1979:* Margaret Crawford, "World in a Shopping Mall," 130.

**95** *"they will visit again in the future":* Leslie Stoel, Vanessa Wickliffe, and Kyu Hye Lee, "Attribute Beliefs and Spending as Antecedents to Shopping Value," *Journal of Business Research*, 57, no. 10 (October 2004): 1067–73.

**95** *all but abandoned by their parents:* Sara B. Miller, "At Shopping Malls, Teens Hanging Out Is Wearing Thin," *Christian Science Monitor*, August 11, 2005.

**95** *but does a quickie through the drive-through:* For insight into this and other tricks of the fast-food trade, see Ellen Ruppel Shell, *The Hungry Gene* (New York: Atlantic Monthly Press, 2002).

96 *would at a fully loaded regional mall*: A. Coughlan and D. Soberman, "A Survey of Outlet Mall Retailing: Past, Present, and Future," INSEAD Faculty & Research Working Paper Series, 2004.

96 *"recreational model of consumption"*: Marianne Conroy, "Discount Dreams: Factory Outlet Malls, Consumption, and the Performance of Middle-Class Identity," *Social Text* 54 (Spring 1998): 63–83.

98 *Lightning McQueen remote-control vehicles*: This helpful symbiosis came to an end when K. B. Toys went bankrupt for the second time in late 2008.

98 *manipulate customers' willingness to buy*: Interestingly, after leaving Las Vegas I learned that the Penney high/low pricing strategy had been exposed years earlier. In July 1992 the North Carolina attorney general's office charged the company with inflating its jewelry prices with markups as high as five times cost and then advertising discounts of 60 percent off the regular price. The judge ruled that Penney had not violated any state laws and, in fact, it would be unfair to single out the department store for bad practices because fully 80 percent of jewelry competitors promoted sale prices based on inflated regular prices.

101 *mattress tagged as such*: Paul N. Bloom and Gregor T. Gundlach, eds., *Handbook of Marketing and Society* (Thousand Oaks, Calif.: Sage Publishing, 2001), 251.

101 *"They don't want their product shopped"*: The bedding industry is notorious for its pricing tactics, which several experts discussed with me at length. For a good press summary of the issue see Kimberly Janeway, "Why Consumer Reports doesn't rate specific models of mattresses," *ConsumerReports.Org*, January 26, 2008.

102 *"encrusted with sapphires, diamonds, silver and gold"*: Dana Thomas, *Deluxe: How Luxury Lost Its Luster* (New York: Penguin Press, 2007), 22.

103 *"It was about making money, a lot of money"*: Ibid., 34

103 *sold it to the Sara Lee Corporation in 1985*: Telephone interview with Miles Cahn, December 10, 2007. After selling his company, Cahn "retired" to a farm in upstate New York and built up a second successful business in goat cheese, which he sold in 2007. When I asked him about his next venture, the ninety-year-old entrepreneur deadpanned, "Toilet paper. If I could sell one roll to every asshole out there, I'd make a fortune."

104 *manufactured specifically for these stores*: Sandra Jones, "Coach's New Purse Line Makes Play for High End," *Chicago Tribune*, February 19, 2007.

105 *"Past, Present, and Future"*: Anne T. Coughlan and David A. Soberman, "A Survey of Outlet Mall Retailing: Past, Present and Future," 2004, available online at http://library.nyenrode.nl/INSEAD/2004/2004-036.pdf.

**105** *"in isolated single-store locations"*: Ibid.

**105** *warehouse in Reading, Pennsylvania*: Alexander Gavin, *The American City, What Works, What Doesn't* (New York: McGraw Hill Professional, second edition, 2002), 143.

**106** *to ancient Egyptian seals*: See, for example, David Wengrow, "Prehistories of Commodity Branding," *Current Anthropology* 49, no.1, February 2008. Wengrow intriguingly argues that while we generally associate the rise of brands with the rise of modern-day consumerism, "comparisons between recent forms of branding and much earlier modes of commodity marking associated with the Urban Revolution of the fourth millennium B.C. suggest that systems of branding address a paradox common to all economies of scale and are therefore likely to arise (and to have arisen) under a wide range of ideological and institutional conditions, including those of sacred hierarchies and stratified states."

**107** *Dior items peddled on the site were counterfeit*: Dana Thomas, *Deluxe*, 292.

**107** *only through selected retailers with trained staff*: Thierry Leveque, "LVMH Wins Compensation from eBay Over Counterfeits," *Reuters*, June 30, 2008.

**107** *manufacturers appear willing to do*: Mylene Mangalindan and Vanessa O'Connell, "eBay Wins in Fight Over Tiffany Counterfeits," *Wall Street Journal*, July 15, 2008, B1.

**107** *"and the most extreme conditions"*: As stipulated on The North Face Web site at www.thenorthface.com.

**107** *different prices under the same brand*: Lisa Lockwood, "Guess' Retail Gambit Pays Off," *Women's Wear Daily*, 192, no 90, October 30, 2006.

**108** *Harvard is diluting its brand and in a sense counterfeiting itself*: Thanks to my colleague Patrick Kaufman, chairman of marketing at Boston University, for his thoughts on the self-counterfeiting of name brands.


## CHAPTER FIVE: MARKDOWN MADNESS

**109** *entire cold weather line*: Maureen Tkacik, "Markdown-Economics," *New York Magazine*, January 14, 2006.

**110** *"pants down—and their coats off"*: Michael Barbaro, "In Shirt-Sleeve Holiday Season, Overcoats Linger on the Racks," *New York Times*, December 23, 2006.

**110** *he said, is "off its axis"*: Guy Trebay, "Luxury Prices Are Fallling; the Sky, Too," *New York Times*, December 4, 2008.

**110** *"What I'm worried about is the creativity"*: Ibid., quoting Beth Buccini, an owner of the chic Manhattan (SoHo) boutique Kirna Zabete.

**110** *financial risk of marketing their goods*: This is not to imply that retailers had no power, particularly in regional markets. For example, in 1904, Marshall Field & Company employed eight thousand to ten thousand workers and served as many as a quarter of a million customers a day, and had grown into a powerhouse for both retail and wholesale. By 1920 the company controlled factories in the United States, China, and the Philippines, producing everything from underwear and neckties to lamps, rugs, and linoleum.

111 *toy stores, and hardware stores*: For example, I grew up in Syracuse, New York, shopping at Dey Brothers, a family-owned chain of nine stores founded in 1877. Dey's, as we called it, became part of Allied Stores holding company, which was bought out by the Campeau Corporation in 1986. In 1987, Campeau sold Dey's to May Company which merged it with another of my favorite stores, Addis Company. After another merger, with Sage-Allen stores, all Dey's stores were closed by 1993. May Company also owned Sibleys, Famous-Barr, Filene's, Foley's, Hecht's, The Jones Store, Kaufmann's, L. S. Ayres, Marshall Field's, Meier & Frank, Robinsons-May, and Strawbridge's. Today, only Macy's and Bloomingdale's retain their names.

111 *slack if and when the sales went south*: Tracie Rozhon, "Markdown Money Sparks a Clothing War," *International Herald Tribune*, February 25, 2008. Rozhon quotes one retailer: "As Lauren's product line got bigger, and the volume increased, he lost some of his exclusivity. Now even Ralph pays markdown money."

111 *were absorbed into even larger chains*: The history of the decline of department stores is well told in a number of books, including Jan Whitaker's excellent and comprehensive *Service and Style: How The American Department Store Fashioned the Middle Class* (New York: St. Martin's, 2006). There are also several well-maintained Web sites on the subject: http://www.dshistory.com and http://www.deadmalls.com.

111 *chains sold 72 percent of American clothing*: Robert J. S. Ross, *Slaves to Fashion: Poverty and Abuse in the New Sweatshops* (Ann Arbor: University of Michigan Press, 2004), 131.

111 *"The manufacturers and contractors are stuck"*: Edna Bonacich and Richard P. Appelbaum, *Behind the Label: Inequality in the Los Angeles Apparel Industry* (Berkeley: University of California Press, 2000), 90.

111 *Critics call it extortion, and sometimes it is*: Tracie Rozhon, "3 Saks Executives Fired Over Vendor Payments," *New York Times*, May 10, 2005.

112 *Oscar de La Renta and Michael Kors*: Tracie Rozhon, "First the Markdown, Then the Showdown," *New York Times*, February 25, 2005.

112 *and paid no fine*: Michael Barbaro, "Saks Settles with SEC on Overpayment," *New York Times*, September 6, 2007.

112 *smaller vendors and manufacturers*: Edna Bonacich and Richard P. Appelbaum, *Behind the Label*, 91–94. The authors write: "Small manufacturers are more likely to have difficulty meeting the complex demands of large retailers, each one of

whom has a different set of specifications, some running to shipping and packing guides the size of telephone books."

112 *by experience told them what to stock*: See, for example, Adam Gopnik, "Under One Roof," *The New Yorker*, September 22, 2003. Gopnik's charming and prescient essay on the life and death of the New York City department store quotes Bloomingdale's founder Marvin Traub as saying that today "the buying is all done on a corporate level, and so the connection between the customer and the product is damaged. They order from the central headquarters with, say, twenty to thirty per cent for the individual store. The department store depends on trust and belief, and if you knock down the reasons for belief, you damage it."

112 *department store sales was a paltry 5.2 percent*: B. Peter Pashigian and Brian Bowen, "Why Are Products Sold on Sale?: Explanations of Pricing Regularities," *The Quarterly Journal of Economics*, November 1991, 1015.

112 *to a startling 18 percent in 1984*: Ibid.

112 *merchants ended up eating their bad calls*: See, for example, Susan Kaiser and Karyl Ketchum, "Consuming Fashion as Flexibility," in S. Ratneshwar and David Glen Mick (eds.), *Inside Consumption: Consumer Motives, Goals, and Desires* (New York: Routledge, 2005), 125.

113 *"goods from other countries"*: Richard Freeman, "The U.S. Import Bubble Is Bursting," *Executive Intelligence Report*, January 19, 2001.

113 *$1.2 trillion in 2000*: Ibid.

113 *store merchandise sold at full price*: Edna Bonacich and Richard P. Appelbaum, *Behind the Label*, 94.

113 *had grown to an astonishing 33 percent*: Scott C. Friend and Patricia H. Walker, "Welcome to the New World of Merchandising," *Harvard Business Review*, November 2001.

113 *within two months of its launch*: Rhys Blakely, "Apple cuts third off price of its iPhone 68 days after launch," Times Online, September 7, 2007, see http://business.timesonline.co.uk/tol/business/industry_sectors/technology/article2398965.ece.

114 *fashion in transport*: B. Peter Pashigian and Brian Bowen, "Why Are Products Sold on Sale?", 1018.

114 *for the next Christmas season*: Interview with Rama Ramakrishnan, Cambridge, Massachusetts.

114 *than the Asian imports*: Ibid.

114 *lap them up, or they don't*: B. Peter Pashigian and Brian Bowen, "Why Are Products Sold on Sale?"

115 *"June 13 sale followed by the June 14 sale"*: Amy Merrick, "Priced to Move," *Wall Street Journal*, August 7, 2001, A1.

115 *many are quickly discounted*: This is true not only of fashion but of electronics, furniture, and even books. The "window" for a new book title today is roughly six to eight weeks. If a title doesn't take off during that time, it is likely to move from the shelves to the bargain bin.

116 *has been available since at least the mid-1980s*: ProfitLogic, Inc., formerly known as Technology Strategy, Inc., was an early player in this space. Founded in 1983, it was based in Cambridge, Massachusetts, and is now part of Oracle.

117 *"They are the price makers, not the price takers"*: Robert J. S. Ross, *Slaves to Fashion* (Ann Arbor: University of Michigan Press, 2004), 129. Ross is a sociologist at Clark University.

118 *a combined savings of $3 billion*: "Rebates, Coupons and Discounts," *NPD Insights*, no. 2 (May 2005), available at http://www.npdinsights.com/corp/enewsletter/html.archives/May2005/index.html.

118 *nearly half of all computer sales—involved them*: Matthew A. Edwards, "The Law, Marketing and Behavioral Economics of Consumer Rebates," *Stanford Journal of Law, Business & Finance* 12, (2007), 362.

119 *redemption rate data:*: Redemption rates are equal to the number of successful redemptions divided by the number of units sold.

119 *make public this side of their business*: See Tim Silk and Chris Janiszewski, "Managing Mail-In Rebate Promotions: An Empirical Analysis of Purchase and Redemption," Sauder School of Business, University of British Columbia, working paper, 24.

119 *"what the manufacturer had in mind"*: Catherine Greenman, "The Trouble with Rebates," *New York Times*, September 16, 1999, G1.

119 *consider their time too valuable*: Widespread speculation that a subgroup of consumers choose not to bother because they don't want to take the time doesn't qualify as an explanation.

120 *is considered an abject failure*: Timothy Guy Silk, "Examining Purchase and Non-Redemption of Mail-In Rebates: The Impact of Offer Variables on Consumers' Objective and Subjective Probabilities of Redeeming," dissertation, University of Florida, 2004, 6.

120 *"without encouraging redemptions"*: Ibid., 7.

122 *to buy the product*: Carrie Heilman, Kyryl Lakishyk, Sonja Radas, "The Effectiveness of In-Store Free Samples on Sample Takers," 2006, available online at http://www.commerce.virginia.edu/faculty__research/Research/Papers/FreeSamples__July26__2006.pdf.

123 *"five shillings besides"*: From the essay "Advice to a Young Tradesman Written in the Year 1748," in *Autobiography of Benjamin Franklin* (New York: Macmillan Company, 1921), 188.

123 *"an opportunity cost"*: Diip Soman, "The Mental Accounting of Sunk Time Costs:

Why Time Is Not Like Money," *Journal of Behavioral Decision Making* 14, no 3 (2001), 169–85.

**123** *we tend to underestimate its value:* Richard Thaler, "Mental Accounting Matters," *Journal of Behavioral Decision Making* 12 (1999), 183–206.

## CHAPTER SIX: DEATH OF A CRAFTSMAN

**125** *"let's pull the legs off":* Oliver Burkeman, "The Miracle of Almhult," *The Guardian*, June 17, 2004.

**125** *among the world's richest men:* In March 2008, *Forbes* magazine estimated Kamprad's fortune at U.S. $31 billion, making him the seventh richest person in the world, while other sources, such as the Swedish business weekly *Veckans Affärer,* argue that he is in fact the wealthiest. Company finances are cryptic, making it very difficult to sort this out, but it is largely agreed that in 2008 he was the world's wealthiest European-born man.

**126** *"And the new one is much bedder":* This commercial first ran in 2002 and is available on YouTube at http://www.YouTube.com/watch?v=Io7xDdFMdgw.

**127** *Bomull twin fitted sheet:* See IKEA 2008 catalog, "Home Is the Most Important Place in the World."

**127** *why does it sell a wok named after a girl?:* IKEA sells a wok for $6.99 called Pyra. See the 2007 catalog, page 73, under "cookware."

**128** *"let alone build the thing":* I was fortunate to spend a most informative morning with Peter Korn, founding director of the The Center for Furniture Craftsmanship in Rockport, Maine. Peter is a master craftsman and a master teacher.

**128** *the short, dark winter days:* Thanks to Michaele Weissman, author of the excellent *God in A Cup: The Obsessive Quest for the Perfect Coffee* (Hoboken, N.J.: Wiley, 2008) for filling me in on the coffee-drinking habits of Swedes.

**129** *"to low prices in its stores":* Author unnamed, "Flat Pack Accounting," *The Economist*, May 11, 2006.

**129** *they poached was acquired legally:* "No Questions Asked: The Impacts of U.S. Market Demand for Illegal Timber—and the Potential for Change," Environmental Investigation Agency, November 2007.

**130** *felling trees and hauling logs:* Peter S. Goodman and Peter Finn, "Corruption Stains Timber Trade: Forests Destroyed in China's Race to Feed Global Wood-Processing Industry," *Washington Post*, April 1, 2007, A01.

**130** *rate unprecedented in human history:* Steve Kemper, "Forest Destruction's Prime Suspect," *Yale Magazine*, Spring 2008.

**130** *industrial manufacturing sectors:* "No Questions Asked," Environmental Investigation Agency, November 2007.

130 *provenance of their wood products:* In June 2008 the United States became the first country in the world to ban the import and sale of illegally-sourced softwood and softwood products as part of the 2008 Farm Bill. How and when this law will be enforced remains to be seen, but it is certainly a hopeful first step.

130 *made by other discount retailers as well:* For example, Home Depot pledges "to give preference to wood that has come from forests managed in a responsible way and to eliminate wood purchases from endangered regions of the world by the end of 2002." This message was still on the company Web site in the early months of 2009. Lowe's states on its Web site that it will "aggressively phase out the purchase of wood products from endangered forests." And in 2007, Wal-Mart released a comprehensive progress report on its Sustainability Initiative, in which it proclaimed a goal of selling products "that sustain our natural resources and the environment." Wal-Mart's "Wood and Paper Network" describes "good wood" as "first and foremost, not illegally harvested." Yet it is hard to take such rhetoric seriously in light of documented evidence that, in the words of the Environmental Investigation Agency, "the company's current supply chain includes suppliers who speak openly about paying protection money to the Russian mob, and do their logging in some of the most high conservation value forests in the world." (See Environmental Investigation Agency, "Attention Wal-Mart Shoppers: How Wal-Mart's Sourcing Practices Encourage Illegal Logging and Threaten Endangered Species," 2007.)

131 *75 million cubic meters of timber:* Mikael Toll, "The Storm Gudrun," *Swedish Energy Agency News*, April 2006.

132 *installed a factory in Danville, Virginia:* IKEA press release, "IKEA Opens 1st Swedwood Factory in United States as Virginia Governor and Local Officials Welcome New Facility, Jobs," Business Wire, May 21, 2008. Also see Ylan Q. Mui, "IKEA Helps a Town Put It Together," *Washington Post,* May 31, 2008, A01. What is striking in this celebration of the new IKEA factory is the mention of a worker whose previous factory job paid $16.95 an hour. Her job in the IKEA factory pays $11.50, far closer to the median wage of a Wal-Mart greeter than that of an experienced manufacturing worker.

132 *"that the masses could afford to buy them":* "Welcome to Almhult and Linnebygden," *Almhult Tourist Information Office,* Almhult, Sweden.

134 *mountain bikes for Christmas:* Julia Finch, "Democratic by Design," *The Guardian,* June 1, 2002.

134 *IKEA soothes its few fitful critics by acknowledging flaws:* In 1994 a Swedish newspaper exposed Kamprad's earlier ties to the neo-Nazi movement. Rather than deny it, Kamprad went on national television and tearfully repudiated his youthful indiscretion.

134 *Save the Children and UNICEF:* Olivier Bailly, Jean-Marc Caudron, and Denis Lambert, "The Secrets in IKEA's Closet," *CounterPunch,* December 29, 2006.

135 *1.1 million customers visit an IKEA store every single day:* Joanna Vallely, "IKEA: The Swedish Revolution in Your Home," *Edinburgh Evening News,* April 16, 2008.

135 *IKEA verge on the hagiographic:* Among the more glaring examples is Bertil Torekull, *Leading by Design: The IKEA Story* (New York: HarperBusiness, 1998). Torekull, a retired business journalist, portrays Kamprad as equal parts Father Christmas and Bill Gates—a benevolent and generous business genius committed to fellowship, fair play, and family values. While the business arrangement between them is unspecified, Kamprad handpicked Torekull to write the book.

135 *"We sell a philosophy and a mission":* Daniel Birnbaum, "IKEA at the End of Metaphysics," *Frieze Magazine,* November 11, 1996.

136 *$6 apiece on the Internet:* For example, see Green Earth Inc., which lists four banana leaves for $24 plus shipping at http://www.greenhousebusiness.com/balefr.html.

136 *in exchange for employing more Vietnamese:* "Mr Ingvar Kamprad from IKEA meets the Vietnamese Prime Minister," *Embassy of Sweden News,* April 3, 2008.

137 *illegally logged timber:* "Vietnam, Hub for Illegal Timber," BBC News, March 19, 2008. The BBC reported on findings of two charitable organizations, U.K.-based Environmental Investigation Agency (EIA) and Indonesia's Telapak, that Vietnam was "exploiting the forests of neighbouring Laos to obtain valuable hardwoods for its outdoor furniture industry, which contravenes Laotian laws banning the export of logs and sawn timber."

137 *six-day workweek:* Keith Bradsher, "As Labor Costs Soar in China, Manufacturers Turn to Vietnam," *New York Times,* June 18, 2008.

137 *"with advanced economies":* Harold Meyerson, "Why Were We in Vietnam?," *Washington Post,* July 9, 2008, A15.

137 *Vietnam and other low-wage nations:* See Anna Eriksson and Margareta Przedpelska, "The Impact of Swedish Investment and Trade in Labour Conditions in Vietnam," a master's thesis online at www.ep.liu.se/exjobb/eki/2001.nek/018.

138 *seven times the area of a football field:* A football field is a bit less than 58,000 square feet in area.

138 *500-kilometer radius:* Karin Lundstrom, "Will IKEA Make the Arctic Bloom?" *This Europe,* November 29, 2007; see http://www.thiseurope.com/node/191.

138 *charging extra for plastic bags:* Avis Thomas-Lester, "IKEA Puts a Price on Throwaway Plastic," *Washington Post,* March 16, 2007, B01.

139 *"enforce a distinct process of adaptation":* Joseph Schumpeter, *Business Cycles* (New York: McGraw-Hill, 1939), 101.

140 *"that could be moved around at will":* Richard Sennett, *The Craftsman* (New Haven, Conn.: Yale University Press, 2008).

143 *consumer electronics shop members*: Carol Stocker, "The Fix Is in Decline," *Boston Globe*, February 10, 2005, H1.

143 *young viewers were unlikely to encounter one*: The Fix-It Shop was converted to a Mail-It Shop with a fax machine and shipping service. Interestingly, the Fix-It Shop was revived without comment in August 14, 2006, in episode 4,109 of the series.

143 *"unintelligible to direct inspection"*: Matthew B. Crawford, "Shop Class as Soulcraft," *The New Atlantis*, no. 13 (Summer 2006): 7–24. This is a stunning, well-thought-out essay on the place and purpose of craft. I spoke with Crawford at length on the issue of craftsmanship, and some of his thoughts are undoubtedly reflected in these pages.

144 *"to meeting the housing need be accomplished"*: Richard U. Ratcliff, review of *American Housing, Problems and Prospects*, American Economic Review 34, no. 3 (September 1944): 635.

144 *"cannot be limited to the construction industry"*: Ibid.

144 *"how many you can sell for how little"*: Eric Pace, "William J. Levitt, 86, Pioneer of Suburbs, Dies," *New York Times*, January 29, 1994.

144 *Levitt and Sons at the age of twenty-two*: Both William and Alfred Levitt attended New York University, but neither graduated.

144 *"he didn't know what a two-by-four was"*: "Up from the Potato Fields," *Time* magazine, July 3, 1950.

145 *thought they had any chance of finding one*: Randall Bennett Woods, *Quest for Identity: America Since 1945* (New York: Cambridge University Press, 2005), 10.

145 *"but it is not good enough for us"*: Geoffrey Mohan, "Levittown at Fifty," accessed August 8, 2008, at http://www.newsday.com/community/guide/lihistory.

145 *finish four to five homes a year*: *Levittown, NY— A Brief Survey. Levittown History Collection*, appended September 1, 1987.

146 *"the masses are asses"*: "Up from the Potato Fields."

146 *"discarded fashions and attitudes"*: Christopher Lasch, *The Culture of Narcissism*, 24.

146 *immersed in the "cult of the new"*: See, for example, M. Keith Booker, *The Post Utopian Imagination* (Westport, Conn.: Greenwood Publishing Group, 2002), 21.

## CHAPTER SEVEN: DISCOUNTING AND ITS DISCONTENTS

150 *were forced to quit their jobs*: Clifford Krauss, "Rural U.S. Takes Worst Hit as Gas Tops $4 Average," *New York Times*, June 9, 2008.

151 *"or $2,329 per household"*: Jason Furman, "Wal-Mart: A Progressive Story," November 28, 2005, online at http://www.americanprogress.org/kf/walmart__progressive.pdf.

151 *study of the impact of Wal-Mart on food prices:* Jerry Hausman and Ephrain Leibtag, "Consumer Benefits from Increased Competition in Shopping Outlets: Measuring the Wal-Mart Effect," M.I.T. and Economic Research Service, USDA, revised draft, 2005. Find online at http://www.businessweek.com/pdfs/2005/jerry__hausman.pdf.

152 *the demand tends to go down:* William G. Farang and Karl W. Einolf, *Management Economics: An Accelerated Approach,* M.E. Sharpe, 2006, 122.

152 *the country's leading "Wal-Martologist":* Justin Wolfers, "Are Wal-Mart's Products Normal?" writing in the *New York Times*–sponsored blog "Freakonomics," May 29, 2008. Wolfers is an associate professor of business and public policy at the Wharton School at the University of Pennsylvania.

152 *was either weak or nonexistent:* Emek Basker, "Selling a Cheaper Mousetrap: Wal-Mart's Effect on Retail Prices," *Journal of Urban Economics* 58 (2005): 203–29.

153 *carrying a savings of no more than 2 cents:* See, for example, Fred Crawford and Ryan Matthews, *The Myth of Excellence: Why Great Companies Never Try to Be the Best at Everything* (New York: Crown, 2001), 48–49.

153 *that everything in the store is cheap:* A study conducted by Zenith Management Consulting between July 2003 and January 2005 concluded that "only *15% to 20% of the items Wal-Mart sells are actually priced lower than competing retailers. 80% to 85% of the items Wal-Mart sells are more expensive than other retailers.*"

154 *some of which was organic in name only:* Mark Alan Kastel, "Wal-Mart: The Nation's Largest Grocer Rolls-out Organic Products—Market Expansion or Market Delusion?" *Cornucopia Institute,* September 27, 2006, available online at http://www.cornucopia.org/WalMart/WalMart__White__Paper.pdf.

154 *"more competitive retail environment":* Gene Koretz, "Wal-Mart vs. Inflation," *Business-Week,* May 13, 2002.

154 *China, and elsewhere around the globe:* See, for example, Keith Bradsher, "High Rice Cost Creating Fears of Asia Unrest," *New York Times,* March 29, 2008; and Robin McKie and Heather Stewart, "Hunger. Strikes. Riots. The Food Crises Bites," *The Observer,* April 13, 2008.

154 *are all too familiar with its dangers:* See, for example, Brad Delong, "America's Only Peacetime Inflation: The 1970s," National Bureau of Economic Research Working Paper No. H0084, May 1996. Available online at http://papers.ssrn.com/sol3/papers.cfm?abstract__id=225048.

154 *"perseverance devoted to few other tasks":* James K. Galbraith, *Balancing Acts: Technology, Finance, and the American Future* (New York: Basic Books, 1989), 83.

155 *most workers to demand an increase in wages and benefits:* Louis Uchitelle, *The Disposable American: Layoffs and Their Consequences* (New York: Knopf, 2006), 125.

155 *"different baskets of goods":* Christian Broda, "China and Wal-Mart: The True Cham-

pions of Equality," online at the Financial Express, http://www.thefinancial express-bd.info/print__view.php?news__id=36662, from a report he coauthored with fellow University of Chicago economist John Romalis: "Inequality and Prices: Does China Benefit the Poor in America?" March 2008.

155 *"close to a record low"*: Ibid.

157 *in almost anyone's book*: Reed Abelson and Milt Freudenheim, "Even the Insured Feel the Strain of Health Care Costs," *New York Times*, May 4, 2008.

157 *18 percent less on food*: In 1947, economist Jesse J. Friedman put today's food costs into even starker perspective, writing: "As every housewife knows, the most important single item in the family budget is food. In the Labor Department's cost of living index, food carries a weight of more than 40 per cent of the total for moderate income families." See Jesse J. Friedman, "That Key Man, the Consumer," *New York Times* Magazine, March 16, 1947.

157 *incurring record levels of credit card debt*: Elizabeth Warren, "The Coming Collapse of the Middle Class: Higher Risks, Lower Rewards, and a Shrinking Safety Net," invited lecture in the Jefferson Memorial Lecture Series, University of California at Berkeley, March 8, 2007. This lecture is available for view at YouTube at http://www.YouTube.com/watch?v=akVL7QYoS8A.

158 *$12 million loss in 2007*: Jim Geraghty, "Hillary vs. Circuit City: An Exercise in Empty Populist Tub-thumping," *National Review online*, April 18, 2007, http://hillaryspot.nationalreview.com/post/?q=M2YzMzg4MjMxYzM3ZTZhOWJlMTA4YThhN2Q1NjZlMGY=.

158 *regardless of seniority*: Ylan Q. Mui, "Circuit City Cuts 3,400 'Overpaid' Workers," *The Washington Post*, March 29, 2007, D01.

158 *or had their commissions cut*: Robert Spector, *Category Killers: The Retail Revolution and Its Impast on Consumer Culture* (Cambridge, Mass.: Harvard Business School Press, 2005), 67.

159 *8.1 percent growth in transportation costs*: U.S. Department of Labor, Bureau of Labor Statistics, Consumer Price Index, May 2008; available online at: http://www.bls.gov/CPI.

159 *becoming dangerously obese*: Adam Drewnowski and S.E. Specter, "Poverty and Obesity: The Role of Energy Density and Energy Costs," *American Journal of Clinical Nutrition*, 79, no. 1 (January 2004): 6–16.

159 *by eating out less*: The National Restaurant Association estimates that the typical U.S. adult averaged 5.8 "restaurant occasions" *per week* in 2007. This figure includes homemakers and people who work at home.

159 *for most of us is substantial*: The Environmental Protection Agency reports that about 25 percent of food in America goes to waste (see http://www.epa.gov/epaoswer/non-hw/reduce/wastenot.htm). But others, such as journalist

Jonathon Bloom who is writing a book on food waste, put the figure even higher, at 40 percent. Check out Bloom's excellent blog: http://wastedfood .com.

160 *raised the minimum wage to $7.25 over two years:* U.S. Department of Labor, Employment and Standards Administration, Wage and Hour Division, online at http://www.dol.gov/esa/whd/flsa.

160 *minimum wage of 1960:* Adam Cohen, "After 75 Years, the Working Poor Still Struggle for a Fair Wage," *New York Times,* June 17, 2008.

160 *and crushing homelessness:* David Levinson, *The Encyclopedia of Homelessness* (Thousand Oaks, Calif.: Sage Publications, 2004), 83.

161 *the final major reform of the New Deal:* Jerold L. Waltman, *The Politics of the Minimum Wage* (Champaign: University of Illinois Press, 2000), 28.

161 *"ever adopted here or any other country":* A bit of hyperbole offered during one of Roosevelt's customary "fireside chats," June 24, 1938. Cited in, for example, Conrad Black, *Franklin Delano Roosevelt: Champion of Freedom, Public Affairs,* 2003, 455.

161 *Model T's his workforce assembled:* William C. Richards, *The Last Billionaire: Henry Ford* (New York: Charles Scribner's & Sons, 1948), 13.

161 *veritable blip on our historical screen:* German philosopher and social theorist Friedrich Engels first introduced the notion of the "labor aristocracy" in a number of letters to Karl Marx stretching from the late 1850s through the late 1880s. Engels was grappling with the growing conservatism of the organized sectors of the British working class. He argued that those British workers who had been able to establish unions and secure stable employment—skilled workers in the iron, steel, and machine making-industries and most workers in the cotton textile mills—constituted a privileged and "bourgeoisified" layer of the working class, a "labor aristocracy."

161 *cheap goods cannot be had without "cheap help":* Howard Zinn, Dana Frank, and Robin D. G. Kelly, *Three Strikes, Miners, Musicians, Salesgirls, and the Fighting Spirit of Labor's Last Century* (Boston: Beacon Press, 2001), 70.

161 *"Does Wal-Mart Sell Inferior Goods?":* Emek Basker, "Does Wal-Mart Sell Inferior Goods?" University of Missouri Department of Economics Working Paper 08-05, April 2008.

161 *beating Wall Street estimates:* "Wal-Mart June Sales up; Raises Earnings Forecast," *Reuters,* July 10, 2008.

161 *also enjoyed sales growth:* Michael Barbaro, "Discounters Fared Well in Quarter," *New York Times,* May 14, 2008.

162 *benefit both its workers and its core clientele:* Interview with Nelson Lichtenstein, July 2006.

162  *"is market potential unrealized"*: Larry Copeland, "Wal-Mart's Hired Advocate Takes Flak," *USA Today*, March 15, 2006.

## CHAPTER EIGHT: CHEAP EATS

163  *from their exploits in the New World*: Jeff Chapman, "The Impact of the Potato," *History Magazine*, January 2000.

163  *such as leprosy and syphilis*: C. Graves (ed.), *The Potato, Treasure of the Andes from Agriculture to Culture* (Lima, Peru: International Potato Center, 2001).

164  *cheap fuel for cheap labor*: Redcliffe N. Salaman, William Glynn Burton, and John Gregory Hawkes, *The History and Social Influence of the Potato* (Cambridge, Mass.: Cambridge University Press, 1985), 420.

164  *with one or two herring on the side*: Leslie A. Clarkson and E. Margaret Crawford, *Feast and Famine: Food and Nutrition in Ireland, 1500–1920* (New York: Oxford University Press, 2001), 74–75.

164  *"Women boiled hardly anything but potatoes"*: Cecil Woodham-Smith, *The Great Hunger: Ireland, 1845–1849* (New York: Penguin Group, 1992, reissue edition).

164  *into a foul-smelling black slime*: Redcliffe N. Salaman et al., *History and Social Influence*, 163.

164  *food exporter, shipping meat and grain*: See, for example, Kenneth F. Kiple, *A Movable Feast: Ten Millennia of Food Globalization* (Cambridge: Cambridge University Press, 2007), 216.

164  *staggering 925 million worldwide*: U.N. News Centre, "High food prices plunge another 75 million people into hunger, says UN agency"; http://www.un.org/apps/news/story.asp?NewsID=28099&Cr=Food&Cr1=Crisis. This is a conservative estimate. International relief organization Oxfam estimates that at least 100 million additional people were added to the hunger roles due to the food crises. See *Another Inconvenient Truth*, Oxfam Briefing Paper, June 2008.

165  *families in the developing world—to the brink*: See, for example, Bart Minten, "The Food Retail Revolution in Poor Countries: Is It Coming or Is It Over?" *Economic Development and Cultural Change*, 56 (July 2008): 767–89. Minten points out that food prices offered by global retailers in the developing world tend to be much higher—in fact, 40 to 90 percent higher—than prices in traditional retail markets, and therefore the poor do not benefit.

165  *than it was a generation earlier*: See, for example, "The End of Cheap Food," The Economist.com, December 6, 2007.

166  *Europe, Saudi Arabia, Mexico, and Cuba*: See company Web site at http://www.riceland.com.

166  *$554,343,039 in government handouts*: See the Environmental Working Group Farm Subsidy Database at http://farm.ewg.org/farm/top__recips.php?fips=00000&progcode=total.

166 *less than what it cost the average U.S. farmer to grow:* IATP, "United States Dumping on the World Markets," 2005.

167 *"into the cities to burgeoning slums":* Jane Regan, "Some Areas Really Miss Tariff," *Miami Herald,* October 26, 2003.

167 *all-time high of over 37 million in 2007:* Julia Preston, "Immigration at Record Level, Analysis Finds," *New York Times,* November 29, 2007.

167 *"de-peasantization" of the developing world:* Walden Bello, professor of sociology at the University of the Philippines, well represents the views of this breed of social critic in "Manufacturing a Food Crisis," *The Nation,* May 15, 2008. Oxford University researcher Deborah Bryceson is credited with coining the phrase "de-peasantization" in her article "African Rural Labour, Income Diversification and Livelihood Approaches: A Long-term Development Perspective," *World Development* 24, no 1: 97–111.

168 *75 percent of the world's poor:* Tiina Huvio, Jukka Kola, and Tor Lundström, eds., "Small-Scale Farmers in a Liberalized Trade Environment," proceedings of a Seminar at Haikko, Finland, 2005. Available online at http://www.mm.helsinki. fi/MMTAL/abs/Pub38.pdf.

168 *enough land to support the string of generations:* Naturally, this is just one scenario. There are many others—for example, the oldest son being the only one to inherit the land. But often that son hires his siblings to work the farm, and they and their children must live off the proceeds. It is a slightly different scenario but with a similar outcome.

168 *multinational interests into play:* See, for example, Henry Bernstein's superb analysis: "Who Are the 'People of the Land?' Some Provocative Thoughts on Globalization and Development, with Reference to Sub-Saharan Africa," delivered at the conference *Environments Undone: The Political Ecology of Globalization and Development,* University of North Carolina, February 29 to March 1, 2008.

169 *high-value foods such as meat and dairy products:* Philip C. Abbot, Christopher Hurt, and Wallace E. Tyner, "What's Driving World Food Prices," *Farm Foundation Issue Report,* Oak Brook, Illinois. Available at http://www.farmfoundation.org/ news/articlefiles/404-FINAL%20WDFP%20REPORT%207-28-08.pdf.

169 *a staple for more than half the world's population:* Keith Bradsher, "High Rice Cost Creating Fears of Asia Unrest," *New York Times,* March 28, 2008.

169 *20.6 million metric tons it bought the year previous:* Ibid.

170 *Suddenly, rice was unaffordable:* C. Peter Timmer, "Causes of High Food Prices," *ADB Economics Working Paper 128,* Asia Development Bank, October 2008.

170 *The price of meat, milk, wheat, and corn skyrocketed:* Walden Bello, "Manufacturing a Food Crisis," *The Nation,* May 15, 2008.

170 *average prices throughout the 1960s:* Milan Brahmbhatt, "The Run on Rice," *World Policy Journal,* Summer 2008.

170 *stuttering decline for nearly a century:* The downward slope of cereal prices was disrupted by brief spurts followed by steep declines during the two world wars and during the oil crises of 1974. The 1974 event prompted the formation of the International Fund for Agricultural Development and the Committee on World Food Security to address food issues on a global scale.

170 *"productivity growth and poverty reduction":* Personal email correspondence, October 13–15, 2008. Dr. Timmer also shared with me a draft of a paper he presented at the Asian Agricultural Economics Association meeting in Manila in September 2008. I was also privileged to learn a good deal about the international rice market in Professor Timmer's course in agricultural economics at Harvard.

170 *supporting farmers, but reducing surpluses:* Kenneth Baltzer, Henrik Hanzen, and Kim Martin Lind, "A Note on the Causes and Consequences of the Rapidly Increasing International Food Prices," *Institute of Food and Resource Economics,* University of Copenhagen, May 2008.

171 *just-in-time approach to getting food to markets:* Ronald Trostle, "Global Agricultural Supply and Demand: Factors Contributing to the Recent Increase in Food Commodity Prices," United States Department of Agriculture, May 2008.

172 *"The other was Wal-Mart":* Andrew Martin, "At McDonald's, the Happiest Meal Is Hot Profits," *New York Times,* January 10, 2009.

172 *or fruit salad or even orange juice:* Melanie Warner, "U.S. Restaurant Chains Find There Is No Too Much," *New York Times,* July 28, 2006.

173 *"shrimp products" distributed to hospitals and schools:* "The True Cost of Shrimp," January 2008. A comprehensive report prepared by the Washington-based Solidarity Center, with funding from United States Agency for International Development and the National Endowment for Democracy. Available online at http://www.solidaritycenter.org/files/pubs__True__Cost__of__Shrimp.pdf.

173 *than canned tuna fish:* See press release from the National Oceanic and Atmospheric Administration: "Shrimp Overtakes Canned Tuna as Top U.S. Seafood; Overall Seafood Consumption Decreases in 2001," August 2, 2002. http://www.publicaffairs.noaa.gov/releases2002/aug02/noaa02113.html.

173 *the world's largest full-service restaurant company:* See the Darden Web site at http://www.darden.com.

174 *on the unofficial Red Lobster blog:* http://rlserver.blogspot.com/search/label/Food%20 Service.

174 *chicken, pasta, and farm-raised shrimp:* Peter Keegan, "Red Lobster Casts $9.95 Value Menu," *Nation's Restaurant News,* May 27, 1991.

174 *and 80 percent of that was shrimp:* See the report "Shrimp Stockpile: America's Favorite Imported Seafood," Public Citizen's Food Program, available online at http://www.citizen.org/cmep/foodsafety/shrimp/articles.cfm?ID=12798.

175 *89,000 pounds per acre*: Fisheries Statistics and Economics Division, National Marine Fisheries Service, www.st.nmfs.gov/st1/index.html.

175 *from 33,000 metric tons in 1987*: John Hambrey and C. Kwei Lin, "Shrimp Culture in Thailand." Paper presented to the Asian Institute of Technology, Bangkok, Thailand, 1996.

175 *to an astonishing 240,000 metric tons in 1995*: "Thai Shrimp Exporters to Seek Reduced U.S. Tariffs," SeafoodSource.com, July 22, 2008.

176 *waste from the shrimp itself*: Thamrong Mekhora, "Rice Versus Shrimp Production in Thailand: Is There Really a Conflict?" *Journal of Agricultural and Applied Economics*, April 2003.

176 *stirred by the winds and tides*: See, for example, F. J. Slim et al., "Tidal Exchange of Macrolitter Between a Mangrove Forest and Adjacent Seagrass Beds," *Aquatic Ecology* 30, nos. 2–3 (October 1996) and I. Nagelkerken et al., "Importance of Mangroves, Seagrass Beds and the Shallow Coral Reef as a Nursery for Important Coral Reef Fishes, Using a Visual Census Technique," *Estuarine, Coastal and Shelf Science* 51, no. 1 (July 2000): 31–44.

176 *leaving millions of others homeless*: Eric Chivian and Aaron Bernstein, eds., *Sustaining Life: How Human Health Depends on Biodiversity* (New York: Oxford University Press, 2008), 91. Thanks also to Drs. Chivian and Bernstein for a stimulating discussion of the importance of mangroves during an evening seminar at the Center for Health and the Global Environment at Harvard Medical School.

176 *contributed significantly to this tragic outcome*: "In the front line: shoreline protection and other ecosystem services from mangroves and coral reefs." United Nations Environment Programme World Conservation Monitoring Centre, Cambridge, England, 2006.

177 *resulting in 5,000 deaths*: The Centers for Disease Control maintains a database on foodborne disease, which can be accessed online at http://www.cdc.gov/ncidod /dbmd/diseaseinfo/foodborneinfections_g.htm#howmanycases.

177 *are likely to be as yet unknown*: Paul S. Mead et al., "Food-Related Illness and Deaths in the United States," Centers for Disease Control and Prevention, Atlanta, Georgia. Available online at http://www.cdc.gov/ncidod/eid/Vol5no5/mead. htm.

177 *important role in digestion and vitamin synthesis*: See U.S. Food and Drug Administration Center for Food Safety and Applied Nutrition Web site http://www .cfsan.fda.gov/~mow/chap15.html.

178 *where the real damage is done*: In his courageous best-seller, *Fast Food Nation* (Boston: Houghton Mifflin, 2001), author Eric Schlosser gives a stomach-wrenching description of the symptoms of E.coli 0157:H7, outbreaks of which he links to the industrialized food chain.

178 *number of foodborne disease outbreaks:* The International Society for Infectious Diseases sponsors a list-serve for members that lists outbreaks of infectious disease around the globe. The list-serve can be accessed at http://www.pro medmail.org/pls/otn/f?p=2400:1000:712869436458594.

178 *bagged baby spinach tainted with the bacterium:* See Food and Drug Administration press release: "FDA Finalizes Report on 2006 Spinach Outbreak," P07-51, March 23, 2007.

179 *fertile breeding grounds for infection:* J. Van Donkersgoed et al., "Environmental Sources and Transmission of Escherichia Coli 0157 in feedlot cattle," *Canadian Veterinary Journal* 42, no. 9 (September 2001), 714–20.

179 *Atlanta, Boston, Denver, and St. Louis combined:* Eric Schlosser, *Fast Food Nation*, 150.

179 *get sucked back into crops—and into us:* Kevin Pickering and Lewis Owen, *An Introduction to Global Environmental Issues* (New York: Routledge, 1997), 198.

180 *"after you've stopped smelling it":* Jeff Tietz, "Boss Hog," *Rolling Stone Magazine,* December 2006.

180 *U.S. rejection of Chinese processed foods:* David Barboza, "China Blocks Some Imports of U.S. Chicken and Pork," *New York Times,* July 14, 2007.

180 *"billions of dollars of food exports":* Audra Ang, "China Shuts 180 Food Factories," *Associated Press,* June 27, 2007.

180 *have quadrupled in the past decade:* Geoffrey S. Becker, "Food and Agricultural Imports from China," CRS Report for Congress, September 26, 2008.

180 *antibiotic that has been linked to cancer:* Rick Weiss, "Tainted Chinese Imports Common," *Washington Post,* May 20, 2007, A01.

181 *"look beyond their emphasis on low prices:"* "U.S., Chinese Leaders Try to Advance Trade, Food Safety Issues," Agri-Pulse, May 30, 2007.

181 *"preceding generations would have found bewildering":* Paul Roberts, *The End of Food* (Boston: Houghton Mifflin, 2008), xi.

182 *two Egg McMuffins for three-fourths of the price:* Mike Hughlett, "In a Bad Economy, Many Rediscover the Value Meal," *Chicago Tribune,* October 17, 2008.

183 *to die younger than their parents:* S. Jay Olshansky et al., "A Potential Decline in Life Expectancy in the United States in the 21st Century," *New England Journal of Medicine* 352, no. 11: 1138–45.

183 *most of us have come to think of as pork:* For a comprehensive, fascinating, and on many levels hilarious account of pig farming in America, see Nathan Johnson, "The Swine of the Times," *Harpers,* May 2006.

184 *as of our simply averting our eyes:* Julie Guthman, "Embodying Neoliberalism: Economy, Culture, and the Politics of Fat," *Environment and Planning D: Society and Space* 2006, vol. 24: 427–448.

186 *American markets with cheap Chinese garlic:* See, for example, Sophia Huang and Fred Gale, "China's Rising Fruit and Vegetable Exports Challenge U.S.

Industries," *Electronic Outlook Report from the Economic Research Service*, U.S. Department of Agriculture, 2006.

186 *of transporting the California variety:* "Garlic: Buying Local Helps Reduce Pollution and Protects Health," National Resource Defense Council, November 2007. Online at http://www.nrdc.org/health/effects/camiles/garlic.pdf.

186 *therefore requiring that we use more of it:* California-grown fresh garlic is heavier than the average imported bulb because of a higher density of soluble plant solids and lower water content. In laboratory tests the American Dehydrated Onion and Garlic Association found that American garlic is 42 percent solid, Chinese garlic about 37 percent solid. The association also measured allicin, the odiferous compound in garlic that is released when the bulb is crushed. It is thought that allicin is behind garlic's purported health benefits. California garlic had more than 4,400 parts per million of allicin compared to 3,500 for Chinese garlic. See, for example, Sue Kovach Shuman, "At the Market: How to Sniff Out Where Your Garlic Came From," *Washington Post*, June 20, 2007, F07.

## CHAPTER NINE: THE DOUBLE-HEADED DRAGON

189 *so cheap as to be essentially free:* Marc Levinson, *The Box: How the Shipping Container Made the World Smaller and the World Economy Bigger* (Princeton, N.J.: Princeton University Press, 2006). In this remarkable book, Levinson quotes economists Edward L. Glaeser and Janet E. Kohlhase: "It is better to assume that moving goods is essentially costless than to assume that moving goods is an important component of the production process."

189 *China and the containers they carry:* Joseph Tarnowski, "NONFOODS: HBC/GM: Dueling for Dollars," *Progressive Grocer,* September 15, 2006.

189 *the vast bulk of them from China:* See "About the Port," Web site: the Port of Los Angeles at http://www.portoflosangeles.org.

190 *only one-twentieth of the world's manufactured goods:* Ted. C. Fishman, *China, Inc.: How the Rise of the Next Superpower Challenges America and the World* (New York: Scribner, 2005), 13.

190 *can match China's efficiency and reach:* See, for example, China expert Orville Schell addressing this issue on the radio show "On Point," http://www.onpointradio.org/shows/2004/07/20040714__a__main.asp.

190 *no developed nation can touch:* See, for example, Ted C. Fishman, *China, Inc.,* 177–201.

190 *her household with Chinese imports:* Sandra Bongiorni, *A Year Without Made in China,* (New York: Wiley, 2008).

191 *poverty line is drawn at $156 a year:* Wang Zhuoqiong, "New Poverty Line Raises Number of Poor," *China Daily,* December 23, 2008.

191 *poverty limit of $456 a year:* The World Bank poverty line was adjusted from $1

to $1.25 a day in 2008. Interestingly, more than half the people in the world live on $2 a day. For an excellent synopsis of global inequality, see Anup Shah, "Poverty Around the World," at http://www.globalissues.org/article/4/poverty-around-the-world.

191 *"combination of capitalism, socialism, feudalism and slavery"*: Howard French, "Ideals and Reality Conflict on Chinese Child Labor," *International Herald Tribune*, June 16, 2007.

192 *the world's biggest shopping mall*: As of early 2008, eight of the ten largest malls in the world were in Asia. Informed speculation has it that within the next few years China alone will be home to seven of the ten largest shopping malls in the world.

192 *clueless in matters of labor law*: Aris Chan, "The Children of Migrant Workers in China," China Labour Bulletin. This remarkably comprehensive report is available online at http://www.clb.org.hk/en/node/100316.

192 *his seventeen-year-old son to sign on*: Lauren Keane, "Chinese Migrants Return to Rural Roots," *Washington Post Foreign Service*, January 2, 2009, A08.

192 *717,938 workplace accidents and 127,089 deaths*: http://www.china.org.cn/english/government/177529.htm.

193 *actual numbers are thought to be much higher*: For example, at least six workers died while working on construction sites of the 2008 Summer Olympics in Beijing. Chinese officials at first denied the deaths until forced to acknowledge them after a British newspaper investigation sparked international outrage. See Maureen Fan, "China Acknowledges 6 Deaths in Construction Work," *Washington Post Foreign Service*, January 29, 2008, A16.

194 *are made by migrant workers in Chinese factories*: See Eric S. Lipton and David Barboza, "As More Toys Are Recalled, Trail Ends in China," *New York Times*, June 19, 2007, and http://www.toy-tia.org/Content/NavigationMenu/Press__Room/Industry__Statements/Toys__Made__in__China/Toys__Made__in__China.htm. Interestingly, President Obama called for a ban on Chinese toy imports in a New Hampshire campaign rally on December 9, 2007.

194 *Chinese use themselves, including food*: For example, the fake milk powder scandal has been widely reported in the Chinese media for years. See, for example, Dwight Daniels, "Fake Milk Powder Case Sounds Alarm . . . Again," *Shanghai Star*, April 21, 2005.

194 *forage for it themselves in the wild*: Fuchsia Dunlop, "Garden of Contentment: In a Toxic Era, A Hangzhou Restaurant Pursues Purity," *The New Yorker*, November 24, 2008.

194 *taking bribes from drug companies*: Daniel Chinoy, "Chinese Buyers Beware," *Fortune*, July 12, 2007.

**195** *artificially boost its protein content:* "China Milk Scandal Claims First Victim Outside Mainland," *USA Today (AP),* September 22, 2008. Among the many suppliers cited for contaminated milk was The Dairy Farm, a China-based vendor for Swiss-based multinational Nestlé, although at first Nestlé denied this allegation. The World Health Organization determined that delays in releasing critical information on the contamination had hampered Beijing's ability to deal rapidly with the problem and further endangered consumers.

**195** *"distancing themselves from their own product":* David Leonhardt, "Outsourcers Could Learn a Thing or Two from Thomas," *New York Times,* June 20, 2007.

**195** *American Girl Doll is made in China:* Maria Halkias, "American Girl Dolls Get Party Started," *Dallas Morning News,* November 3, 2007.

**196** *shirts are made by Oxford Industries:* At this writing the shirts were on sale on the IslandTrends Web site for $30.

**197** *"and show monitors falsified books":* Dexter Roberts et al., "Secrets, Lies and Sweatshops," *BusinessWeek,* November 27, 2006. The article reports on Nignbo Beifa Group, a top supplier of pens, mechanical pencils, and highlighters to Wal-Mart stores and other discounters. The company had already failed three audits when the managers learned that Wal-Mart was sponsoring a fourth. Flunking the fourth audit would cost the factory Wal-Mart's business, so it apparently hired a consultant to help tamper with the books and prepare managers to falsely answer questions. The factory passed the fourth audit but improved none of its labor practices.

**198** *that figure had leaped to 40 percent:* Louis Charbonneau, "Half of the World to Live in Cities by the End of 2008 UN," Reuters, February 26, 2008.

**198** *"should campaign in favor of sweatshops":* Nicholas D. Kristof, "In Praise of Maligned Sweatshop," *New York Times,* June 6, 2006. Kristof, a generally insightful and sensitive reporter and columnist, has been promoting sweatshops for some time. Following the East Asian financial crises of the late 1990s, he reported the story of an Indonesian recycler who, picking through a garbage dump, dreamed of her son growing up to be a sweatshop worker. He and his wife, Sheryl WuDunn, penned "Two Cheers for Sweatshops: They're dirty and dangerous. They're also a major reason Asia is back on track," which appeared in the *New York Times Magazine* September 24, 2000. Two years later Kristof's column advised G-8 leaders to "start an international campaign to promote imports from sweatshops, perhaps with bold labels depicting an unrecognizable flag and the words 'Proudly Made in a Third World Sweatshop' " ("Let Them Sweat," *New York Times,* June 25, 2002).

**198** *"difficulty of competing internationally":* Nicholas D. Kristof, "Where Sweatshops Are a Dream," January 15, 2009.

199 *in the history of New York City for ninety years:* For this I relied on David Von Drehle's authoritative account in *Triangle, the Fire That Changed America* (New York: Atlantic Monthly Press, 2003).

199 *several small producers have taken up the challenge:* A list of sweatshop-free manufacturers and distributors can be found online at http://www.state.ct.us/ott/PolicyAndEducation/YDYW2008/Track3HumanRights/Background%20Resources,%20Best%20Practices%20and%20Further%20Reading/Sweatshop%20-%20Free%20Clothing.pdf.

200 *due in part to the decline in farming:* China's land mass is similar to that of the United States (about 9.4 million and 9.6 million square kilometers respectively), but per capita has fewer farms than do most other countries. It is staggering to learn that China feeds 20 percent of the world's population on only 7 percent of the world's farmland. Even that percentage is threatened thanks to government policies that make land development far more lucrative than farming, so local officials rigorously pursue development whenever possible. See Chengri Ding, "Farmland Preservation in China," *Lincoln Institute of Land Policy,* July 2004. See also Anthony Kuhn, "China's Food Prices Rise as Population, Wealth Grow," National Public Radio, April 2008; available online at http://www.npr.org/templates/story/story.php?storyId=89642147.

201 *live in nations with growing income disparity:* Human Development Report, United Nations Development Program, November 27, 2007, 25.

201 *urban growth by a wide margin:* Ibid.

201 *with Wal-Mart being the largest:* If Wal-Mart were a country, at this writing it would be China's eighth largest trading partner.

201 *that ensures timely payment at a minimum rate:* "Comments and Suggestions on Revision to Labor Contract Law," American Chamber of Commerce in Shanghai, April 19, 2006; accessed at http://www.amcham-shanghai.org/NR/rdonlyres/A18F268D-6EE8-4221-B075-4F00282E8623/1427AmChamShanghaihailaborcontractlawcommentstoNPCApr2006.pdf.

202 *if the new law was implemented:* Fergus Naughton, "China to Revise Employment Law, Tighten Employee Safeguards," *AFX International Focus,* February 13, 2007.

202 *"not going to have a long-term impact":* Robert Gavin, "In Low-Priced Imports, Worrisome Costs. Chinese Toy Recall Is Latest Sign of Risk," *Boston Globe,* August 3, 2007.

202 *hard-won gains of American workers:* For an eye-opening discussion of worker conditions (in particular for white collar workers) in China, see Andrew Ross, *Fast Boat to China: Corporate Flight and the Consequences of Free Trade; Lessons from Shanghai* (New York: Pantheon, 2006).

204 *total manufacturing workforce of the United States:* "300 million Chinese Farmers to

Enter Cities Amid Urbanization in the Next Two Decades," *China Daily*, March 21, 2006.

**205** *to less than $83 per year:* Richard McGregor, "China's Poor Worse Off After the Boom," *Financial Times*, November 21, 2006. See http://www.ft.com/cms/s/ e28495ce-7988-11db-b257-0000779e2340,dwp__uuid=9c33700c-4c86-11da-89 df-0000779e2340.html.

**205** *as adults refused to accept the growing injustices:* Reported in Cao Deshen, "Diseases at Work Haunt Migrant Workers," *China Daily*, February 17, 2006.

**205** *no health or safety controls at all:* See Section 301, Petition of American Federation of Labor and Congress of Industrial Organizations, presented by U.S. Representative Benjamin L. Cardin and U.S. Representative Christopher H. Smith. China Petition MB final 6-6, p. 9, available online at: http://www.aflcio.org/issues/jobs economy/globaleconomy/upload/china__petition.pdf.

**206** *global procurement headquarters in Shenzhen:* Stacy Mitchell, *Big Box Swindle* (Boston: Beacon Press, 2006), 50.

## CHAPTER TEN: THE PERFECT PRICE

**207** *"every capitalist concern has got to live in":* Joseph A. Schumpeter, *Capitalism, Socialism and Democracy* (third ed.) (London: Allen and Unwin, 1950), 83.

**209** *"lag far behind productivity growth in the U.S.":* Lawrence Summers, "The Global Middle Cries Out for Reassurance," *Financial Times*, October 29, 2006.

**211** *"But the economy overall benefits":* Mankiw responding to a questioner on "Ask the White House," an online interactive forum available at http://www.whitehouse .gov/ask/20040122.html.

**211** *"displace old ones as they always have":* Jonathan Weisman, "Bush Report Offers Positive Outlook on Jobs," *Washington Post*, February 10, 2004, E01.

**211** *down from 50 percent in 1975:* These statistics—and some of the thoughts reflected by them—once again come thanks to Harvard Economist Richard B. Freeman, who was kind enough to speak with me at length on the topic of international labor markets.

**211** *surpass their American rivals:* "Foreign Science and Engineering Graduate Students Returning to U.S. Colleges," National Science Foundation press release, January 28, 2008.

**211** *"and that is a good thing":* Thomas L. Friedman, *The World Is Flat* (New York: Farrar, Straus & Giroux, 2005), 233.

**212** *"there is no strong labor response":* Richard B. Freeman, "Labor Market Imbalances: Shortages or Surpluses or Fish Stories," delivered to the Boston Federal Reserve Economic Conference, "Global Imbalances—As Giants Evolve," in Chatham, Massachusetts, June 14–16, 2006.

212 *working conditions for the rest of us:* Interview with Richard B. Freeman.

213 *plus $9 in benefits:* Louis Uchitelle, "Two Tiers, Slipping into One," *New York Times,* February 26, 2006, sec. 3, 1.

213 *"But it chooses not to":* Ibid.

213 *a jump of 17 percent from the previous year:* Dave Carpenter, "Caterpillar's Owens Got $14.8 Million in 2007, Up 17 Percent," Associated Press, April 22, 2008.

213 *dig foundations for new homes:* Peter S. Goodman, "Specter of Deflation Lurks as Global Demand Drops: Consumer Cutbacks Could Lead to Falling Prices, a Tough Problem to Cure," *New York Times,* November 1, 2008, A1.

214 *70 percent of the nation's gross domestic product:* This is a widely quoted statistic, but for a recent accounting see: Mark Skousen, *EconoPower: How a New Generation of Economists Is Transforming the World* (New York: John Wiley, 2008), 221. Skousen takes the unusual precaution of pointing out that gross domestic product is not the same as economic activity, as journalists often mistake. Rather, it represents only the final output of goods and services.

214 *the economy came to a crashing halt:* A widely accepted assertion. See, for example, William R. Childs, Scott B. Martin, and Wanda Stitt-Gohdes, *Business and Industry* (Tarrytown, N.Y.: Marshall Cavendish, 2004), 318.

214 *"kind of environment that Sam Walton built this company for":* Stephanie Rosenbloom, "For Wal-Mart, a Christmas That Was Made to Order," *New York Times,* November 5, 2008.

214 *Dollar stores, too, were booming:* Jason Asaeda, "Tough Times Favor Family Dollar Stores," *BusinessWeek,* October 28, 2008.

215 *for its 1.3 million employees:* Kris Maher, "Wal-Mart Seeks New Flexibility in Worker Shifts," *Wall Street Journal,* January 3, 2007.

215 *entitled "Obama's Biggest Challenge":* Bob Herbert, "Obama's Biggest Challenge," *New York Times,* January 9, 2009.

216 *"whether carrots were grown without chemical fertilizers":* Andrew Martin, "Budgets Squeezed, Some Families Bypass Organics," *New York Times,* November 1, 2008.

216 *is trucked in from huge California farms:* In *Omnivore's Dilemma,* author Michael Pollan writes that Cascadian Farms founder Gene Kahn, now a vice president of General Mills, acknowledges his farm is essentially a "PR farm." See Michael Pollan, *The Omivore's Dilemma: A Natural History of Four Meals* (New York: Penguin, 2006), 145.

218 *"need be employed in dissuading them from it":* Adam Smith, *The Wealth of Nations,* Books IV–V; Andrew S. Skinner, ed. (New York: Penguin Books, 1999), 32.

218 *"tolerably well fed, clothed and lodged":* Adam Smith, *The Wealth of Nations,* Books I–III; Andrew S. Skinner, contributor, (New York: Penguin Books, 1970), 181.

220 *B-grade versions of national brands:* Charles Fishman offers a great example of this in *The Wal-Mart Effect.* In 2002, Wal-Mart sold an estimated $3 billion worth of

its house brand "Faded Glory" jeans—more jeans than any other retailer. Iconic jean maker Levi Strauss, looking for a way to revive its fading business, agreed to become a Wal-Mart supplier. But their own line was too expensive, so the company developed a cheaper "value" line—Adult Levi Signature—specifically to sell at Wal-Mart and later to Target and Kmart. "The only thing truly 'Levi' about them," Fishman writes, "is the name."

221 *an alternative route to progress:* "67,000 Chinese Factories Closed in 6 Months," UPI, Beijing, November 14, 2008.

224 *bar coding to the supermarket sector in 1974:* "Robert Wegman, 87, Leader in Supermarket Innovation," *New York Times,* April 22, 2006.

224 *"difficult for your competitors to emulate":* Jon Springer, "Robert Wegman," *Supermarket News,* December 3, 2007.

224 *"one stinks of Zen, the other doesn't":* S. S. Fair, "Two on the Aisle," *New York Times,* November 7, 2004.

228 *Wegmans as a "Living Poem to Capitalism":* Radley Balko, "The Living Poem to Capitalism," Techcentralstation.com, May 31, 2005.

229 *"hot" word of the year: frugalista:* William Safire, "Frugalista," *New York Times Magazine,* November 23, 2008.

229 *less class-bound society:* Simon Nelson Patten, *The New Basis of Civilization* (New York: Macmillan, 1907).

230 *"capital as a means to a particular end":* Simon Nelson Patten, *The Development of English Thought: A Study of Economic Interpretation of History* (New York: Macmillan Company, 1899), 37.

# BIBLIOGRAPHY

Abernathy, Frederick H., et al. *A Stitch in Time: Learn Retailing and the Transformation of Manufacturing—Lessons from the Apparel and Textile Industries.* New York: Oxford University Press, 1999.

Ashby, LeRoy. *With Amusement for All.* Lexington: University Press of Kentucky, 2006.

*Autobiography of Benjamin Franklin.* New York: Macmillan Company, 1921.

Babson, Steven. *Working Detroit: The Making of a Union Town.* Detroit, Mich.: Wayne State University Press, 1986.

Barmash, Isidore. *More Than They Bargained For: The Rise and Fall of Korvettes.* New York: Lebhar-Friedman Books, 1981.

Bean, Jonathan J. *Beyond the Broker State: Federal Policies Toward Small Business, 1936–1961.* Chapel Hill: University of North Carolina Press, 1996.

Best, Joel. *Damned Lies and Statistics: Untangling Numbers from the Media, Politicians, and Activists.* Berkeley: University of California Press, 2001.

Black, Conrad. *Franklin Delano Roosevelt: Champion of Freedom.* New York: Public Affairs, 2003.

Bloom, Paul N., and Gregory Thomas Gundlach. *Handbook of Marketing and Society.* Thousand Oaks, Calif.: Sage Publications, 2001.

Bonacich, Edna, and Richard P. Appelbaum. *Behind the Label: Inequality in the Los Angeles Apparel Industry.* Berkeley: University of California Press, 2000.

Brion Davis, David. *In Human Bondage: The Rise and Fall of Slavery in the New World.* New York: Oxford University Press, 2006.

Brown, Stephen. *Revolution at the Checkout Counter: The Explosion of the Bar Code.* Cambridge, Mass.: Harvard University Press, 1997.

Céline, Louis-Ferdinand. *Death on the Installment Plan.* New York: New Direction, 1971.

Childs, William R., Scott B. Martin, and Wanda Stitt-Gohdes. *Business and Industry.* Tarrytown, N.Y.: Marshall Cavendish, 2004.

Chivian, Eric, and Aaron Bernstein, eds. *Sustaining Life: How Human Health Depends on Biodiversity*. New York: Oxford University Press, 2008.

Clarkson, Leslie A., and E. Margaret Crawford. *Feast and Famine: Food and Nutrition in Ireland, 1500–1920*. New York: Oxford University Press, 2001.

Cohen, Lizabeth. *A Consumers' Republic*. New York: Knopf, 2003.

Crawford, Fred, and Ryan Matthews. *The Myth of Excellence: Why Great Companies Never Try to Be the Best at Everything*. New York: Crown, 2001.

Damasio, Antonio R. *Descartes' Error: Emotion, Reason, and the Human Brain*. New York: Harper Perennial, 1995.

Dehaene, Stanislas. *The Number Sense: How the Mind Creates Mathematics*. New York: Oxford University Press, 1997.

Dickson, Paul, and Joseph C. Goulden. *There Are Alligators in Our Sewers and Other American Credos*. New York: Delacorte, 1984.

Economy, Elizabeth C. *The River Runs Black: The Environmental Challenge to China's Future*. Ithaca, NY: Cornell University Press, 2005.

Featherstone, Liza. *Selling Women Short: The Landmark Battle for Workers' Rights at Wal-Mart*. New York: Basic Books, 2004.

Fishman, Charles. *The Wal-Mart Effect*. New York: Penguin Books, 2006.

Frank, Dana. *Buy American: The Untold Story of Economic Nationalism*. Boston: Beacon Press, 1996.

Freud, Anna. *The Ego and Mechanisms of Defense: The Writings of Anna Freud*. Madison, Conn.: International Universities Press, reprint edition, 1967.

Friedman, John. *China's Urban Transition*. Minneapolis, Minn.: University of Minnesota Press, 2005.

Friedman, Thomas L. *The World Is Flat*. New York: Farrar, Straus & Giroux, 2005.

Galbraith, James K. *Balancing Acts: Technology, Finance, and the American Future*. New York: Basic Books, 1989.

Galbraith, John Kenneth. *The Affluent Society*. Boston: Houghton Mifflin, 1958.

Gavin, Alexander. *The American City: What Works, What Doesn't*. New York: McGraw Hill Professional, second ed., 2002.

Gilovich, Thomas, Dale Griffin, and Daniel Kahneman. *Heuristics and Biases: The Psychology of Intuitive Judgment*. New York: Cambridge University Press, 2002.

Greenhouse, Steven. *The Big Squeeze: Tough Times for the American Worker*. New York: Knopf, 2008.

Halberstam, David. *The Fifties*. New York: Villard Books, 1993.

Hardwick, M. Jeffrey. *Mall Maker: Victor Gruen, Architect of an American Dream*. Philadelphia: University of Pennsylvania Press, 2003.

Hounshell, David. *From the American System to Mass Production, 1800–1932*. Baltimore, Md.: The Johns Hopkins University Press, 1985.

Isaacson, Walter. *Benjamin Franklin: An American Life.* New York: Simon and Schuster, 2003.

Kanigel, Robert. *The One Best Way: Frederick Winslow Taylor and the Enigma of Efficiency.* New York: Viking, 1997.

Kiple, Kenneth F. *A Movable Feast: Ten Millennia of Food Globalization.* New York: Cambridge University Press, 2007.

Klein, Naomi. *The Shock Doctrine: The Rise of Disaster Capitalism.* New York: Henry Holt, 2007.

Lakwete, Angela. *Inventing the Cotton Gin: Machine and Myth in Antebellum America.* Baltimore, Md.: Johns Hopkins University Press, 2003.

Landman, Janet. *Regret: The Persistence of the Possible.* New York: Oxford University Press, 1993.

Lasch, Christopher. *The Culture of Narcissism: American Life in an Age of Diminishing Expectations.* New York: W. W. Norton, 1979.

Lebhar, Godfrey. *Chain Stores in America, 1859–1962.* New York: Chain Store Publishing, 1963.

Levinson, David. *The Encyclopedia of Homelessness.* Thousand Oaks, Calif.: Sage Publications, 2004.

Levinson, Marc. *The Box: How the Shipping Container Made the World Smaller and the World Economy Bigger.* Princeton, N.J.: Princeton University Press, 2006.

McGovern, Charles. *Sold American: Consumption and Citizenship, 1890–1945.* Chapel Hill: University of North Carolina Press, 2006.

McKee, Robert. *Story: Substance, Structure, Style and the Principles of Screenwriting.* New York: HarperCollins, 1997.

Medding, Peter Y. *Coping with Life and Death: Jewish Families in the Twentieth Century.* New York: Oxford University Press, 2000.

Meyer, Stephen, III. *The Five-Dollar Day: Labor Management and Social Control in the Ford Motor Company, 1908–1921.* Albany: State University of New York Press, 1981.

Miles, Malcolm, and Tim Hall with Iain Borden, eds. *The City Cultures Reader.* New York: Routledge, second edition, 2004.

Mitchell, Stacy. *Big Box Swindle.* Boston: Beacon Press, 2006.

Mohammed, Rafi. *The Art of Pricing.* New York: Crown Business, 2005.

Mokyr, Joel. *The Lever of Riches: Technological Creativity and Economic Progress.* New York: Oxford University Press, 1992.

Naughton, Barry. *The Chinese Economy: Transitions and Growth.* Cambridge, MA: MIT Press, 2007.

North, S.N.D., and Ralph H. North. *Simeon North, First Official Pistol Maker of the United States: A Memoir.* Concord, N.H., 1913.

Patten, Simon Nelson. *The New Basis of Civilization.* New York: Macmillan, 1907.

————. *The Development of English Thought: A Study of Economic Interpretation of History*. New York: Macmillan, 1899.

Paulos, John Allen. *Innumeracy: Mathematical Illiteracy and Its Consequences*. New York: Hill and Wang, 2001.

Pickering, Kevin, and Lewis Owen. *An Introduction to Global Environmental Issues*. New York: Routledge, 1997.

Plato. *Socratic Discourses—Plato and Xenophon*. Borzon Press, 2007

Pollan, Michael. *The Omivore's Dilemma: A Natural History of Four Meals*. New York: Penguin, 2006.

Pursell, Carroll W., Jr., ed. *Technology in America: A History of Individuals and Ideas*, second ed., 1990.

Ratneshwar, S., and David Glen Mick, eds. *Inside Consumption: Consumer Motives, Goals and Desires*. New York: Routledge, 2005.

Reich, Robert. *Supercapitalism: The Transformation of Business, Democracy, and Everyday Life*. New York: Knopf, 2007.

Richards, William C. *The Last Billionaire: Henry Ford*. New York: Charles Scribner's & Sons, 1948.

Roberts, Paul. *The End of Food*. Boston: Houghton Mifflin, 2008.

Ross, Andrew. *Fast Boat to China: Corporate Flight and the Consequences of Free Trade; Lessons from Shanghai*. New York: Pantheon, 2006.

Ross, Robert J. S. *Slaves to Fashion: Poverty and Abuse in the New Sweatshops*. Ann Arbor: University of Michigan Press, 2004.

Ruppel Shell, Ellen. *The Hungry Gene*. New York: Atlantic Monthly Press, 2002.

Salaman, Redcliffe N., William G. Burton, and John G. Hawkes. *The History and Social Influence of the Potato*. Cambridge, Mass.: Cambridge University Press, 1985.

Schlosser, Eric. *Fast Food Nation*. New York: Houghton Mifflin, 2001.

Schumpeter, Joseph A. *Capitalism, Socialism and Democracy*. London: Allen and Unwin (third ed.), 1950

Skousen, Mark. *EconoPower: How a New Generation of Economists Is Transforming the World*. New York: John Wiley and Sons, 2008.

Smiley, David J., ed. *Sprawl and Public Spaces: Redressing the Mall*. New York: Princeton Architectural Press, 2002.

Smith, Adam. *The Theory of Moral Sentiments*. 1790, sixth ed.

Spector, Robert. *Category Killers: The Retail Revolution and Its Impact on Consumer Culture*. Boston: Harvard Business School Press, 2005.

Thaler, Richard. *The Winner's Cure: Paradoxes and Anomalies of Economic Life*. New York: The Free Press, 1992.

Thomas, Dana. *Deluxe: How Luxury Lost Its Luster*. New York: Penguin, 2008.

Torekull, Bertil. *Leading by Design*. New York: Harper Business, 1998.

Uchitelle, Louis. *The Disposable Americans: Layoffs and Their Consequences*. New York: Knopf, 2006.

Von Drehle, David. *Triangle: the Fire That Changed America*. New York: Atlantic Monthly Press, 2003.

Waltman, Jerold L. *The Politics of the Minimum Wage*. Champaign: University of Illinois Press, 2000.

Watts, Alan. *The Book: On the Taboo Against Knowing Who You Are*. New York: Collier Books, 1996.

Winkler, John K. *Five and Ten: The Fabulous Life of F. W. Woolworth*. New York: Robert M. McBride, 1940.

Wood, Diana. *Medieval Economic Thought*. New York: Cambridge University Press, 2002.

Woodham-Smith, Cecil. *The Great Hunger: Ireland 1845–1849*. New York: Penguin Group, 1992.

Wright, C. D. *Rising, Falling, Hovering*. Port Townsend, Wash.: Copper Canyon Press, 2008.

Zinn, Howard, Dana Frank, and Robin D. G. Kelly. *Three Strikes*. Boston: Beacon Press, 2001.

Zola, Emile. *Au Bonheur des Dames*. New York: Penguin Classics, 2002.

# INDEX